Vicious Loops and Pendulums.

Contents.

Chapter 1. Introduction. –Page 8.
Vicious loops and pendulums.
Negative feedback loops
Damped feedback
Positive feedback loops
Bistable loops
Negative to positive loops
Over riding influences
Positive to negative loops
Summary.

Chapter 2. Pendulums –Page 21.
Waves and tsunamis
Delay of feedback and hunting
Modelling
Rigidity or flexibility
Some social aspects
Summary.

Chapter 3. Vicious loops –Page 32.
Introduction
The scoldent list
Controlling a potential disaster
A beneficial loop
The effect of change in loop gain
Sigmoid response
Negative to positive loops
Monopoly and the remainder problem.
Summary

Chapter 4. Maximisation of inequality. –Page 46.
The tournament ploy
Inequality and management
Maximisation of unfairness
Physical conflict
Monopoly
Compensation for inequality
Summary

Chapter 5. Feedback in the home. –Page 54.
Central heating.
The Kitchen.
The Bathroom.
The Door..
The Garden.
A stitch in time.
Self-compensating systems.
Summary.

Chapter 6. The Problems of no feedback. –Page 62.
Absolute power and absence of feedback
Remoteness between cause and effect
Sharing the cost of a decision
Advancing of technology and complexity
Media hype and distorted data
Accountability and feedback
Summary
References.

Chapter 7. Crime and the devil's advocate. -Page 72.
The Devil's Advocate.
Role of the Media
Role of Fashion
Role of Judiciary
The Synergy of Minds
Motivation.
Delay in the feedback loop
Feedback and organised crime.
A look at the other side.
Immediacy of Feedback.
Power and influence.
Summary
References.

Chapter 8. Social relations and Organisations. –Page 85.
Clubs and societies
The ratchet effect
The confidence loop
Social interaction & partnerships
Gearing
Argument
Generation sequences.
Summary
References.

Chapter 9. Psychology. –Page 96.
Self confidence
Crowd behaviour
Reinforcement
Motivation
Chaos and development
Group think
The increase in understanding
Observations on alcoholism
Summary
References.

Chapter 10. Sociology. –Page 110.
Living with change
Compensating factors
The aspiration for riches
Crowd behaviour
Social stability
Swing of pendulum to liberalism.
Minorities in a democracy
Vicarious behaviour
Warren Buffett and Social Capital.
Summary
References.

Chapter 11. Education. - Page 125.
The pendulum of curriculum
The pendulum of discipline
The inequality of human rights.
Higher education
The pendulum of requirement
Private schools and unequal opportunities
Education and accelerating change.
Summary
References.

Chapter 12. Companies. – Page 138.
Profit or loss
Start-up companies.
Investment or subsidy.
Forecasting the market.
Summary
References.

Chapter 13. Employment. – Page 147.
Management
Delay of accountability
Parkinson's law
Government
Rate of change
Matching employer and employee
Decline of employment in manufacturing
Loop distortion
Summary
References.
Appendix: Optimising Employment in the Microelectronics Age.

Chapter 14. Economics. – Page 161
The free market
Monopoly
State control
Credit and money supply
Butterfly economics
The problem of rising costs.
Pensions and social security issues.
Summary
References.

Chapter 15. Industry. – Page 176.
Capital risk
Forecasting trends
Cultural differences
Evolving industry
Success factors
Counteracting effects
Fashion
Summary
References.

Chapter 16. Finance. – Page 188.
Vulnerability
Insolvent thrifts
The crisis of 2008
Delay in response to credit
Some positive loops
Negative feedback
The poverty trap
Summary
References.

Chapter 17. Financial systems. – Page 204.
Bonds
The stockmarket
The crash of 87
Arbitrage
Derivatives
Options
Covered warrants
Gearing
Summary
References.

Chapter 18. Legislation. – Page 216.
Legislative problems.
Data delay and future perception.
Complexity and diminishing returns.
Litigation.
The further compensation culture.
Excess legislation.
Human rights.

Summary
References.

Chapter 19. Physiology. – Page 231.
Muscle control
Homeostasis
Temperature control
Water concentration
Unstable conditions
Biofeedback
Neurofeedback
Summary
References.

Chapter 20. Environment. – Page 242.
Natural hazards.
Global warming
Hurricanes typhoons cyclones
Road congestion or public transport
The motorway
Disincentives for the car
Counter measures
The total picture
Population issues
Survival issues.
Summary
References.

Chapter 21. Information Technology. –Page 261.
Information loops
Stockmarket
System over-load (or chaos breeding chaos)
Beneficial effects
Data overload
Counteracting influences
Summary
References.

Chapter 22. Matching - Page 271.
Efficiency issues
Optimisation
Connectivity
Price of perfection
Summary
References

Chapter 23. The Future - Page 280.
Legislation and planning
Trend in litigation
Consumption
Resources
Human rights
Religious conflict
Movements in democracy
Protectionism
Complexity & interdependence
Summary.

Index. Page 291.

Chapter 1.   Vicious loops and pendulums.

Introduction.

A beginner cyclist falls over; a fire rages out of control; a snowball runs down hill gaining in speed and size. Alternatively a motorist drives down the centre of a traffic lane; supermarket queues are the same length; an experienced cyclist appears to defy gravity. What do these situations have in common? They are all examples of two kinds of feedback loop. It is not, perhaps, a phrase that is used in everyday conversation but it has an important influence on our daily lives. It comes in various forms. Some are benign while others can cause serious problems. The motorist and the experienced cyclist use a compensating loop. It provides an influence that is used to maintain stability whether keeping the car in the centre of the lane or helping the cyclist to remain upright. It occurs when errors or deviations are used to correct wrong behaviour. The positive feedback loop on the other hand magnifies problems such as a raging fire or the balance of the beginner cyclist; but in other situations it can enhance benefits.

It is important to distinguish between feedback and a feedback loop. The word positive is normally associated with something good. Positive feedback usually means getting good advice from a friend or mentor. A positive feedback loop on the other hand acts upon itself so as to accentuate an effect. Its behaviour is added to the influence that started it and this behaviour is circulated with increasing effect. Sometimes known as the vicious circle, it can, when used in a controlled manner, be beneficial, but if applied inadvertently it can have dramatic consequences. Not only does it apply to a fire raging out of control; or a business that is going bankrupt - but also to the successful business and numerous other applications. These will be discussed in later chapters.

The negative feedback loop should not be confused with negative feedback as a form of criticism. This type of feedback loop provides neither criticism nor compliment; it simply acts to compensate for unwanted change. To prevent confusion this form of loop is, perhaps, better described as a compensating loop; however, it too has its problems if the compensation arrives too late. Delay in the compensating influence is a factor in rising and falling economies, minority influences, sociological perturbations and especially the banking crisis of 2008.

The feedback loop, in its many forms, has been extensively investigated by scientists and engineers. It plays an important role in the design of many systems. The Design Engineer and particularly the Control Systems Design

Engineer has to be careful that a system is stable. Heavy machinery, which is controlled to move to a new position must do so without overshooting or oscillating backwards and forwards. Electronic systems are also subject to these criteria and much design and development effort goes into ensuring that feedback is stable when incorporated into electronic amplifiers and operating equipment. Sophisticated mathematics is used to check that there is an adequate margin in stability to cope with any situation that might arise.

Compensating loops.

This concept is better illustrated by means of an example such as the steering of a car where the human being is part of the loop. The experienced driver continually corrects the steering wheel with a barely perceptible movement to maintain the car in the centre of the lane. As the car deviates from the centre so the correction to the wheel is increased, the correction (i.e. error) is subtracted from the original behaviour and so it is a compensating loop. The effect of delay in the loop is important. This is evident with a learner driver who typically applies the correction too late and then with greater emphasis thereby generating more of a zigzag motion down the road.

The effect may be more exaggerated if the driver is drunk. The delayed response of the drunken driver causes the movement to one side to be greater than is prudent and accordingly a greater correction has to be applied. The car then goes further over to the other side of the road and it is possible the car will be steered on an increasingly erratic course. It is important that the feedback is applied in time otherwise the departure from the desired state increases.

Delay in response is a problem in shipping when, for example, a large oil tanker is being steered along a narrow channel. The time for the tanker to respond to the steering can be so long that the movement is not noticeable for several miles. If an amateur were at the helm then it is certain that a correction applied to the steering would be too much and too late. It would not be seen to have any effect for so long that an excessive change in steering would be applied. Accordingly the ship would eventually respond with a course too far in the other direction. The course would oscillate with increasing diversions until the tanker eventually ran aground. Systems with delayed feedback tend to oscillate, and the greater the delay the greater the oscillation about the desired position.

In practice, computer systems can be used to help control the movement of such a ship since it can not only assess smaller changes in direction, it can also be programmed to predict the ship's response and so modify the steering appropriately. The computer in this case is a part of the feedback loop.

A familiar example of a compensating loop is the temperature control in a central heating system (Figure 1.1a).

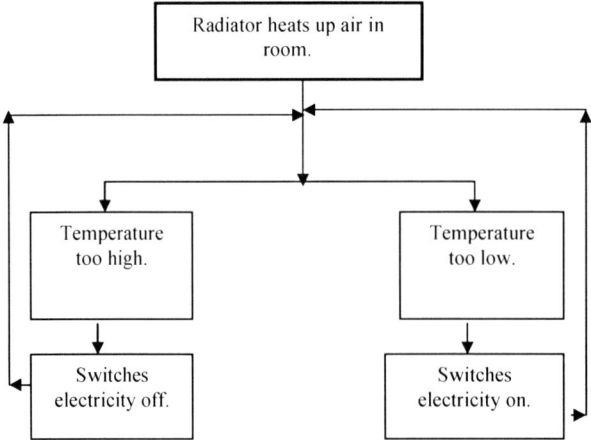

Figure 1.1a Control of central heating system.

As the temperature rises the heated air warms the thermostat until it cuts off the electricity (or other fuel) to the heaters. The air, and consequently the thermostat, then cools until the thermostat reaches the temperature set for switching the heating on again. There is a delay while the radiator heats the air - and the heated air travels to the thermostat - before any change is detected. Consequently the radiator heats air to a higher temperature than set for the thermostat before it responds. Similarly when the radiator is turned off the thermostat is again late in responding. The effect is to cause the temperature of the room to fluctuate above and below the temperature desired. This is a very basic design in which the control simply switches on or off. (It will be seen that there is some similarity to the delay in steering a ship.)

One of the early applications of compensating loops occurred in the design of the steam engine. It is a good illustration of automatic control, which is a basic theme found in all walks of life.

It is necessary that the speed of a steam engine be controlled so that it does not run so fast as to destroy itself or the equipment it is driving. Whereas this can notionally be done by a person using a form of throttle, or accelerator, it is much better to use an automatic control that maintains a constant speed.

A mechanical device known as a governor is used. It consists of a couple of heavy balls, which are attached to a rotating spindle by hinged rods. As the spindle rotates, the balls fly out sideways and pull up a sleeve. The faster the machine rotates the further the balls swing out, and the further the sleeve rides up the spindle. The height of the sleeve is therefore a measure of the speed of the machine and it can be used to control the steam entering the cylinders.

If the engine slows down, the balls become closer together, the sleeve drops down causing a larger aperture to open up in the steam pipe and accordingly the engine speeds up again. It is not desirable to have the engine continually speeding up and slowing down so it is necessary that the response of the governor be fast compared to the rate at which the engine can change speed (this will be found to be important in other systems also). It is expected that the governor will settle at some mean position that allows the right amount of steam necessary for the speed desired.

This is a compensating loop because as the engine increases in speed above a certain amount, it causes an effect that reduces the speed or prevents the trend of increasing speed; i.e. "it compensates for the error in speed". Figure 1.1b shows the behaviour in diagrammatic form.

These types of steam engine are often on display at summer fairs where they chug away, contentedly, all day. The owners will doubtless be happy to illustrate the working of the governor.

The steam engine has two important differences compared with the control of a central heating system. Firstly the delay round the loop is small so that the response is immediate and secondly the valve controlling the flow of steam can be partly turned on (rather than switched on or off). This means that the degree to which the valve is opened can be proportional to the flow required.

In order to discuss how this behaviour, in general, applies to other situations I shall want to use words which are more general such as "trends" and influences". If it is a compensating loop then, when a trend goes beyond the level desired, it is necessary to introduce an influence, which counteracts the trend, so as to maintain sufficient stability.

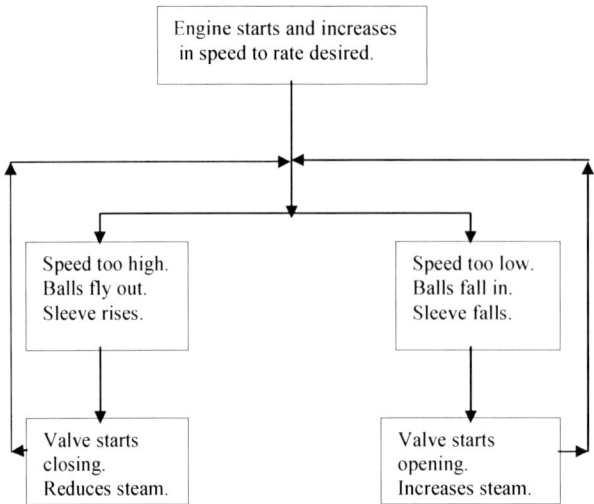

Figure 1.1b control of steam engine.

To put this in terms of the steam engine; the trend is the change in speed; the influence is the response of the balls (and therefore the sleeve) to the change in speed, which in turn alters the amount of steam applied to the engine.

In the example of steering a car, the trend was the deviation from the centre of the road and the influence was the human moving the steering wheel to counteract the trend.

Sometimes the compensating loop is called a self-righting system. Nature has provided us with the autonomic nervous system. This is an effective physiological system for compensating for changes in the demands on the body such as temperature, heart rate etc.

It is important to consider these trends and influences in other spheres such as sociology, ecology or the effects of legislation where the compensating influence of a free market is sometimes removed.

The compensating loop is found in the following situations:

- stable systems;
- automatic control;
- good management;
- physiology;
- the free market;
- social behaviour.

Delayed compensating loops contribute to:

- traffic jams;
- educational problems;
- crime;
- vibrations, waves and wobbles.

Damped feedback.

As mentioned above it is a characteristic feature that delay in a compensating loop causes oscillation. Whereas this is a natural feature which we learn to live with, there are many cases when it is necessary to bring the system back to rest immediately or as soon as possible without the inconvenience of it wobbling about its centre. If a simple system such as a pendulum is considered then a simple way of damping it would be to immerse it in water. The friction from the water stops it from moving so fast that it overshoots. A yacht is an analogy to a damped pendulum. A deep keel or centre-board attempts to shovel water from side to side as the yacht rolls. The water resists this and makes the boat more stable. Erecting the sails can increase the comfort of the crew since the air resistance over such a large area is also effective in damping the rolling movement of the boat.

Oil is used to dampen the spurious movements of magnetic compasses. Electronic systems are often used to control physical systems and optimise the return to the norm with minimum oscillation. Other systems - in the social and financial spheres - may need control to minimise fluctuations and these will be considered in later chapters.

Positive feedback loops.

The systems described so far are compensating loops in which the influence on the system (if applied in time) is such as to reduce variations. There are more dangerous conditions where the feedback accentuates the variation - the vicious circle.

A familiar example will be the microphone amplifier where the sound coming out of the loudspeaker feeds back into the microphone. If the gain of the amplifier is set too high then any slight sound into the microphone will be amplified and emitted by the loudspeaker as a much louder sound. If this amplified sound reaches the microphone at a louder level than the original, then it too will be amplified and come out of the loudspeaker even louder. This loop from the amplifier to the loudspeaker through the air to the microphone and again to the amplifier is a positive feedback loop. The initial sound increases to a deafening crescendo and is heard rather like a scream.

A further example is the spread of a fire which, when the temperature is high enough to ignite the surroundings, increases the fire and accentuates the rate of ignition of further objects. The ultimate case is an explosion where the pressure wave

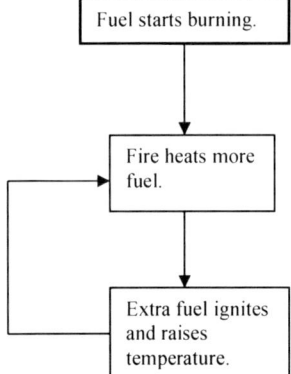

Figure 1.2 A positive feedback loop.

The positive loop is to be found in the following situations:

- population explosion;
- crowd psychology;
- media influence;
- stock market;

- self confidence;
- Parkinsons law;
- healthy businesses, etc.

Bistable positive loops.

Systems can sometimes be in one of two extremes depending on circumstances caused by external events. The bonfire will have given a clue to this category, which occurs quite frequently in everyday life. When a system can settle into one of two situations then it is likely that one of those situations is infinitely preferable to the other. A successful baker sells loaves and uses the income to buy more flour to sell more loves to buy more flour – etc. If less flour is bought then less loaves are sold and flour is bought -etc. and the business declines.

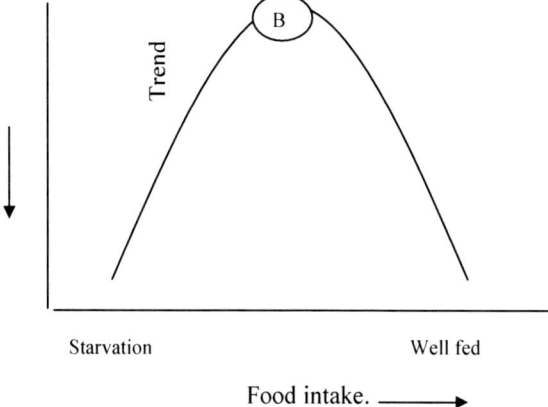

Figure 1.3 Bistable positive loop.

Consider for example a starving chicken that is less able to compete for food in competition with well fed ones. If it is so starved as to be too weak to compete against the other chickens then it will starve further and become weaker - a positive feedback loop. On the other hand if the chicken has sufficient strength to get some food then it becomes stronger and is able to get yet more food - also a positive loop.

It is like positioning a ball (B) at the top of a hill as shown in figure 1.3; it might run down one side or the other. It will never return of its own accord. It is important for the chicken to be on the "right side of the hill".

This kind of situation will also be seen in:

- commerce
- marriage
- education
- mental illness.
- war.
- electric switches
- judo

Negative to positive feedback loops.

Is it possible for a compensating loop to become a positive one? Two possibilities are:
    i. Due to a change in circumstances:
    ii. Due to influences that overcome the compensation.

i. A change in circumstances.

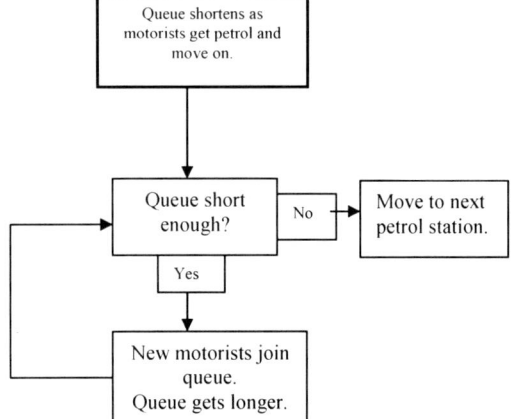

Figure 1.4 Compensating loop.

What change in circumstances will change this to a positive feedback loop? An international oil crisis or a problem in the petrol distribution network, which creates a petrol shortage (or even a virtual shortage created by media hype), are candidates. As soon as a garage received its allocation of petrol a queue would rapidly form as motorists tried to get their share. A lengthening queue now meant that it was worth joining and this is represented by Figure 1.5.

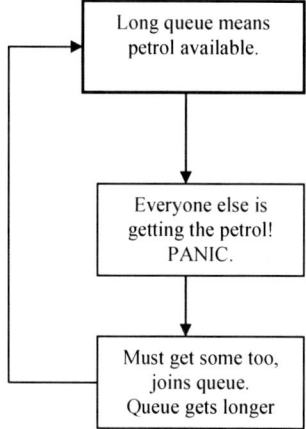

Figure 1.5 Change to positive loop.

Alternatively the change in circumstances might occur because of interference in the regulation of the loop. The control on an electric blanket is turned up if it is too cold or turned down if it is too hot - until it reaches the right temperature. This is a compensating loop since the trend of change in temperature is used to compensate for the error in temperature.

It is illustrated in Figure 1.6

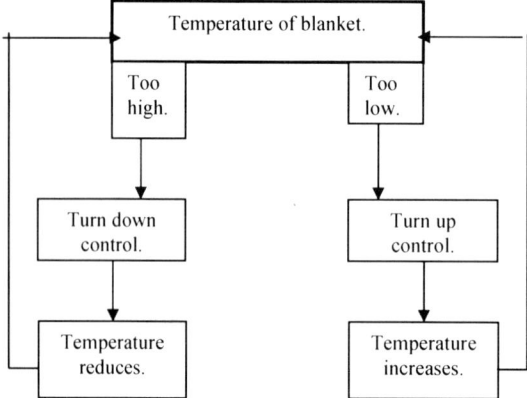

Figure 1.6 Compensating loop.

What change in circumstances will make this into a positive feedback loop? Consider a double blanket used by husband and wife. It is quite easy to get the controls mixed up when changing the blanket. If the control, inadvertently used by the wife, controls the husbands side of the bed (and similarly the husband's

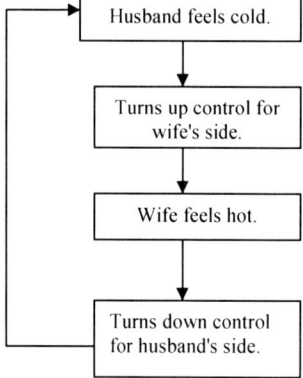

Figure 1.7 Change to positive feedback loop.

control controls his wife's side) then the following actions will follow: Husband feels cold and turns up the control. Wife feels hot and turns down the control. Husband now feels colder and the cycle repeats - a positive feedback loop represented by Figure 1.7.

ii. **Over-riding influences**

Returning to the scenario of the starving chicken, which is progressively becoming weaker. This time, however, it has the good fortune to meet a farmer. He counteracts the trend towards starvation by feeding the chicken until it is strong enough to look after itself. This moves the chicken to the positive loop on the beneficial side of the "hill". The influence of the farmer is a compensating loop, which counteracts and overcomes the trend of the positive starvation loop.

A chair, which is tipped back, will recover its position (up to a certain point) because gravity opposes the tipping (a compensating loop) and acts to move the chair back to its stable position. Beyond the balance point, gravity acts in support of the tipping force and increases its effect as the chair falls over - a positive loop.

A tree in a storm bends but has the strength to oppose the wind and recover its position. If the wind is strong enough to uproot the tree then wind and gravity combine to make it fall over.

Positive to Compensating loops.

In general a positive feedback loop which is left to continue its expansion, will create problems. Even a successful business, itself an example of a positive loop, will end up as a monopoly if it continues to expand indefinitely.

Fortunately there tend to be influences that act to oppose the positive feedback loop. These opposing forces are usually designed into the system at the outset. An example is the domestic fire that is contained within a stove. Whereas there is sufficient fuel and oxygen at the beginning for the fire to increase, as discussed previously, a point is reached when the restrictions on the intake of air, or fuel, limit the further increase of the fire.

The successful family business is likely to reach a point when sufficient funds are generated for the needs of the family. There is no need to expand the business further and the family work less hard, perhaps channelling some of the profits into holidays instead of feeding so much back into the business. This compensating loop arises due to the lack of further incentive and opposes the expansion beyond the level necessary for family funding.

In other situations it may be necessary to learn to cope with the problems resulting from a positive loop. The beginner cyclist wishing to turn right will steer the handlebars to the right and fall to the left. If the cyclist attempts to recover by turning the handle bars further to the right then the fall to the left is accentuated and a positive loop is in being. On the other hand the experienced cyclist, wishing to turn right, makes a momentary turn to the left (to initiate a fall to the right) and then compensates by steering to the right sufficiently to recover from the fall - a compensating loop.

Summary.

This chapter has introduced a few of the examples where a phenomenon known to science and engineering is relevant in everyday life. The further chapters will consider these and other situations in more detail and discuss how to recognise problem areas and correct them. Economic and social systems are complex and there are many influences that disguise a trend. Provided we have enough information, and a system responds slowly, then we can monitor it and alter a trend before problems occur, but this may not always be the case. Further problems may arise in the future in a computer controlled environment, but forewarned is forearmed and it will be important to be aware of the possibility of feedback loops whether in legislation, economics or social systems.

Chapter 2.   Pendulums.

Waves and tsunamis.

We were sitting beside the River Thames ready to watch the Oxford and Cambridge boat race. We had found a good position at the water's edge; our lunch box and cameras were on the ground beside us. Presently the race came by followed by an armada of motor launches intent on achieving a good view. As they passed, the water started receding from the bank revealing the mud on the river's bottom. It kept on receding as I looked at it. We were no longer at the edge of the water but now about ten feet away. I sat there contemplating how remarkable it was that the water should go so far back. Would it never stop, I wondered. Suddenly I realised that, like a pendulum, it would not only stop but return and travel further up the river's bank by a similar amount to the drop.

Quickly we gathered our chairs, cameras and lunch box and retreated up the bank. Soon the water came pounding back soaking the ground where we had been sitting a few moments before. It was caused by the propellers of the armada of motor boats which had drawn the water down stream, causing the trough of a large wave; there had been a delay until the peak of the wave had replenished the lost water - overshooting its previous position.

Many years later in 2004 a similar occurrence happened on a much larger scale when a tsunami devastated islands in the Indian Ocean. On a very small scale the phenomenon is similar to a stone dropping into a pond. It does not matter whether the disturbance is the entry of an object into the water or the collapse of a section of the bottom of the ocean. A sudden dip in the level of the water initiates the same wave motion as the level recovers and goes beyond its stable level.

Pendulums and waves have similar properties. They are two instances of a phenomenon known as simple harmonic motion. The motion of a pendulum (and analogous systems) is determined by the force causing it to return to its central position. The force by itself will never stop the motion at its stable position because it comes too late. It only starts acting when the object has passed the central point.

A familiar example of a pendulum is the child's swing. When it is at the bottom of the swing there is no force affecting its motion but the momentum (due to its speed) carries it up the other side. As it ascends, gravity plays an increasing affect in opposing the swing until it has slowed to its maximum height. Gravity then causes it to accelerate in the opposite direction until the speed of the pendulum reaches its maximum when it is again at the bottom of the swing.

A small movement can be increased by applying a nudge each time the swing approaches. It in fact stores the energy that is applied in small doses over a period of time. This is evident if we try to stop it suddenly. When it is swinging high it can be dangerous both to adult and child. It is a property of oscillating systems that they store energy and for a large system care is needed when attempting to arrest the movement. Taming such a system is best undertaken in easy stages, whether it is a physical one like a swing or a sociological one like a commercial company.

These systems tend to have a constant period of oscillation, which is of course utilised in the pendulum clock. To maintain the motion a small nudge analogous to pushing a child's swing is applied to the pendulum every cycle. (A cycle is the time between the same point on successive waves or the time for a pendulum to perform a complete swing.) In the case of the clock the nudge is likely to be a mechanical push energised by a spring or heavy weights, or the pull of an electromagnet if it is battery powered. There are other devices, which have equivalent properties to a pendulum, such as the hairspring in a watch.

Oscillating systems are all around us but they need energy to maintain the motion that would otherwise die out because of friction. The wave machine in a swimming pool may be energised by paddles which push the water at the same point in every wave so that relatively little energy is required to build up a significant movement. It is important to realise that the paddles have no control over the period of the waves. If they tried to control it, then their energy would be dissipated uselessly by opposing the natural forces of the wave motion. An analogy would be the parent who tried to control the period of the child's swing by pushing it at a different time in each swing; the effect would be counterproductive and simply waste energy. By contrast, a periodic thrust adds to the energy stored in the swing which becomes greater as the swing moves higher.

An army of soldiers marching across a bridge traditionally breaks step. The concerted effect of so many steps taken at the same time and repeated at regular intervals could cause dangerous oscillations in a bridge should its natural period of oscillation correspond to the marching feet.

The Millennium Bridge in London suffered in a similar way. In this case civilians walking across the bridge fell in with the slight swing of the bridge and accentuated it to the point where people felt unsafe. Had they walked out of step the swing would not have been a problem.

The movement of the bridge is an example of excited oscillation, in this case unwanted. Similar unwanted excitations occur in the vibration of a part of the car at certain engine speeds. In other spheres attempts are made to excite oscillations to achieve greater benefits for industry. The fashion industry is one example and car manufacture another. Illegal behaviour on the stock market has been known to have similar effects, which benefited the instigator.

The examples given represent a simple movement with one axis. Many of the systems to be discussed in this book are more complex; perhaps analogous to several pendulums being buffeted in different directions.

In physical systems it is usually desirable to limit the movement to acceptable levels to prevent damage; but a rigid control to prevent any movement at all may be unduly expensive and introduce stresses on the system's structure. The point has been established in the fable of the rush, which survived the storm by bending with the wind, while the tree, which tried to withstand the force, was blown down.

The delay of feedback and hunting.

Numerous systems suffer from the problem of delay in the corrective action that negative feedback is supposed to supply. In a mechanical system a delay can be caused by slack in the links of the feedback chain. In chapter 1, the governor of the steam engine relied upon mechanical linkages to control the amount of steam fed to the engine. If there is slack in the links then the engine could increase its speed significantly before the slack is taken up and the valve actuated to reduce the speed. Similarly, as the engine reduces speed, the change in valve position would again be too late and the engine would lose too much speed. The result would be an engine changing its speed up and down continuously and never staying at the optimum. This endeavour to achieve the optimum but always shooting beyond it, is known as hunting and is characteristic of systems with a large corrective force which arrives late.

If the feedback is delayed extensively, a system can become unstable. The point can be illustrated by a ridiculous example, which nevertheless helps to clarify the point. A very rich man has dealings on the stock market, which are large enough to influence the market trend. Suppose that this very rich man (VRM) wants to get away from it all and finds a spot in the deepest jungle without mobile phone, radio or television. The only way to contact him is by messenger who flies to foreign parts and takes two weeks to navigate the jungle to reach him. During this time the stock market is wavering up and down every two months, at month 1 it is low and at month 2 it is high - and so on. VRM has instructed his secretary to advise him when the market is at a low or high.

At month 1 the messenger is dispatched and advises VRM the market is at a low. VRM sends back instructions to buy. The messenger takes two weeks to renegotiate the jungle paths and buy his air ticket, and arrives back at month 2 when the market is at a high. The buy order, being of substantial size, influences the market to go higher. The messenger is again dispatched with the news that the market is at a high. VRM sends instructions to sell. These arrive at month 3 when the market is at a low and depress the market further. The effect of the delay in timing, of the substantial dealings of VRM, is to cause the market swings to be greater than they would otherwise be; not to mention the squandering of VRM's fortune. The effect of the delay, caused by the messenger service, is to alter the phase relationships between market swings and VRM's intentions so that the action is the opposite of that intended. The analogy to delay in a negative feedback loop will be clear. If the delay is equal to half a cycle then the negative loop changes to a positive one.

Control of a country's economy suffers from a similar problem. Here the delay is not caused by the jungle messenger but by the time it takes to collect the data representing the state of the economy. By the time sufficient data has been gathered, and a change in bank rate is announced, the economy may have moved on to a new situation for which the bank rate change is not appropriate. Bureaucracy is a further factor, suffered not only by governments but also companies. If an urgent decision is seen to be necessary by those intimately in touch with a situation, then a long approval procedure may delay action until it is too late.

William Gosling in his book: "Helmsmen and Heroes" refers to "The Celebrated Pig Cycle". Here it is postulated that if pigs are scarce then the price of pork, ham and bacon will be high. Accordingly farmers will be encouraged to breed more pigs. Breeding however takes several years and by the time the meat is ready for market there may be a glut of pig meat since many farmers had noted the opportunity. The price is then low and farmers turn to other produce. Accordingly there is a scarcity a few years later and the cycle is repeated.

This swing in demand has been seen in the supply of candidates for the professions. If a profession is overcrowded so that salaries are low then students will be encouraged to study for other professions. Since the message is received by a large number of students the effect is significant and can lead to a disproportionate reduction in numbers for the next generation; the converse also applies. These are situations, however, in which the consequences can be anticipated and plans prepared to compensate - a process known as modelling.

Modelling.

The problem of controlling a large oil tanker was mentioned in chapter 1 as an example of the problem of delay in receiving information about the helmsman's actions and the disastrous consequences that ensue. Gosling mentions a similar experience when he was invited to drive a submarine simulator. The response of the submarine, when diving, is so slow that the inexperienced operator is likely to move the diving controls to an extreme position. When the submarine does respond it is too late to compensate for the excessive movement of the control wheel and it crashes onto the bottom of the sea.

These are examples where it is possible to measure the response of the steering system accurately and, in consequence, forecast the effect of moving the controls. By utilising this information a mathematical model can be prepared and used by a computer to modify the instructions of the helmsman to provide the control necessary to achieve the helmsman's intentions. It would otherwise be necessary for the helmsman to know the delay in response of the system and also be able to measure the smallest of movements of the vessel in order to assess the ultimate response.

Figure 1 shows the curve of thermometer reading against time. Since the formula for this graph can be calculated, it is possible to design an electronic system that simulates the curve. The rate at which the curve is changing near the beginning can be used to indicate the final reading the thermometer will reach. In other words it is possible to forecast the performance of the thermometer and read the ambient temperature with little delay. The electronic system is a model of the thermometer. The system could have been modelled on a computer equally well but at greater cost.

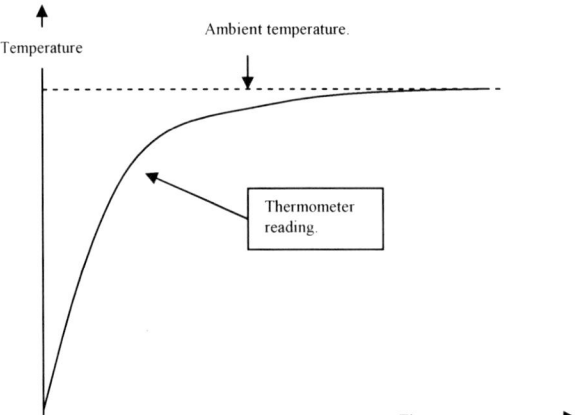

Figure 1.   A Simple model.

Similarly the oil tanker and submarine can be modelled so that the response to an action by the helmsman can be forecast in adequate time.

Rigidity or Flexibility.

The amount of control that is possible over a system depends a great deal on the degree of access. Very often the controller is separated from the item to be controlled by levers, flexible connections or other people. A flexible connection such as a rubber steering wheel in a car would be worrying and would require practice to determine how to steer around a corner. A car's brakes and steering, however, are controlled by rigid hydraulic systems and give confidence in the outcome. A driving instructor, telling a pupil how to drive, lacks the same conviction.

This issue of rigidity versus flexibility determines how systems behave. Suppose a weight (Figure 2a) is suspended from P1 by a piece of string and its position can only be controlled by moving the top of the string. If the string is moved sharply from P1 to P2 then initially the weight moves only slightly. A short time later it overshoots the line P2 and then the free weight swings like a pendulum on either side of P2 (solid line in Figure 2b).

To make the weight follow the string, it must be moved sufficiently slowly so that the difference is not detectable (as shown by the dotted line for the damped weight in Figure 2b). It is not possible to move the string quickly and expect the weight to follow exactly. To do this the string must be replaced with a rigid bar so that the weight is forced to follow.

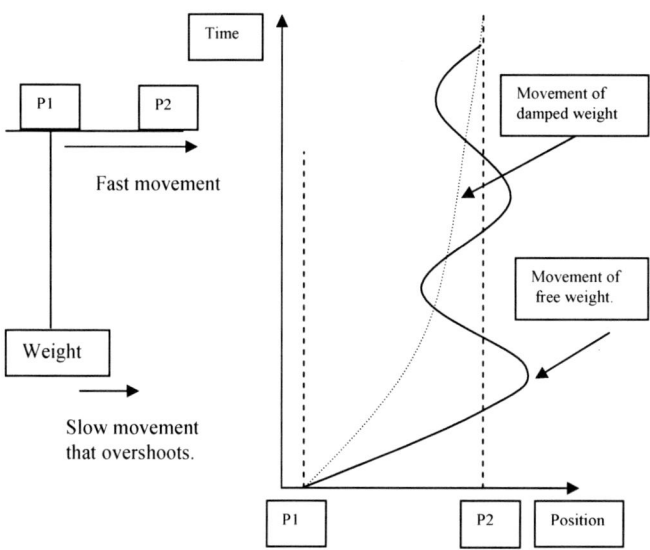

Figure 2a **Figure 2b.**

It would be easier to get hold of the weight and move it directly but in everyday life this is often not possible. This example has many analogies. We do not usually control the end product of a situation but instead set in motion the activities that are necessary to bring about the desired end. This may require a communications chain involving a number of people - all of whom introduce delays and modifications based on their interpretation of the event. It will take time to implement the changes. If management attempts to force through a major change too quickly then staff may overreact and require corrective actions to be taken later. The situation is even more critical in a voluntary organisation where force must be replaced by a velvet glove, perhaps analogous to moving the weight slowly.

A more rigid structure can be seen in the armed forces when it is necessary for orders to be carried out immediately regardless of circumstances. In the less hectic environment of civilian life this would be equivalent to putting staff into an intellectual straitjacket with no options to make decisions. The ultimate in a rigid structure is a computer system in which the only flexibility is provided by the options foreseen by the programmer at the design stage. Rigid systems can have problems of their own.

There are many situations where it is desirable to switch a situation quickly without it going into oscillation like a pendulum. The desired position is the optimum and there is less benefit if the system fluctuates.

Fluctuations can be minimised by damping as discussed in chapter 1 where a pendulum-like action can be restrained from swinging too far by immersing it in water or oil, for example in a yacht where rolling is reduced by the resistance of the keel moving laterally through the water. An improvement in stability, and more comfort for the crew, is achieved if a sail is hoisted so that the force of air on the sail further limits the rolling of the vessel. In many other situations, damping is a costly way of achieving stability, as manifested in a bureaucracy where resistance to change can be so prevalent that little happens to upset the status quo.

Is it possible to move the point of suspension of the pendulum (the fulcrum) quickly without causing subsequent swinging? An answer is to be found in the schoolboy's game of conkers. After the conker has been hit, it swings violently on the end of its string. With practice the schoolboy can quell the swing by moving his hand so as to counteract it. This method might not be as quick as steadying the conker with the other hand, but it is nevertheless effective. There is evidence of this skill in the crane driver who lifts a heavy load through the air and expertly moves it in an arc to a waiting receptacle with no noticeable swing of the load. The essence of the problem is to understand the rules for moving the fulcrum of the suspended pendulum so that the pendulum stops swinging.

I saw a graphic illustration of the problem many years ago at the Institution of Electrical Engineers. Instead of a pendulum, a voltmeter with an undamped needle was used. A voltage was applied by switching on the connection to a battery. The needle overshot its position and then oscillated wildly (normally a voltmeter needle is damped so that it reaches its position smoothly in a short time). Switching on a voltage is an exceptionally rigorous test since the voltage rises instantly and it is not conceivable that a mechanical device could follow so quickly, a damped needle being comparatively slow. In order, however, for the voltmeter to accurately record the voltage applied, the needle would have to move instantly to its position and stay there without fluctuation. The interesting question posed at the seminar was: whether it is possible to modify the shape of the voltage waveform at the input to make the needle step immediately to the final position and stay there without oscillating. The problem is equivalent to the one of the schoolboy quelling the swing of the conker, or moving the weight in Figure 2 by moving the fulcrum in such a way that the weight does not subsequently swing.

Going back to the problem of the meter, the answer lay in calculating the inverse mathematical function of the needle's behaviour and using this to modify the switched voltage waveform. Referring to figure 2 it will be seen that in order to make the weight move quickly at the beginning, it is necessary to move the top of the string beyond the point P2. As the weight approaches the line P2 it needs to be slowed down by moving the string back towards P1. Subsequent potential swings of the weight would be counteracted by moving the string in opposition as illustrated in Figure 3. The movement of the weight is now improved and if the movement of the string is calculated correctly, the weight will arrive at destination P2 more quickly and without further swing. (It would be possible for the weight to be moved even more quickly (i.e. more horizontally on the graph) by moving the string further beyond P2 (off the paper) but there are usually limits to the practicable extent of the movement. This is a technique that is learned, perhaps unconsciously, by the schoolboy and no doubt by fishermen with rod and line.

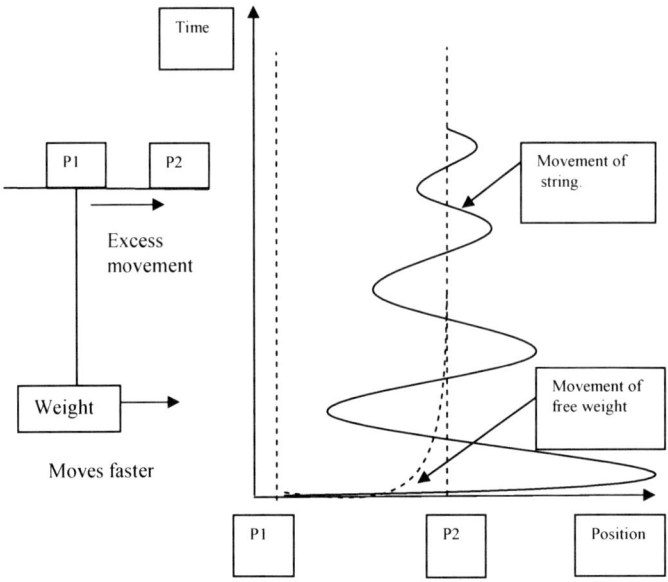

Figure 3. Changing the movement of the string to optimise movement of weight.

Some social aspects.

There are analogies in other walks of life. A company starts a production line and needs to step up sales to equal the rate of production. It is in the nature of markets that they are slow to respond especially to a new product. A counter to this slow start in sales is to launch an initial aggressive advertising campaign, which is way beyond the level appropriate for continued business. Increasing the number of sales representatives would also achieve an initial boost to sales. The campaign must then be reduced to prevent sales exceeding the production capability but it is clear that the campaign cannot be calculated with the mathematical precision applied to the meter needle. Whether the campaign can be fine-tuned to generate a constant demand must depend on the experience of the management. The advertising campaigns in the 20th century, for soap powder and detergents, had these characteristics.

A further example occurs when a manager, and especially a leader, takes over a reluctant group of people and has to get them up to speed. If leadership is by example, then the leader must initially put in an effort that exceeds the level that can be maintained. When the group is working effectively then the leader can be more relaxed.

There is some similarity in the technique used by the union negotiator when presenting a case to management for a pay rise. A demand in excess of that expected is made and the management counteracts with an offer below the expected. Subsequent bargaining reduces the "swing of the offers" but the level of increase was probably decided by both sides in advance of the negotiation and the expectation remains the same provided the negotiators perform the ritual correctly.

The analogy of the schoolboy moving the string, to compensate for the swing of a conker, can be taken further. Let the swing of the pendulum represent an argument between two people, which sways back and forth, and suppose the amount of swing represents the degree of anger on each side. When the pendulum is at one extreme, the amount of swing can be reduced by moving the fulcrum in the direction of the pendulum weight. In this analogy movement of the fulcrum, towards some middle point, represents a degree of appeasement by the other side which reduces the heat of the argument. The skill of the professional negotiator lies in assessing the optimum middle ground and steering the fulcrum towards it.

Summary.

The pendulum has been discussed in this chapter because of its familiarity. It has a similar action to the delayed negative feedback loop. Delayed negative feedback causes a system to oscillate and it is desirable to find ways of reducing the swing or oscillation to a minimum. Damping is effective and cheap in some situations but costly in others. If a system is well known and can be analysed, then it is likely it can be modelled so that changes in behaviour can be anticipated in sufficient time for corrective action to be taken. Exceptional delays in feedback can turn the negative loop into a positive one with the instability that that implies.

A system can be made to react more quickly by providing excessive influence and then correcting it to a moderate level before the system moves too far. The swing in a situation might be subdued by moving the fulcrum to reduce its energy. These observations apply also to other situations, which will be explored in subsequent chapters.

CHAPTER 3.   VICIOUS LOOPS.

Introduction.

The vicious loop is perhaps one of the more important positive feedback loops that will be encountered. Usually termed a vicious circle or a vicious spiral, it is associated with systems that run out of control with the potential for a disaster unless efforts are taken to counteract the trend. The positive loop does not have to be a disaster; it is sometimes beneficial. It is then often termed a virtuous circle. The mechanism in both cases is identical; it is the quantity that is circulating around the loop that is usually different. The more important criterion, however, is whether or not it is under our control.

A simple example is a snowball. Rolling a snowball in the snow so that it gathers up more snow to make a bigger snowball (strictly a snow cylinder) is a good way to start the base of a snowman. The snow ball does not get bigger indefinitely because the person pushing it (the "engine" of the loop) is unable to push it further when it becomes too heavy to move. It is a different matter if the ball is rolling down a mountainside and gathering speed and weight as it goes. This is a potentially dangerous situation that might end with the ball crashing into people but hopefully a tree or a rock that is stable enough to withstand the onslaught. A crash of some kind is the likely end to a vicious loop. The snowball might spin so fast that it flies apart but it is possible that it arrives at the end of the slope and settles in a valley where gravity (the "engine" of the loop) ceases to have effect - analogous to a system designed to be self-limiting.

A positive loop is valuable when good planning and design keep it under control. The control may be inherent in the design, or it might be achieved by introducing a negative feedback loop at a suitable stage in its growth. Thus a fire is beneficial in the home but a disaster if it gets out of control. Here there is a positive loop as burning fuel heats up adjacent fuel until it ignites. It is kept under control by limiting the amount of fuel and oxygen available so that it burns at the rate required for comfort. A forest fire might not stop until there is no more forest left to burn, Figure 1a illustrates the loop.

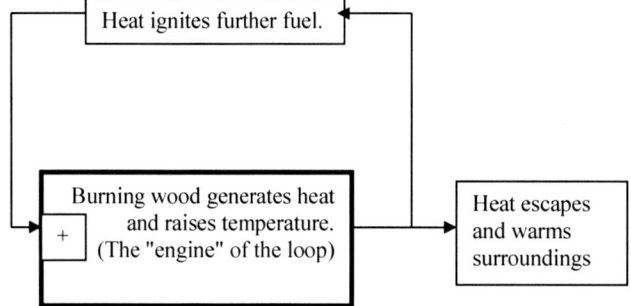

Figure 1a.

The Scoldent list..

There are various ways in which a positive loop may be controlled, either by design or by force of circumstances. Taking an analogy from electronic systems in which the theory is well developed the following methods can be considered:

1. Saturation;
2. Cut-off;
3. Open-loop;
4. Low gain;
5. Delay in feedback;
6. External force or influence;
7. Negative feedback loop;
8. Theme change.

The first letters of this list spell out "scoldent", in future these criteria will be called the scoldent list.

1. Saturation implies that a necessary ingredient for the "engine" of the loop has reached a maximum and cannot be supplied at a greater rate to satisfy the increasing demand. Thus a car engine draws fuel to generate power, a part of which is used to pump more fuel to the engine. The supply of fuel, however, is limited by the rate at which the fuel pump can supply fuel to run the engine at

an increasing speed (this is in part restricted by the diameter of the fuel pipes) and the supply line eventually becomes saturated.

2. Cut-off as the term implies occurs when a necessary ingredient is unavailable. Switching off the fuel pump for the engine is an example.

3. An open loop occurs when none of the output is fed back to the input (it ceases to be a loop). If a baker stopped reinvesting some of the profits from the business to buy flour then the business would cease to function and no further profits would be generated.

4. Low gain will occur when the loop's "engine" is inefficient. This may be due to poor quality of ingredients such as damp wood that does not burn well or dry snow that does not stick together well enough to make a large snowball. In the case of a business, siphoning off money for taxes or other expenses may lower the gain. A bureaucracy in a business is a likely candidate for low efficiency and so is excessive government regulation whether from Brussels or elsewhere.

5. Delay in the feedback loop will slow down the rate of increase of the loop. If customers are late in paying invoices then the company's investment in resources will be slower and a degree of business opportunity will be lost.

6. An external force will be any outside influence that is in opposition to the mechanism of the loop. It might be a legal restraint on a monopoly; a rock in the path of the runaway snowball or the fire brigade dealing with a house fire.

7. The negative feedback loop needs to be of sufficient influence to overcome the gain of the positive one and come into play before the system gets out of hand. The governor, on the steam engine mentioned in chapter 1, must be set to reduce the volume of steam before the engine runs at too high a speed. There may be innate negative loops. The friction in a car engine, and the wind resistance which increases as the square of the speed of the car, are factors determining its top speed. The engine will have been designed with these forces in mind and full throttle without these opposing forces (because the engine is out of gear) is likely to damage the engine. The feedback loop of a successful family business will become subject to a negative loop when the income is sufficient and they can reduce their workload to maintain a level income.

8. A theme change could be met by a change in the control method as a result of experience. A system will have been designed by anticipating the situations that are likely to occur. Some of these forecasts will be wrong and accordingly

the system can be improved by modification.

A feature of the positive loop is that it may be insignificant at the early stages in a system's lifetime and other features dwarf its effects so that it is not recognised. In the course of time, however, the loop may go on increasing until it achieves a dominant position unless steps are taken to keep it under control. A positive loop that continues indefinitely must end in disaster; whether it is a revving car engine; a population explosion; or a successful business that grows into a monopoly.

The well-known proverb that a stitch in time saves nine is, in effect, a cautionary tale about a positive loop. As each stitch breaks, the strain on the remaining stitches increases so that another stitch is likely to break and so on. The strands of a rope suffer a similar fate; when the first strand breaks the strain on the remaining strands is increased. It is interesting to note that simple knitting is an example of a positive loop with a gain of 1. As each stitch unravels the next becomes a candidate for unravelling but each must unravel, in turn, one at a time. On the other hand damage to paint, which lets in the weather, is a further example where early correction saves much effort later on. If the rate of damage is proportional to the area of damage to a painted surface then it is a candidate for an exponential increase in the cost of repair.

Controlling a potential disaster.

It will be useful to consider two examples of positive loops and how corrective action can be applied. A fire is an example where it is important to maintain a satisfactory degree of heat generation so that the fire is contained within safe limits. The Scoldent list will be examined for controlling a fire. (Figure 1b, which illustrates the methods, is Figure 1a with the seven controlling methods added in boxes).

1. Saturation would occur if the delivery system for essential ingredients were restricted from supplying the ingredients above a safe limit. This might be the pump for an oil burner, or a narrow tube that restricts the rate of oil flow. A similar argument will apply to a gas fire. The supply of the oxygen necessary for combustion of all normal fuels can also be restricted. A conventional stove does this by closing off the air intake to keep the rate of burning at a slow level. It is important in the case of a house fire to keep the doors and windows shut so as to restrict the flow of air to the fire to be as small as possible.

2. Cut-off is a more dramatic form of 1. Whereas saturation implies that

flow is restricted but maintained at an appropriate level, cut-off implies removing combustible material altogether. A fire blanket prevents air, and in consequence oxygen, from reaching the fuel. A fire extinguisher, which aims to block oxygen from reaching the fire, is a preferred method for petrol and oil fires. In the case of a gas fire or an oil burner it will mean simply turning off the tap.

3. An open-loop system occurs when the feedback line is cut. The feedback loop in a fire is the heat flowing from the burning material to other combustible material and causing it to burn. A wall of fire retardant could be used to interrupt the path. For a wood fire this could be achieved by separating the wood so that further wood does not get heated sufficiently to ignite. A forest fire might be arrested by chopping down a swathe of trees that is wide enough to prevent sparks flying across the gap to the forest beyond.

4. Low gain in a fire is the bug bear of the gardeners bonfire or the Boy Scout trying to light a campfire with one match. Damp wood will ensure that the gain, and in consequence the loop gain, is low. Various woods burn slowly even when dry. The fire that is out of control needs the gain reduced in order to limit the spread of the fire. Water on the fuel is the usual candidate. If houses are in the path of a dangerous fire then wetting the surface, especially in the case of a thatched roof, is a deterrent provided the heat is not so intense as to evaporate the water.

5. Delay in feedback prevents a fire from being an explosion. A feature of explosives is that the combustible material is in intimate contact with the chemicals required for a reaction to take place. Such reactions are so fast that the rise in temperature and pressure is considerable and these factors further accelerate the reaction.

6. An external force is likely to be in the form of the fire engine with a copious supply of water and extinguishing foam. Alternatively the combustible material might be moved away from the heat.

7. Some of the methods described in this section could be considered to fall under more than one category. A negative loop might incorporate several of them. For example an automatic mechanism that separates wood fuel, if the temperature rises above a threshold, would accomplish the task of a negative feedback loop. The action could be performed by a human being who then forms part of the loop. Automatic methods are used in gas or electric ovens that incorporate a

thermostat to control the supply of gas or electricity so as to maintain the temperature required. A thermostat to control the airflow may be preferred for solid fuels.

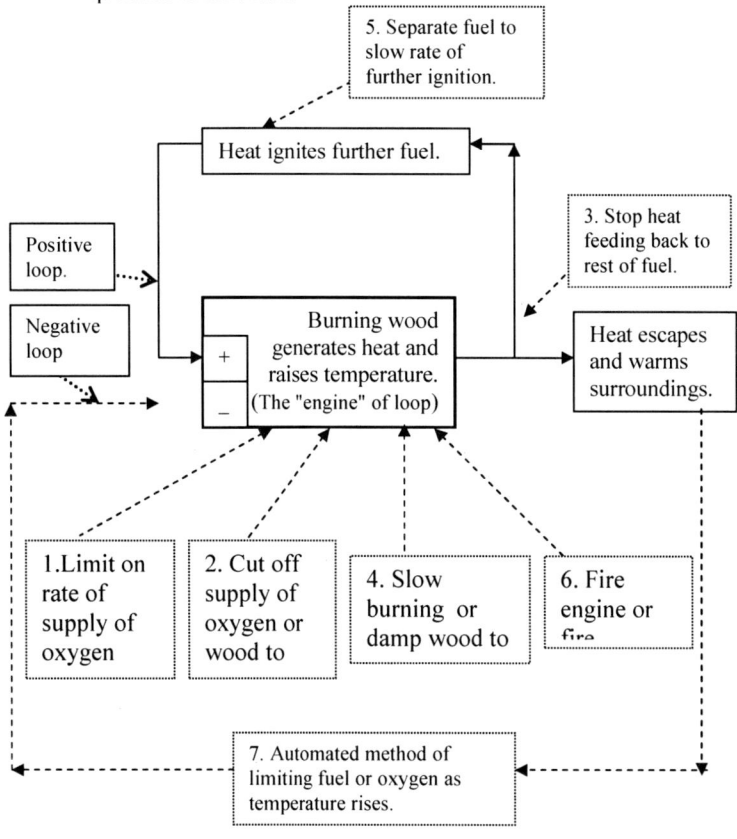

```
                              ┌─────────────────────┐
                              │ 5. Separate fuel to │
                              │ slow rate of        │
                              │ further ignition.   │
                              └─────────────────────┘
                    ┌──────────────────────────┐
                    │ Heat ignites further fuel│
                    └──────────────────────────┘
                                              ┌──────────────────┐
                                              │ 3. Stop heat     │
  ┌──────────┐                                │ feeding back to  │
  │ Positive │                                │ rest of fuel.    │
  │ loop.    │                                └──────────────────┘
  └──────────┘
                    ┌──────────────────────────┐  ┌──────────────┐
  ┌──────────┐      │ Burning wood generates   │  │ Heat escapes │
  │ Negative │      │ heat and raises          │  │ and warms    │
  │ loop     │  +   │ temperature.             │  │ surroundings.│
  └──────────┘  –   │ (The "engine" of loop)   │  └──────────────┘
                    └──────────────────────────┘

  ┌────────┐ ┌────────┐ ┌────────┐ ┌────────┐
  │1.Limit │ │2. Cut  │ │4. Slow │ │6. Fire │
  │on rate │ │off     │ │burning │ │engine  │
  │of      │ │supply  │ │or damp │ │or fire │
  │supply  │ │of      │ │wood to │ │        │
  │of      │ │oxygen  │ │        │ │        │
  │oxygen  │ │or wood │ │        │ │        │
  └────────┘ └────────┘ └────────┘ └────────┘

             ┌────────────────────────────┐
             │ 7. Automated method of     │
             │ limiting fuel or oxygen as │
             │ temperature rises.         │
             └────────────────────────────┘
```

Figure 1b. The application of the first seven methods to control a fire.

8. A theme change in this example implies changing the design

of the fireplace; maybe changing from a wood fire to a gas fire with artificial logs. For a forest fire it might come about by planning new forests with extra spacing between trees or by interspersing them with slow burning woods.

A Beneficial loop.

The rate at which a positive loop increases is dependent on the loop gain and it is necessary for there to be an impulse or a nudge to get the loop started. A seed farmer can illustrate this. Suppose that the farmer starts with one seed, which produces a flower that generates 100 seeds. The farmer sells 90% of the crop and retains 10% for planting the next year. 10 seeds are then planted producing a crop of 1000 seeds and 100 are retained for planting, and so on. The "engine" of the loop is the seed drawing on sunlight and nutrients to increase by 100 times Figure 2a.

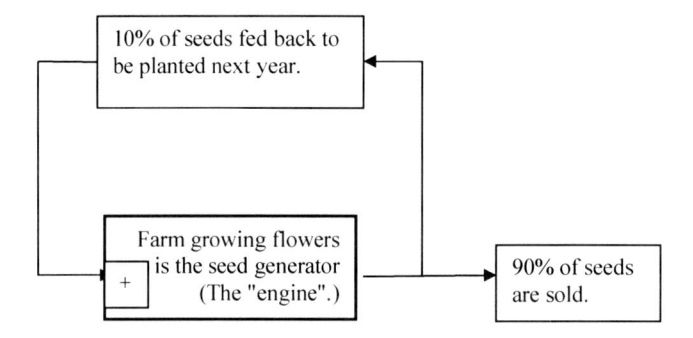

```
          ┌──────────────────────────┐
          │ 10% of seeds fed back to │◄────┐
   ┌─────►│ be planted next year.    │     │
   │      └──────────────────────────┘     │
   │                                       │
   │      ┌──────────────────────────┐     │
   │      │   Farm growing flowers   │     │   ┌──────────────┐
   │      │   is the seed generator  │─────┴──►│ 90% of seeds │
   └──────│ +    (The "engine".)     │         │ are sold.    │
          └──────────────────────────┘         └──────────────┘
```

Figure 2a.

The gain of the "engine" is 100. Since only 10% are fed back around the loop, the loop gain is 10. Accordingly the rate of increase is 10 times per year. (In practice of course the farmer is likely to take out a loan to tide him over the first few years and plant 100% of his seeds each year. The loop gain would then be 100 and the turnover a million seeds after three years; more than sufficient to repay the loan with interest.).

There are three points to be noted about this example. Firstly the business required the "impulse" of the first seed to activate the loop. Secondly the rate of increase of the business depends directly on the proportion of the output that is fed back around the loop and thirdly it depends on how quickly the output is fed back. If the farmer found a seed which flowered and produced seed in six months, and the farm benefited from a climate which allowed the seed to be sown twice a year, then the million would be achieved in 18 months. In practice it is doubtful that this rate of increase would continue since various difficulties would arise that, in effect, would modify the loop.

Methods for restricting the runaway expansion of a positive loop are important when the potential outcome is dangerous. When, however, the loop is performing a useful function for an expanding business, such as the seed farmer, the scoldent list represents situations to be avoided. (Figure 2b, which illustrates the system, is Figure 1b with the Scoldent situations added in boxes).

1. Saturation implies that the throughput of the seed farm cannot be increased due to limitations in the ingredients whereby the seeds germinate and become flowers. The area of the farm is such a limitation since the seeds must be spaced appropriately to receive their share of sunlight and fertiliser. The purchase of more land as the farm becomes successful (which implies modifying the loop) will increase the yield to a higher saturation level.

2. Cut-off in which the "engine" of the loop ceases to function could arise if the flowers were not pollinated because, for example, bees could not gain access to the crop.

3. An open loop system, in which none of the seed is replanted, would imply that all the seed is sold and the farmer is probably retiring, or changing to farm a different crop.

4. Low gain might be caused by a reduction in the effectiveness of any of the ingredients of the farming process: e.g. diseased seed in which only a portion of the seed is viable; insufficient sunlight or water to support the full potential of the seed.

5. Delay in the feedback might be caused by planting the seed too late in the year to obtain a crop that year but could also arise if the crop were a biennial variety which only flowers every second year.

6. An external force or influence could take a variety of forms. Taxation at a level that causes the farmer to reduce the work force, or a bureaucracy that takes up much of the time the farmer could otherwise apply to running the farm. In the case of a poppy farmer feeding the illegal drug industry, the external force might be the intervention of

government or a foreign power intent on destroying the poppy fields.

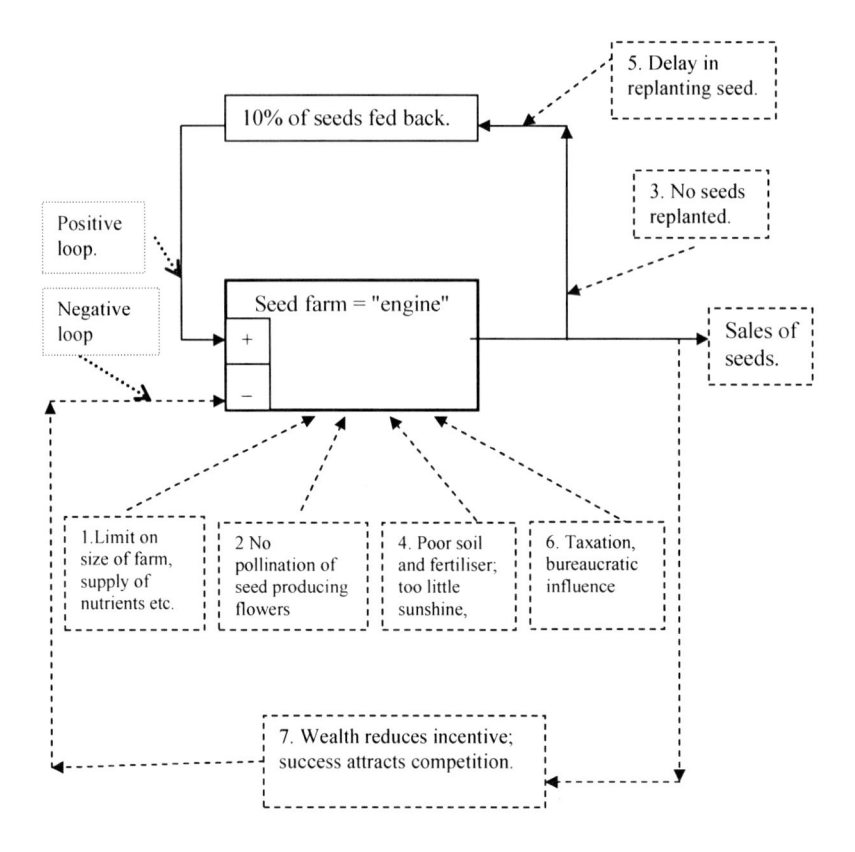

Figure 2b. Example of factors which reduce the effect of a beneficial positive loop.

7. Negative feedback is likely when the farmer has reached a level of prosperity at which the incentive to work hard is reduced. If output

reduces too much then in the nature of negative loops to maintain a stable condition the farmer increases the amount he works to compensate for the reduction.

8. A theme change may be needed if the seed farmer chose the wrong seed for the climate. Either the seed type would need changing or the farm should be set up elsewhere. Alternatively it may be more viable to build glass houses to contain more heat.

The effect of change in loop gain.

It is possible to have a positive feedback loop that does not increase in value. This occurs if the loop gain is less than or equal to one. Thus if the seed farmer keeps only 1% of the crop for replanting (the loop gain is 1% of 100 = 1) it will just replace the quantity required to maintain the output at 100 seeds (based on a gain of 100 - giving 100 seeds per flower).

If the loop gain is reduced below one then the farm will decline. Suppose, for example, the farmer has reached an output of 800 seeds. If he then reduces the number of seeds replanted to 1/2% of the crop (the loop gain is 1/2% of 100 = 1/2) then 4 seeds will be sown (1/2% of 800 = 4). The yield the next year will be 400; then 200 the following year and so on until the farm ceases to function.

It is evident that any successful enterprise must have at least one positive feedback loop with significant gain in order to succeed. The seed farmer with a loop gain of only one will not survive since, in reality, there will be many adverse influences which will drain some of the productivity. A proportion of the seed will fail and in adverse conditions so may the flowers. The successful business will have overcome many problems for which it needed a surplus of resources.

There are numerous examples of the positive feedback loop in action ranging from crowd behaviour; fashion and self-confidence to Parkinson's law in administration and survival criteria. These will be discussed in subsequent chapters.

Sigmoid response.

Methods 1 and 7 above are likely to cause the loop performance to follow a sigmoid pattern as shown in figure 3. Method 1 implies that an ingredient, which contributes to the loop, becomes more difficult to obtain. The characteristic will then show a sharp increase initially as the positive loop gets underway, but the loop gain is reduced as the supply of an essential ingredient becomes more difficult and the saturation level is reached.

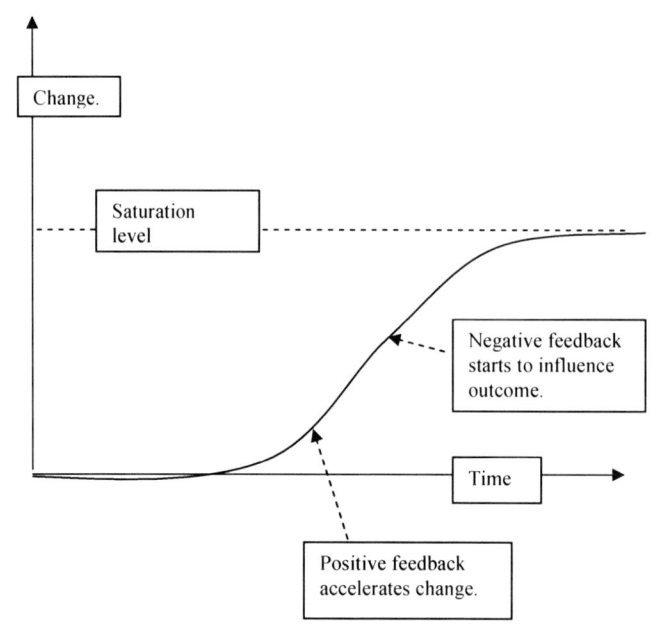

Figure 3. A sigmoid response.

Similarly under method 7, a negative loop will often be a proportional one in which the correcting force is increased as the system departs from optimum. Accordingly the negative loop gradually opposes the positive loop more and more until it becomes dominant and the curve reaches the maximum shown as the saturation level in figure 3. Supposing the baker works in a village then the business will follow this characteristic. As the baker increases the output of loaves, a point will be reached when everyone has enough loaves and the market saturates.

Negative to positive loops.

The electric switch was mentioned in chapter 1. This and similar systems are interesting examples of the transfer from a negative to a positive feedback loop. The diagram in figure 4a illustrates the movement of the switch contact in response to the movement of the knob when there is no spring influencing the movement. A is off and B is on - the transition between the two positions is gradual and there would be no "click" from the switch. It is however important that the contact in an electric switch moves more quickly than the knob to reduce sparking between the contacts.

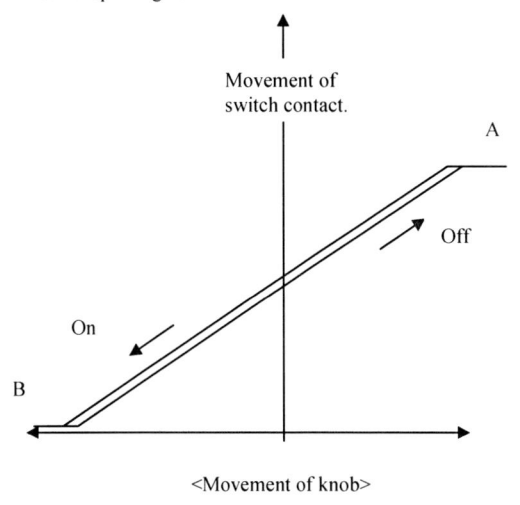

Figure 4a. Switch changeover without feedback.

In order to cause a rapid movement of the contact, even when the knob is moved slowly, a spring is incorporated. This initially opposes movement of the contact but at a critical position of the knob, it reverses and supports the movement. Figure 4b shows the movement of the contact as the knob is moved in response to the action of the spring. Initially the contact moves slowly from the lower position and the spring opposes with increasing resistance (negative feedback). As the force on the knob increases further and the knob moves beyond the mid-point, the spring reverses and helps the knob to move the contact over (positive feedback). In this case the click of the switch can be heard as the spring reverses to cause a sudden transition. The reverse happens on the way back.

The curve traced out is similar to the sigmoid loop in two directions (although in this case with a sharper change). Curves of this nature are known as hysteresis loops, they are familiar in magnetism when the residual magnetism in a material opposes a magnetic field until it is overcome and switched in the same direction. This phenomenon is important for the storage of data on magnetic materials, they played an important role in the memories for early computers.

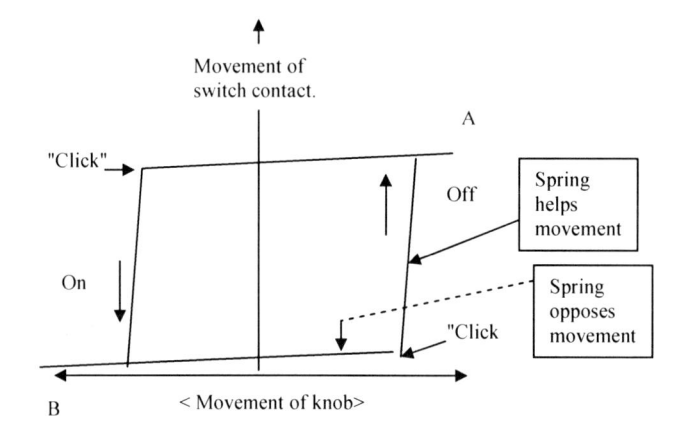

Figure 4b. Change from negative to positive feedback loop.

This characteristic occurs in Judo. The expert initially pushes against the opponent, and then quickly changes to pull in the direction the opponent is moving so that both people are supplying the energy in the direction of the throw. The characteristic also applies to the recognition of data: for example when people try to recognise the words on a signpost. Words that are not readable from a distance become more recognisable as the signpost is approached. On moving away, it is possible to continue recognising the words at a greater distance than previously because of their familiarity until eventually it is not possible to tell whether someone has not changed them while your back was turned. When listening to conversation at a noisy cocktail party it is necessary to stand closer to someone whose accent is unfamiliar, but as their accent becomes more understandable it can be heard from a greater distance. One's own name can likewise be heard from further away than less familiar words.

The first half of this loop is likely to occur in solving a crossword puzzle. As more spaces are filled with letters so previously difficult clues become more solvable.

Similar characteristics are found in the relation between crime and law enforcement, and crowd psychology. These will be discussed in later chapters.

Monopoly and the remainder problem.

The monopoly gives rise to a problem in which the behaviour is comparable to a positive feedback loop. If a near monopoly buys up a scarce resource, such as land, then the remaining land will rise in price significantly as free land becomes scarce. In fact if the cost of the resource increases in proportion to its scarcity then cost increases faster than an exponential rate as the resource is bought up. (If the monopoly has cornered 90% of the market then increasing its share by about 5% to 95% causes the free resource to diminish by 50% (i.e. from 10% to 5%). If value is proportional to scarcity then the resource will double in price.) Another example that would meet the remainder criterion is in the supply of fish in areas where over-fishing has depleted stocks. The cost of catching a fish increases in proportion to the scarcity of fish. If the cost of the fishing boat and crew is constant and the catch of fish halves, then the cost per fish is doubled.

Summary

1. A vicious loop occurs when positive feedback accentuates an undesirable situation.
2. It is important to curtail the expansion of a loop before it gets out of hand.
3. If there is no limitation on the expansion of the loop then a disaster of some kind is inevitable.
4. Measures such as the scoldent list suggest ways of alleviating problems.
5. Positive loops need not be vicious they can also be beneficial in the right circumstances.
6. Switching from negative to positive loops is an essential factor in the efficient operation of some systems.
7. Monopoly is a likely outcome of positive loops in business and in consequence a scarcity of resources for others.

Chapter 4.   Maximisation of inequality.

The Tournament Ploy.

When I was a boy my parents took me on holiday to a hotel which had a tennis court. My opportunities to practise on the public courts at home had been limited due to lack of funds. Accordingly the idea of a free court, with unlimited opportunity to play on it, was an attractive one. My expectations were soon to be squashed however. The experienced players immediately organised a tennis tournament, and of course the players in the tournament had priority over the court. The better players stayed in the knockout tournament longer and consequently had more games. To put this in feedback loop terms: the more experienced the player, the more experience that player would enjoy as shown in the simple diagram - Fig. 1.

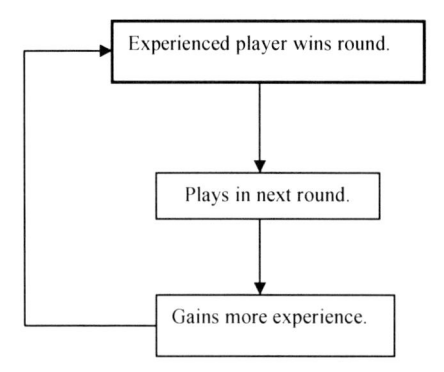

```
    ┌──────► Experienced player wins round.
    │                │
    │                ▼
    │         Plays in next round.
    │                │
    │                ▼
    └─────── Gains more experience.
```

Figure 1. The Tournament Ploy.

This form of loop is not limited to tennis; it will apply to tournaments of other games where the facilities are limited. Cricket provides another example of the positive loop. The better the batsman the longer he is likely to stay at the wicket and accordingly the more likely he is to practise his technique than the less experienced; similarly for the bowler. There is also some degree of "the better player enjoying more of the game" in other team games such as soccer, rugger or hockey. These are situations where others are more likely to pass the ball to the better player.

I am sure we have all felt sympathy for snooker players who stand by watching their opponent clear the table with a high scoring break. The theme for maximising inequality only holds, of course, provided there are limited facilities on which to practise.

This form of positive feedback loop is not confined to team games. Experiences with windsurfing illustrate very well that the better you are the more experience you get at surfing. The beginner gains a lot of experience in climbing back onto the surfboard and becomes expert at that particular manoeuvre. This can be thought of as the ability to clear a hurdle. It is not possible to gain experience in a hurdles race until you can jump over a hurdle. There are many situations in life where this analogy applies: such as passing an examination in order to qualify for a job, or having strength to survive against competition.

It should perhaps be observed that not all competitive games have this characteristic. An exception is golf where inexperienced golfers play more shots than their opponents. Consequently they get more practice - especially, one supposes, in the rough.

It would be possible to plan a form of tournament in which the least experienced player gets the most experience. The rules would have to be changed so that the person who loses a round moves onto the next round, and the winner drops out of the tournament. The last to lose is clearly the worst player. Whereas this may sound ridiculous there is an analogy to this form of organisation in the chapter on education. A partial solution to the problem in cricket has been tried where the weakest batsmen bat first and accordingly get the chance to play before the captain declares.

The tendency of the positive loop to increase inequality is seen in many other situations. If two children in a family have unequal levels of confidence then the difference between them is likely to increase with time. The more confident one may acquire the habit of making the decisions and enjoy an increase in confidence. The converse effect may occur with the other who becomes progressively less confident. It is likely, however, that this loop effect will be neutralised, to some extent, by the parents in order to give the second child a better chance. There has also been evidence of attempts within the education system to hide the differentials between children by the removal of competitive sports. Some educationists have been trying to remove the competition in other spheres.

Inequality and Management.

There may be particular reasons why it is preferable to introduce inequality between people; for example between the governors and the governed. It will be noted that when people within a company are promoted, there is a learning period while they grow into the job. It is usual to send them on courses that increase their management capability. The separation between the ones promoted, and former colleagues, grows as more experience, and confidence in the job, is gained. This is probably a situation where it is important to accentuate the differences in order for the higher management to be accepted by the staff reporting to them.

The system may be unfair if there are candidates of essentially equal ability, but positive loops are not about fairness; they may specifically accentuate unfairness. This could be necessary in the interest of improving efficiency (used here only in the sense of maximising profit or output; rather than other ways of defining efficiency such as the ratio of profit to human stress). The accentuation of differences has been most pronounced in the military services. Here the lines of demarcation have been clearly indicated in order to give the authority required at different levels in the command structure and the attendant discipline that this maintains.

Maximisation of Unfairness.

If employees of a company experience unfairness then so may the companies themselves. In the early 1980s there was a rumour of a policy of "The maximisation of unfairness". It related, I understand, to the funding of Research and Development. Public funding of companies is expected to be channelled where it will do most good. A company which is rich and successful will be a better candidate (other things being equal) to achieve a target than one which is apparently less successful and evidently more in need of the funds. The rich and successful company thereby becomes more so, and the demarcation between these different companies becomes greater. The result may be that the smaller company can no longer compete in that field of endeavour.

The tendency for the differentiation between the rate at which companies and other institutions increase may not be something that is specifically due to merit or fault. There is a natural tendency in a free society for people to congregate amongst like-minded people. This is particularly true of intellectual expertise in science and engineering. Thus a renowned research laboratory will attract high calibre research scientists who will further increase the renown of the laboratory. Similarly professional engineers will only accept contributions from people of similar intellectual calibre. This collection of people introduces the other feedback effect whereby group members trigger further ideas amongst the group. This enhances the creativity of the group. The effect of this symbiosis is to maximise the inequality between that laboratory or institution and others.

Physical conflict.

The normal aim of parties in a conflict is to maximise their advantage in order to overcome the opposition quickly. Such a situation is more likely when both parties believe they have a chance of winning and therefore they are, at the beginning of the conflict, roughly equal in ability. In the physical case there is usually the opportunity to weaken the adversary significantly to the point where he is unable to defend himself.

Boxing is an example where the opponent commences a fight on roughly even terms but is progressively weakened to the point where he is unable to defend himself adequately. The rate of decline in defensive ability is therefore accentuated. Inequality is increased to the point where there is no longer any opposition. In modern times the referee is expected to step in when the result of the fight is clear and before significant damage is done.

This can also be seen in the methods of hunting by wildlife. A pack of hyenas attacking a wildebeest choose the weakest member of the herd. The wildebeest is initially stronger than any member of the pack and it puts up a considerable fight. The pack progressively injures the beast until it gradually has less strength to defend itself. Further attack is therefore easier and victory then follows quickly due to the rapid increase in inequality.

There is an analogy to the starving chicken, which needs to have a certain degree of strength to overcome opposition when competing for food. A progressive loss of strength makes the end more certain.

The particular case where it is important to maximise inequality occurs in war. Initially there is increasing opposition to an intruder as the defending nation mobilises its forces to oppose the invading party. This is a negative feedback effect that arises in trying to maintain the status quo. If the defence can be mobilised fast enough, to prevent outright victory by the invader, then the war enters a more prolonged phase. Each side endeavours to weaken the other to gain the advantage and increase the inequality in its favour.

If nation A is stronger then there will be proportionately more casualties on the side of Nation B. The inequality of the two sides increases thereby increasing the opportunity for Nation A to conquer. The situation may of course be altered by support from other nations, which changes the balance of power. The ultimate in inequality may not be reached since there may be terms for surrender when the outcome is clear. Alternatively one of the higher powers may become a referee to stop the fight and introduce sanctions against further slaughter.

The degree of inequality has often been limited in recent times by virtue of the media coverage. Public opinion has demanded a limitation on the extent of the force that is used. This inequality limitation is one of the effects that a democracy has on hostilities. It may, in effect, prevent a war reaching a final conclusion. The effect has been reported extensively in respect of the American war in North Vietnam. When the slaughter was shown on television the public became increasingly opposed to the war and were eventually influential in stopping it.

Conflicts need not involve physical violence. Economic strength may be an effective weapon in demolishing a competitor as discussed in the section on monopoly. It is likely that future wars will target a nation's computer networks. Media coverage, which in the past has elicited sympathy and outrage against slaughter, may be less effective in limiting the extent of the sabotage. It is possible the media networks themselves will be destroyed.

Many developing countries have been caught in a positive feedback loop that accentuates inequality. In consequence they may be unable to compete with the more capital intensive and efficient nations. Their situations have been exacerbated by loans negotiated by banks from the developed countries. Unable to pay the rate of interest an increasing debt was incurred with no prospect of retrieving the situation. There is a clear analogy to the theme of the profit or loss making business. Profit is needed in order to invest in further business, as discussed in chapter 12.

Monopoly.

The purpose of conflict is often to create the conditions of a monopoly in respect of some quantity. This quantity may be important insofar as it permits the owners to dictate terms to their own advantage. A monopoly and a dictatorship have similarities in their aim at maximising inequality. The commercial monopoly seeks to maximise its access to a resource and thereby eliminate competition. The dictator aims to maximise the differential in power between the dictator and subordinates or at least hold it at a level that eliminates competition. This monopoly on power, and its detrimental effects on society, is recognised in the legislation that limits the power one particular company, or group of individuals, can have on the nation. The quantity that should be looked at in the feedback loop, which arises in the case of the monopoly, is not so much the resources available to the monopoly as the resources left for everyone else. Thus if an industry has monopolised the supply of 90% of raw materials; then an increase from 90% - 95% is only about 6% of the monopoly's resources. It, however, represents a reduction of 50% in the resources available to others. The proportional change in this residual quantity accentuates the effect of the inequality by a factor of about 8. Clearly as a monopoly extends its power even further so this ratio is further increased.

The issue of inequality also has some bearing on the success of a company in addition to the profit loop that is necessary for a business to expand. The competition between companies in the same line of business is likely to be influenced by the economies of scale. If the more successful business produces greater volumes of a commodity then not only are its overheads spread over a greater volume of sales but bulk buying and mass production techniques will give scope for reducing prices. The less successful company therefore falls further behind giving a situation where the loop can lead to a monopoly in the market place.

A central element in this discussion has been the role of competition in inequality. Society is reluctant to accept a monopoly situation except in small things. Depending on a person's political persuasions, greater or lesser degrees of inequality will be tolerated. The advances in science and technology are, however, creating further resources. They are likely to be utilised to a greater extent by people who are informed and educated to exploit the tools that are provided. The tendency will be to widen the gap between these people and the less informed who will be less able to compete.

There has been a startling increase in technology resources and access to information, for example via the Internet to the World Wide Web. This together with the ability to employ advanced computing technology (provided it is properly implemented) give an enterprise a significant advantage over others who do not enjoy such facilities.

Whilst this could result in the unprincipled buying up of all the resources that society has to offer it is evident that government must limit the extent so that there is sufficient left for the less able. The danger of creating a society of no-hopers, in which a feedback loop (and consequently sanctions for bad behaviour) ceases to exist, is discussed in chapter 10.

Compensating for inequality.

Methods for counteracting the effect of the positive loop were discussed in chapter 3. Two of this chapter's topics - the tournament ploy and war - will be considered using the Scoldent list as an exercise.

Counters to the tournament ploy:

1. *Saturation* implies limiting the number of games a guest can play; perhaps placing a limit of two per day.
2. *Cut off* would occur if a player were prohibited from playing another game until all other guests had played.
3. *An open loop* will be achieved if the winner does not qualify for extra games.
4. *Low gain* possibly occurs when players are exhausted.
5. *Delay in feedback* by providing enough other activities to occupy players before returning to the court.
6. *External force or influence* by a directive from the management.
7. *A negative feedback loop* would occur if the number of games played were proportional to the need to practice.
8. *Change of system* – ban the organised tournament, or provide facilities for other types of game.

War has, for centuries, occupied so many minds that it is unlikely that these methods will produce any surprises, but perhaps confirm methods already adopted:

1. *Saturation* occurs when an army is over extended and the supplies of arms and ammunition are limited by the transport services. It would also occur if the manufacture of arms reached saturation or an arms supplier placed a limit on the amount to be provided.
2. *Cut-off* of the arms supply might be either by enemy action or by sanctions by another power.
3. *Open loop* implies no counteraction by either side - due to an armistice.
4. *Low gain* occurs if the weapons are less effective, or by agreement to scale down retaliation - such as President Kennedy's policy of under-retaliation in the build up of nuclear tests.
5. *Delay in feedback* may result from an effective defence or by destroying communication lines to slow down the build up.

6. *External force or influence* typically due to a super power intervening to stop the war, or making effective sanctions.
7. *A negative feedback loop* occurred in the gulf war due to media coverage, which aroused public opinion against further action.
8. *Change of system* would imply diplomatic negotiations or other means of resolving differences.

Summary.

Maximisation of inequality can occur due to different influences:

1. From competition where the resources are limited.
2. By the symbiosis of creative people.
3. By the policy of resource providers who channel the resources where they will have most effect.
4. By the need to generate differentials between people to maintain discipline and authority.
5. By the experienced qualifying for more experience, and learning opening channels to more learning.
6. By confidence breeding greater confidence.
7. In areas of conflict where the aim is to weaken the opponent in order to maximise advantage.
8. By the desire for power by reaching a monopoly situation to limit the resources of the competition.
9. By the imprudent provision of capital to parties who, being unable to utilise them efficiently, incur greater debt.
10. By the provision of more powerful tools incorporating science and technology which enable those people who are able to exploit them to benefit to an ever-greater extent.

Chapter 5.   Feedback in the home.

A house fire is the most damaging feedback loop likely to be experienced in the home. This has been discussed in chapter 3. It should be noted that in this case the most effective application of the scoldent list is by cut-off to remove the supply of oxygen by keeping doors and windows closed if the fire should run out of control. Hopefully the smoke detector will provide early feedback with little delay in order to use a fire extinguisher before the heat escalates.

Whilst the house fire can escalate to a dangerous level, the incandescent light bulb is an example of controlled heating. As the filament heats up its resistance increases more than ten times its resistance when it is cold. This increase limits the current through the bulb to a safe level, so that the filament does not melt.

Central heating.

There are not many heating devices that have the inherent control of the light bulb. Central heating systems and hot water tanks require a thermostat to keep the temperature under control. Such thermostats are a very basic form of negative feedback loop and simply switch on and off as the temperature changes compared to the temperature setting. This on-off action is an insensitive negative feedback loop and is known as a "bang-bang" control. There is a delay before the thermostat senses the hot air coming from a radiator. If the thermostat is a long way from the radiator then the temperature of the room will fluctuate to a greater degree; it increases with the distance from the radiator. To maintain a more constant temperature it is necessary that the rate of heating is slow compared with the time taken for the sensor to operate.

A thermostat will also control the temperature of the hot water tank. The action is similar to a central heating thermostat except that the sensor is closer to the heater and the thermostat responds more quickly and the temperature is controlled more closely.

The control of water level in the cold water tank has an analogy to the thermostat. The float, which is attached to the float valve, rises with the water level. It is mainly a two state control, which is either fully on or off like the thermostat. As the full level is approached however, the valve turns off gradually so that it acts like a proportional control, which is a more sensitive feedback action. This is in contrast to some washing machines that use electrically controlled valves that switch the water flow off suddenly. The result can be hammering of the pipes as a mass of water is brought to a sudden halt.

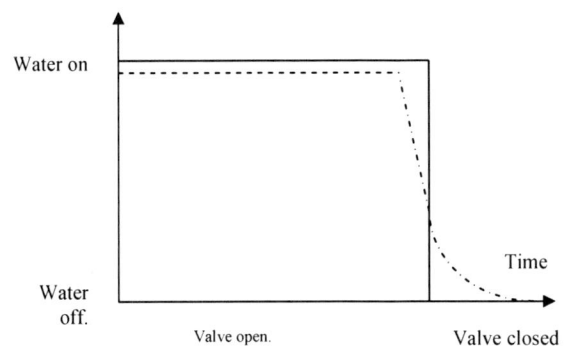

Figure 1. Electrically switched valve – solid line.
Float valve with proportional end control - -dotted line.

The Kitchen.

A gas oven typically has a bimetal strip that curves as it is heated. It can be set to obstruct the gas outlet as the required temperature is reached. It must not, however, be the on/off mode used in central heating since the gas must remain lit, but at a low rate, usually from a small bypass. Since the obstruction increases with temperature it is possible to introduce a proportional element into the control so that the temperature approaches the required level more gradually and remains more constant.

By contrast toast is subject to a positive loop. It has analogies to the more rapid melting of dirty snow in sunlight. As the toast darkens it becomes more absorbent of infrared and consequently darkens more quickly. It explains why it can be difficult to set the timing just right since a positive loop is operating and the time between browning and burning is short compared with the toasting time.

The light switch, mentioned in chapter 1, is a two state positive loop due to the action of the spring in aiding the movement in either direction. This makes a sharp movement to limit electric arcing. Arcing damages the switch contacts and shortens their life.

Another two-state loop occurs in the kitchen and is observed when a cup or saucer is cleaned with a jet of water from the tap. If there is water in the saucer then the tap may be safely turned on slowly without causing the water to be deflected out over the surroundings. The water already in the saucer quells the action of the jet. As the tap is turned on more the stronger jet starts ejecting the water in the saucer. As water is removed there is less resistance so that the rate of water removal is increased until, when the saucer is empty, the jet causes the water to splay out over the surroundings – often including the washer-upper. If the strength of the jet is decreased, a point is reached when water remains in the saucer and the resulting increase in resistance causes more water to be retained - giving a positive loop in the other direction. The same action occurs less quickly in a cup but is more likely if it has sloping sides. A spoon is another well-known candidate. My wife finds it difficult to fill the birdbath from the hose, but a jet of water is a good way to clean it out.

Whilst in the kitchen note should be made of a slippery floor. It is usually possible to recover from a slide if reacting quickly enough but as the balance is lost and a person starts falling over the angle of the leg and foot are progressively less suitable for recovery and the foot is pushed along the slippery surface. The only recovery is by emulating a soldier in studded army boots that are likely to slip on a smooth surface. He will lift his foot and stamp it down vertically below his body. The problem is exacerbated in the elderly since they often do not have reflexes fast enough to react in time. Stiction is another factor; it refers to the apparently greater friction that exists when an object is stationary, as though there is some stickiness. Once sliding commences the friction is less. Irregularities in the sliding surfaces may mesh when stationary, but jump across each other when sliding. The effect is particularly noticeable on cobblestones. Here the angle of a stone may be such as to instigate a slide, which then continues because the friction of subsequent stones in not realised as one's foot, or car tyre, jumps over the surface.

The Bathroom.

In the bathroom the most likely feedback situation to grab our attention is a cold shower when someone elsewhere in the house turns on the hot tap. When water is supplied from a hot tank via a mixer tap the resulting lower pressure of hot water causes the shower to cool rapidly as the cold water predominates. Setting the temperature in the first place can also be a problem. It is an example of a delayed negative feedback loop since the degree of mixing of hot and cold water is not assessed until it has travelled the length of the pipe feeding the shower. We soon learn that we have to be careful not to re-adjust

the tap too much in case the temperature shoots off in the other direction. It is a case where modelling is necessary: judging how much the tap needs to be turned in order to achieve the right temperature is a matter of experience. It is possible to automatically control the mixing of
the two taps, but the temperature sensor has to be placed immediately after the mixer in order to apply the correction in time. Even with such a system the sensor is unlikely to respond to temperature change quite so quickly as a naked human and it is wise to give the system time to settle down.

Whilst in the bathroom a positive loop may have been observed whenever the toilet roll comes to the end of its paper. For most of the life of the roll, the friction due to the weight of the paper on the roller is sufficient to prevent the roll unwinding. As it becomes lighter a point is reached when the weight of paper hanging down is sufficient to start unwinding the roll. Accordingly more paper is now acting to unwind the roll and a positive loop has started as shown in figure 2. It ends when all the paper is on the floor.

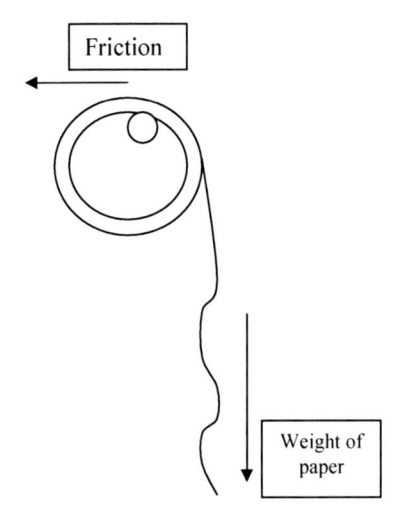

Figure 2. Instability of the nearly spent toilet roll.

This situation may not occur when rolls are bought in bundles where the roll is so squashed that it has a more elliptical cross section. The weight of paper would then have to overcome gravity when the roll is lifted at one extreme of the ellipse.

The Door.

Getting doors to shut automatically is usually accomplished by using a spring to close the door. A problem with this arrangement is that the spring gives the strongest force when the door is wide open and the weakest force when it is about to shut. A door opened wide is then likely to slam while a door barely open has insufficient force from the spring to overcome the resistance of the door latch. The situation is analogous to the pendulum where the force causing it to return to the centre increases with the distance from the centre. Ideally the door needs a strong force when it is about to close and no larger a force than is necessary to start closing the door when it is wide open. A rising hinge performs this action and may give the door (if opened sufficiently) enough momentum to shut it against the latch resistance.

The solution is found in many office doors and entrance doors to commercial buildings. A very strong spring is fitted; enough to shut the door against the latch resistance. The force acting on the door when it is wide open is opposed by a pneumatic or hydraulic system that uses the movement of the door to force fluid through a small hole. The resistance of the fluid to movement increases with speed; if the door tries to move too fast the fluid resistance is considerable. The result is a door that moves slowly to a close. When the door is countering the resistance of the latch and has slowed to almost zero then the fluid resistance essentially disappears and the full force of a strong spring is available to overcome the latch resistance. Often it will be seen that the fluid action is removed as the door is about to close so that the last inch is moved rapidly; adding to its ability to overcome the latch.

A similar action to the fluid occurs when the door is closing in an airtight room. In this case the closing door changes the air pressure in the room, which opposes the movement of the closing door. It is usually sufficient to stop slamming. An open window alters these characteristics since the air pressure can be equalised through the open window and doors frequently slam as a result.

The misconnected double electric blanket has been mentioned in chapter 1 where the husband's temperature control controls the wife's side and vice versa. If the husband gets too hot he reduces the wrongly connected temperature control on his side and cools his wife's side. She in turn turns up the temperature control and heats the husband's side further. Presumably this is a loop that does not go to the extreme since both are likely to realise that something is wrong before one of them roasts or freezes.

The Garden.

The dandelion produces approximately 70 seeds, which as is well known blow all over the garden to propagate the weed. This represents a loop with a high gain of 70 (less those seeds that fall on paving or rock).

A tree in a storm bends but has the strength to oppose the wind and recover its position. If the wind is strong enough to uproot the tree, then wind increases the effect of gravity and the two combine to make it fall over. We had an apple tree that leant away from the adjacent trees towards the light. A full crop of apples weighed down the branches on one side causing the tree to bend over. Since the tree was leaning over the effect of gravity on the extra weight caused it to lean more and was sufficient to pull the roots out of the soil.

An unwanted path in the vicinity of the home is an example of the need to stop a loop "in its tracks". Paths are started by one person. If marks are left on the grass or through bushes then it is more likely that a second person will take the same route. As more people take the route so the path becomes more established. This experience is doubtless the bane of park keepers who want people to keep off the grass!

I had this experience when a footpath was beginning in the wood behind our home. Since I did not want a footpath too close to the garden it was necessary to divert the path further away. This entailed placing some brambles on the track being established and beating a new path through the bushes further away. It soon attracted its adherents whose pounding footsteps established the alternative route.

Unstable systems show similar behaviour to a positive loop as they become increasingly unstable. An example is the chair tilted back by the occupier until it balances on its rear legs. If the occupier overbalances then recovery is possible during the first few moments but otherwise gravity rapidly takes over to force the chair over at an increasing rate. Chairs, like flower vases and many other objects, are only stable whilst their centre of gravity is vertically over the base. As soon as the object is tilted so that the centre is beyond the base then it tilts further to accentuate the instability.

It is not only gravity that shows increasing effect with instability. The wind plays a similar role with open windows and doors. If a door is nearly inline with the wind then the wind force may be insignificant. If the wind starts to blow a door open then the door presents a larger area to the wind and is subject to a greater wind force that forces the door to open further.

A stitch in time.

All these instability problems, in addition to their positive loop nature, have an element of the proverbial "stitch in time". It is necessary to act fast enough to prevent the stresses that increase instability from getting out of hand. If a stitch breaks then the stitches that remain in a garment become subject to a greater stress and accordingly break more easily. The fibres of a rope take on more stress if one of the fibres breaks; and the deterioration is progressive.

The analogy can be taken to deteriorating paintwork. As water penetrates wood or rusting metal, so the exposure to water increases and accentuates the action. The penetration of water is important in cold weather when the water has a chance to freeze. A crack in a tile or paving stone will hold water, which, if it freezes will expand and open the crack further. The next time the larger crack holds more water and freezing pushes the crack open further still.

Dirty surfaces tend to attract dirt more quickly than a shiny one because a rough surface is easier to adhere to. I notice it takes a long time for sediment to deposit on the glass side our fish tank when it is clean, but once the deposit starts it increases rapidly.

Self-compensating systems.

In contrast to the stitch in time issue, many systems are designed to be self-compensating. The auto-exposure system in a camera senses the light intensity and compensates by altering the aperture of the lens so that the film (or other recording medium) receives the appropriate amount of light. Radio and television sets incorporate negative feedback loops to compensate for the variations in strength of transmitted broadcasts signals.

One of the less comprehensible situations, in my view, is the tendency of some people to buy a larger screen television but then sit further away so that the perceived size of screen is the same.
It is similar to the theme of maintaining a constant level of inconvenience, which I discuss in another chapter.

Summary.

1. Numerous negative feedback loops have been engineered into the home to maintain a comfortable environment.
2. It is important to be aware of situations where a loop might operate and organise with those possibilities in mind.
3. Situations where a positive loop operates are often the site of a potential accident.
4. When a positive loop gets out of hand, a quick response is necessary before it becomes dangerous.
5. Positive loops can be beneficial when designed to be self-limiting

Chapter 6. The problems of no feedback.

"Power tends to corrupt, and absolute power corrupts absolutely." Lord Acton

Absolute power and the absence of feedback.

We have considered, so far, various types of feedback and have noticed that negative feedback loops tend to make systems stable whereas positive feedback loops tend to make them unstable - if they are not monitored and correction applied in time. The situation where there is no feedback at all is perhaps the worst scenario if people are not aware that there are no controlling influences to show the trend of a system. Thus the statement that power corrupts and absolute power corrupts absolutely implies that no consideration need be given to other persons, irrespective of the effect which that power is having on them.

The historian will quote many examples where dictators have been disastrous for the people. It is hoped that the idea of democracy quells that power by providing feedback from the people in terms of their ability to vote for a new government of various kinds every few years. Feedback is also necessary during the intervening period. The government may be unaware of the effect that its legislation is having unless there is feedback of some kind, hopefully through the constituency of the elected member. Alternatively opinion polls may indicate dissatisfaction with the government which must be corrected before the next election if it is to be re-elected.

There are however situations in the democratic society where feedback is lacking. Public opinion seems to have been ignored in regard to the punishment of criminals and delinquents and we have been seeing a trend in which there are many delinquents who feel they are above the law and do not feel censored by the actions of the courts. More surprising has been the closure of small post-offices in the UK. The vote was steamrollered through parliament in spite of the protests and hardship caused to the people, particularly in rural areas.

Whereas positive feedback can cause a system to run out of control; it is a situation in which the effects can be observed and measures taken to prevent a disaster. It is perhaps more pernicious when the power receives no feedback and accordingly is unaware of the effect of its actions. Alternatively the feedback is distorted by a minority of people who are not representative of the population. Groupthink, the self-reinforcement of group opinion (discussed elsewhere in this book) may be a factor here.

Remoteness between cause and effect.

A Groupthink situation is to be expected when the source of the action is remote from the effect with consequent desentisitization. War has developed to the point where the operator of a gun or the pilot of a bomber does not see the effect of the shells or bombs on human beings. The fire or explosion may confirm success in hitting the desired target but the effect on people in the vicinity is not seen. Weapons have moved a stage further and now the arsenal includes rockets that navigate their way to the target according to instructions entered into its guidance mechanism at a location remote from the target. Such weapons desensitise the users to the effects. The feedback, if it comes, will probably be via the media that has been taking extensive measures to report on carnage in war. The power of the media in this situation has been seen in recent wars when American citizens (and others) objected to the use of excessive power over other people.

Remote operation is not confined to war. Financial institutions have become increasingly international. Instead of obtaining a mortgage from the friendly local building society, it may be possible to negotiate better terms from an international institution with no connections to the local community. The mortgagee, then, is a mere number on a computer and the institution is less likely to have any compunctions about calling in the loan, consequent on default of payment, no matter what hardship ensues for the mortgagee.

There are many other situations that are less newsworthy, which nevertheless affect the lives of people every day. Many in authority make decisions in situations where they are insulated from the effects of the decision. If they suffered from the effects of their decision then many might change their minds.

Some of these situations are contentious. None more so perhaps than the right to an abortion. The more sympathetic attitude currently taken in regard to a mother-to-be who does not want a child is in sharp contrast to the attitude in former years. The issue is clearly more contentious since the unborn child is not in a position to protest - though others may argue it is more important to conceive another child at a later time when is more wanted.

The right to euthanasia for a person in full possession of their faculties would seem less contentious since such a person is fully able to provide the feedback necessary to inform the decision makers of the suffering being endured. The permission, however, may be withheld by people who have little awareness of the suffering of the person concerned or who have religious convictions that encourage them to ignore it. These are cases where there is an inadequate mechanism for the decision-makers to experience, first hand, the problems of those whose lives they are affecting.

Sharing in the cost of decisions.

There is a case to be made for decision-makers to bear the cost of their decision where this would otherwise fall on the victim. There have been reports in the press of wives in penury because their husbands are suffering from diseases such as advanced Alzheimer's that require costly nursing home treatment. Doubtless the time will come when it will be considered that the quality of life does not justify the cost of treatment to maintain a living vegetable and that euthanasia is justified - especially when the medical resources are insufficient to treat everyone including those whose quality of life would be deemed to be more worthwhile. In the mean time some local authorities may demand the income of one partner to pay for care, leaving the spouse with limited means.

The Child Support Agency in the UK (CSA), at the end of the 20th century, provided a significant example of detached decision making. The absolute powers given to the agency enabled it to penalise many husbands to a degree that in the fullness of time was seen to be unjustified, if not merciless. This was particularly so since the powers of the agency enabled it to give priority to pursuing those men who had kept in touch and were making a contribution for their children's benefit. Other men who reneged on their obligations were often let off due to the time and effort required to pursue them through the courts. The required feedback eventually came when the complaints received by members of parliament, and the coverage given by the press, generated sufficient public concern for modifications to be made to the terms of reference of the Agency.

A further issue arises when an unmarried couple cannot agree on whether to terminate a pregnancy. It would seem appropriate that the party wanting the child, against their partner's wishes, should be the one to provide for it. Such provision might be delegated to a couple wishing to adopt a baby rather than a single mother unable to provide the support.

Reports appear from time to time of nature lovers demanding that building works and other activities be halted because it would destroy the nesting of young birds. The cost of halting a significant project must be considerable, perhaps running into millions of pounds. The question arises as to whether the nature lovers would be so keen on the preservation of the bird's nest if they had to foot the bill.

Advancing technology and complexity.

Alvin Toffler [1] in his book Future Shock debated the effect of ever increasing technology and our ability to control it. This he argues is particularly relevant when the technology advances so rapidly that people cannot keep up with the changes and are therefore unable to comprehend the effects.

> "So long as a society is relatively stable and unchanging, the problems it presents to men tend to be routine and predictable. Organizations in such an environment can be relatively permanent. But when change is accelerated, more and more novel first-time problems arise, and traditional forms of organization prove inadequate to the new conditions."

In support of his case he quotes from Vickers [3]

"The rate of change increases at an accelerating speed, without a corresponding acceleration in the rate at which further responses can be made; and this brings us nearer the threshold beyond which control is lost".

This is evidently another example of lack of feedback to the general population. The feedback might alternatively go to a select group of technologists - who may not pass on the message.

Toffler further suggests
".. many of our social processes have begun to run free resisting our best efforts to guide them."
He believes many welfare programmes today often cripple rather than help their clients. In the USA the Urban Renewal Agency, at a cost of three billion dollars, succeeded in reducing the supply of low- cost housing in American cities.

Why, he asks, do college students riot and rebel? "Can one live in a society that is out of control?". The interesting question is whether society is going out of control. Could it simply be that the authorities, that traditionally control the lives of others, think they are losing control when in fact they are simply losing excessive powers they once had, due to the feedback from the people affected. Riots by students are a form of protest that in former times would not have been viable without the activists being sent down. Students were in any case more conditioned to behave in a manner considered by the authorities as appropriate. (This is not to say that all student demonstrations are useful. Some may be intended to exercise political muscle rather than raise a valid protest.) Nevertheless protest, in a democracy, is a form of feedback that an authority should consider then modify its policy appropriately to take account of the concerns. Figure 1 illustrates the loop. For this to be a negative feedback loop, which compensates for the difficulties being experienced, the information generated by the protest is used to "subtract" those elements from the policy that are not acceptable. The modified policy may be subject to further protest until it achieves an acceptable status. If this were an absolute authority, which ignored protest, then the loop would be broken at B.

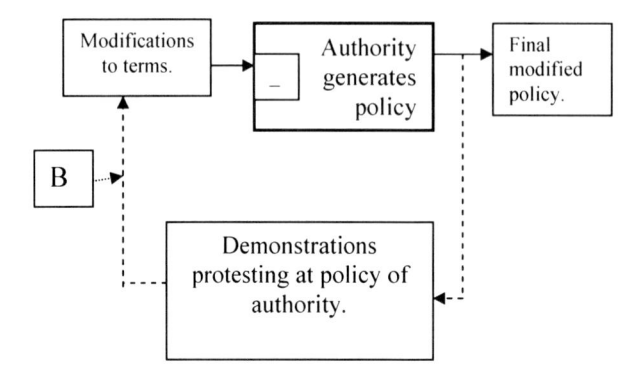

Figure 1. Protest as a form of negative feedback loop.

The effect of this loop is shown in figure 2. The protest starts at point P, in a true democracy conditions would be modified or dropped to a level acceptable to the population.

Is unrest in society an indication of inability to comprehend new technology or simply the view of people who, traditionally, exercise authority over others without the need to consider the views of the general population? Toffler [2] notes that whereas we have measures to guide our control of the economy we have no comparable 'social indicators' to tell whether society as distinct from the economy is healthy. We have no measure of the quality of life and insufficient means of measuring the social impact of our policies.

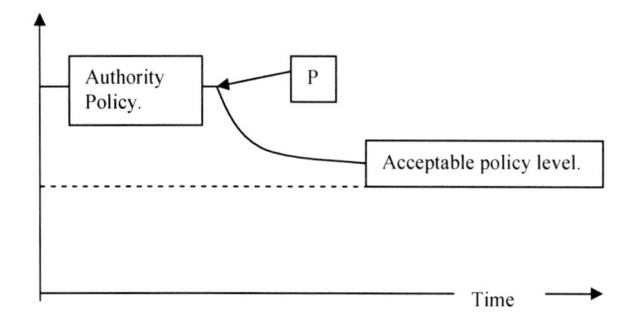

Figure 2 The effect of the feedback loop over time.

Media hype and distorted data.

A significant problem occurs when distorted facts take on the role of feedback. Whereas a genuine feedback loop is beneficial in suppressing distortion in the engine of the loop, it is detrimental if the distortion appears in the feedback path itself since the system then tries to compensate on distorted information. A major cause of distorted feedback is due to misreporting of the facts. Over-hype by the media is evidently one influence that causes people to worry unnecessarily.

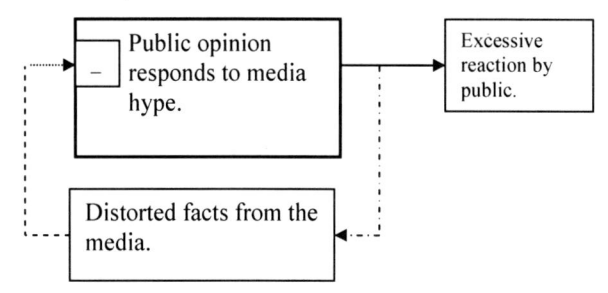

Figure 3. Distortion in the feedback loop.

The block diagram in figure 3 shows a negative feedback loop in which the data fed back to the "engine" of the loop - in this case the formation of public opinion - is erroneous. Since the operation of the loop is to compensate for error, the tendency is to compensate for the erroneous data and move away from the optimum response as shown in figure 4.

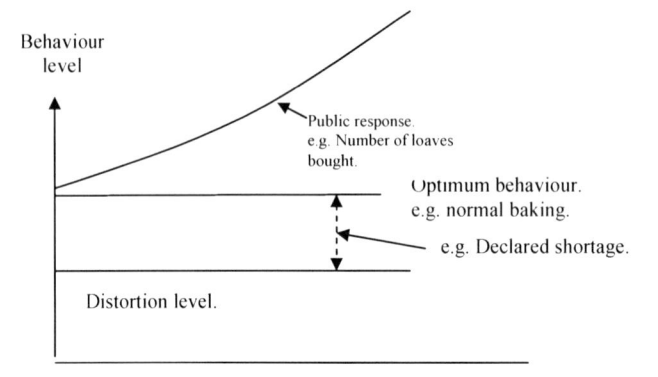

Figure 4. Response to distortion in the feedback loop.

An example of this kind of action would occur if the media wrongly informed the public that there would be a shortage of bread. The response from the public is likely to be an overreaction manifested as the purchase of too much bread and storing it unnecessarily. (This in itself would cause a positive loop if panic spreads at the shortage of bread in the supermarkets).
The use of misleading information to exploit the market is known to have occurred in various fields, including the stock market and the markets for other commodities.

A particular concern is the reporting of crime and its affect on the public who often change their behaviour in undesirable ways to compensate for the perceived dangers. Thus people use the main road rather than a footpath at night, drive rather than walk or stay at home rather than go out to the theatre and meet other people.

According to a survey [4] in 1998 over-anxious parents are preventing children from having the summer holidays they enjoyed when they were young because of panic about their welfare. A study by Mori [5] found that 80% of parents would not let their children play unsupervised in the park during holidays.

Parents believe that the modern world is too dangerous to let youngsters out on their own and this is hampering their development. Mothers ferry their children to school by car increasing the congestion on the roads (especially by the schools where they park) and in consequence increase the likelihood of traffic accidents. Home office statistics show that the chance of a child being killed (other than in an accident) is 1 in 90,000. A spokesman for the NSPCC observed that parents should keep a sense of proportion. "There is not a paedophile behind every lamppost."

At the time of writing there has been extensive legislation to the point where people feel inhibited in giving voluntary help to organise catering for children. One factor is the possibility of being sued for damages if a child is injured. Accordingly outdoor activities and adventures holidays have been curtailed.

A degree of paranoia has arisen to the extent that any adult working with children is deemed a risk unless screened to establish their innocence. The inevitable result will be a shortage of volunteers to help with youth organisations. Even adherents to the policy protested that legislation was going too far when it was suggested that parents sharing the school run should be screened.

Risks to health are in any case significant in the home. Statistics in 1998 show 600 deaths per year from falling down stairs (20 from falling out of bed). 30 - 40% of cases are due to hospital error. It was noted that the death rate has halved in the last 200 years. For every murder today there were ten in the Middle Ages and twenty 100 years ago.

Accountability and feedback.

It is a feature of most organisations that the performance of senior staff cannot be monitored in the short term. It may be many months before the actions of management reveal a change in the performance of the organisation, perhaps up to a year when the audited reports of the company become available. This is in contrast to a small business where the performance of entrepreneurial staff is more immediate and corrective action can be taken before misjudgement steers the organisation too far off course.

In essence the problem is one of experience. Many people will claim it is faster for them to do a job than to ask others to do it. This may be the case but more importantly they know exactly how much progress has been made. The alternative of supervising staff is by its nature less immediate. The supervisor should not be monitoring staff every minute of the day since this negates the purpose of employing staff for the work. As the management structure grows so staff will be given more responsibility and accordingly the checks will be less frequent. The feedback loop is not continuous but is sampled periodically perhaps once a month or every 3 months until finally a shareholder waits for 18 months to see the audited accounts These kinds of delays with no feedback allow significant deviation from the expected path. They may become the cause of wild fluctuations, as dramatic efforts have to be made to get back on course. An analogy to the captain of a ship checking his position infrequently, in spite of not knowing the tidal currents accurately, is relevant. The problem then becomes the topic of oscillating behaviour, or hunting, as discussed elsewhere in this book.

The limited feedback may not be entirely due to the scope of responsibility offered to staff. Senior management is reliant on feedback from middle management in order to fully assess the success of a business and take corrective action when necessary. Failures at junior management level may not be reported upwards, possibly due to the wish to preserve an appearance of competence or perhaps in order to correct problems before they are spotted. Either way there may be delay in reporting problems that need drastic corrective action. A report [6] on the decline of company Marks and Spencer Ltd. In the year 2000 noted that senior management did not receive, in sufficient time, the warning signals of the dwindling popularity of its merchandise.

In addition to the complexity consequent on new technology a problem arises if the information fed back is not understood by the recipient, perhaps when an authority or legislature is not familiar with the activities under its remit. This is not likely to be a problem within the successful company where it is supposed that staffs are promoted according to competence and have the ability to communicate adequately with management levels above and below them. Problems can, however, arise when a merchant bank or venture capitalist is inadequately staffed to assess a new business - perhaps due to its high technology nature.

Legislation is another area of concern. For example legislators, unfamiliar with the problems of small business, may be unaware of the additional burden they place on small companies. Whereas the large successful company has the clout to lobby members of parliament and other people of influence, the small companies may not have the resources to do so. The employment, within the civil service, of people with experience of the commercial world is a move to provide the feedback necessary. A welcome directive was given by the labour government (circa 1999) which required ministers to assess the cost of new legislation.

Summary.

1. Feedback associated with the facility to ensure its application is necessary for a democracy.
2. Absence of feedback removes the corrective action necessary to ensure efficient operation.
3. An effect that is remote from its cause provides no feedback.
4. Wielders of absolute power can ignore feedback
5. People in government with no business experience may not understand the burden their legislation is causing.
6. People in positions of influence who do not understand new developments may not understand the feedback.
7. People with strong moral convictions sometimes ignore the suffering that their decisions cause.
8. Distortion of facts makes for unrealistic feedback that creates an unrealistic response.
9. Media hype often causes unnecessary worry and inappropriate behaviour.
10. Accountability is delayed feedback that may arrive too late to provide necessary correction.

References:

[1] Toffler, Alvin; "Future Shock", p.129
[2] Ibid. p.411
[3] Vickers, Sir Geoffrey; "Ecology, Planning and the American Dream".
[4] Elsworth, C; "Parents' fear of strangers places curbs on children." 9/8/98
[5] Mori study for the Nestle Family Monitor, Circa 1998.
[6] BBC2 Money Programme, October 2000

Chapter 7. Crime and the Devil's Advocate.

The Devil's Advocate.

The public concern over the increase in crime is understandable. Changing legislation and procedures appear to favour the criminal unduly and sometimes burden the honest citizen to an unreasonable extent. Political correctness and human rights have been a factor but this chapter will explore the role that feedback loops can play in accentuating criminal and yobbish activities.

The change in a situation might be caused by a force that has sufficient power to overcome any opposition. In such a case we will be aware of the problem and can plan on a means to correct it. The feedback loop, on the other hand, may be more insidious and less easily recognised. Accordingly when a situation gets out of hand, for no apparent reason, then we should check whether there is such a loop in operation. There might alternatively be other reasons such as a very delayed negative feedback loop or even a complete break in a compensating loop.

As an exercise in the application of feedback, this chapter will look at the role of a Devil's Advocate and consider how he could plan situations so as to maximise the crime rate and increase the antisocial behaviour that now permeates much of society.

Role of the Media

Our Devil's Advocate "the DA" has several resources to draw on. The most powerful of these are the media, which he can use to emulate the problem of feedback in the microphone amplifier described in chapter 2. The media via their outlets of television, radio and newspapers are, in effect, information amplifiers of enormous power. Single items of news which, in earlier times, would have been limited to a few people, are now transmitted to a population of millions. It is an information amplifier with a gain of the order of a million or more *. What is the likelihood that certain information can be fed back to create circumstances that regenerate similar information? Is it likely that when the quirks of some antisocial human are being reported they will be copied? If so will that copycat behaviour spread among other antisocial people?

[* Strictly speaking it is an amplifier of some quantity which represents information multiplied by the number of people it influences]

Several years ago football hooliganism became a problem that reached the headlines.

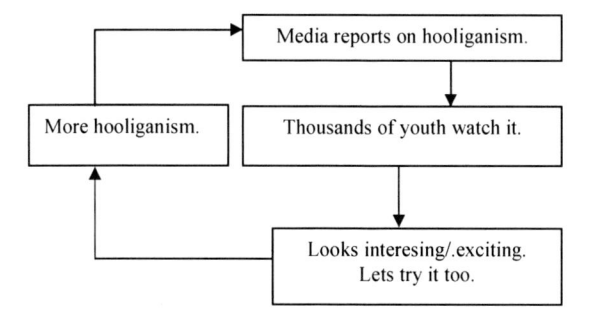

```
            ┌──────────────────────────────────┐
            │  Media reports on hooliganism.   │
            └──────────────────────────────────┘
                           │
                           ▼
┌──────────────────┐  ┌──────────────────────────────────┐
│ More hooliganism.│  │  Thousands of youth watch it.    │
└──────────────────┘  └──────────────────────────────────┘
                           │
                           ▼
            ┌──────────────────────────────────┐
            │  Looks interesing/.exciting.     │
            │  Lets try it too.                │
            └──────────────────────────────────┘
```

Figure 1. The Media loop.

It is clear that the DA could incite football hooliganism quite easily. He would have the co-operation of many news editors whose aim in life is to report headline catching events, figure1. They can be widely advertised on television, so that there is ample opportunity for them to be copied by others when they see what is possible. It is particularly likely to be copied if potential hooligans see it to be fashionable in other parts of the country.

Role of Fashion

Fashion in its various guises is a strong motivant to behaviour. This is evident from the large sums of money expended "in keeping up with the Jones's". Fashion is not, however, confined to the doubtless good behaviour exhibited by the Jones family. There are fashions in hooliganism, mugging and a variety of other antisocial behaviour. The effect has been seen in various crimes where the feasibility has been demonstrated and then broadcast to the population. It can then be picked up and copied by others who might otherwise not have thought of it. It is even possible to show the methods used by criminals in sufficient detail for others to emulate. The actual weapons and methods of penetrating security screens can be described.

Whether video-nasties are a separate issue to the copycat behaviour engendered by newscasting may be subject to debate. The video might well be a trigger to start a mode of behaviour. If the behaviour catches on then it can assuredly be popularised by the media.

For the next experiment the DA could look at the possibilities for using a positive loop to increase mugging. It is clear that from the point of view of using a feedback this is a similar case to football hooliganism but it can be taken further.

The mugger can be encouraged by publishing a series of reports that show him in an unassailable position. For example that no one comes forward to help a victim in a crowded train. Such reports will reinforce the confidence of the mugger to perpetrate further attacks in the knowledge that no one is likely to prevent him. When such events are further reported by the media they will be read by further potential muggers. In parallel with this influence will be the effect on the general public. They will also read that no one is going to assist them if they intervene in such a dispute. If, however, someone does intervene then there is a further factor in favour of the mugger, namely the attitude of the judiciary.

Role of Judiciary

If the DA is to be successful then it is important to give further encouragement to the criminal. This can be done by providing a legal system that appears to favour the criminal compared to the victim. This needs to be reported widely so that the criminal fraternity are aware of their favoured position. In particular they will be encouraged by reports of the punishment meted out to victims who react violently in their own defence. This would follow litigation (with public funding) by the criminal against the victim. We should note that the media might be exaggerating the situation. It is possible that the apparently ludicrous sentencing is not as widespread as the media lead us to believe. Judges [1] have published articles pointing out that the media is very selective in its choice of news items. The punishment meted out to criminals is more severe than the publicity implies. For the advocate's purpose this does not matter. People's reactions are not based on reality so much as what they believe reality to be.

How else can the chances of the mugger be increased? The advantages of creating confusion in the mind of an opponent are doubtless taught in military colleges worldwide. This advantage can be increased by organising a surprise attack and outnumbering the victim by two to one or more. A collection of weapons, hidden about the mugger's person, will be a further advantage.

Having planned how to optimise the advantage, how can the plan be applied? The first issue is to create confusion in the mind of the victim. It is evidently difficult for the average citizen to assess, on the spur of the moment, what is reasonable force to apply in his defence. He will know from media feedback that, even if he has the ability to defend himself, he has to be careful not to hurt his assailants too much in case they sue him for damages. Unlike a court of law, he will not have the opportunity and time to debate his course of action. He will not have the advantage of hindsight to find out the optimum procedure in any circumstance. If this confusion creates indecisiveness on the part of the victim then this is an added benefit for the mugger.

The second weapon in the mugger's arsenal is the element of surprise. Clearly it is the mugger's prerogative to initiate the encounter with all the obvious advantages. Finally there are the unknown factors of support from colleagues and hidden weapons which can be retrieved at a moments notice.

With all these factors against them it is to be expected that people will be reluctant to become involved in opposing a crowd of hooligans - even supposing that they have a chance of winning. The media is in a position to report this further and an information loop is in operation. The predictable result is that it will accentuate the situation.

The Synergy of Minds

The media is not the only ally of the advocate. The prison system has been noted for the opportunity it offers to the seasoned criminal to influence the younger offender. Whereas the punishment is enough to deter some offenders, in others there is a significant recidivism rate. Clearly the system can be used to enlarge the criminal fraternity by providing an environment for learning how to tackle bigger crimes.

The Advocate can draw an analogy from the known benefits of collecting like-minded people together. As we discuss in the chapter on industry there are positive advantages in creating a critical mass of people in a research department. Ideas trigger further ideas; and of course a large research department has the skills to tackle most of the problems which might arise. These industrial success stories can be emulated by collecting criminals into groups. They can then make further contacts with like-minded individuals who influence each other. In order to make this theme self perpetuating, young and inexperienced criminals can be introduced to the group.

Motivation.

We have noted before that there can be alternative positive loops controlling a system. A factor in our system is the motivation for achievement. It is, however, particularly important to start on the right side of the divide in order to achieve the aim.

As discussed in chapter 1 a ball on a peak will roll one way or the other depending on which side it starts. The example of the starving chicken, or the critical finance for a successful business, illustrates the importance of starting on the right side of the hill.

Thus on the one hand children can be introduced to career prospects that motivate them to achieve as honest citizens. On the other hand by restricting them from achieving in the employment market, or other worthwhile activity with which they can be occupied, the conditions can be created to maximise antisocial behaviour. Their achievements may now be by whatever other means they can compete with, and score over, their contemporaries. It should be possible to get advice on this from the psychologists. They will no doubt draw attention to the team spirit amongst muggers and the kudos to be gained by assaulting the normal citizen.

Delay in the feedback loop.

At this point it is appropriate to look briefly at other situations that support the advocate. Delay in a negative feedback loop is such a case. We have observed, in the early chapters, that a negative feedback loop acts so as to counter the occurrence of behaviour that diverges from the optimum. It is also important for the corrective response to act quickly. Is it possible to advocate changes in a feedback loop that could influence events to the advantage of the criminal? The honest community has been deprived of delivering a short sharp shock. The delay in bringing a criminal to court must act in the DA's favour. Most witnesses do not have an infallible memory and the punishment lacks the effectiveness of immediacy.

Society might expect that plans to encourage the criminal could be thwarted by its procedures whereby laws are enforced and criminals are punished efficiently. The advocate, however, does not have so much to worry about in view of the apparently light treatment of criminals by the judiciary and the apparently harsh treatment of some of the victims who defend themselves. Whether or not this is the case does not matter, it is only necessary for the criminal and the citizen to believe it to be so for a feedback loop to operate.

There has been some support for victims by vigilantes but so far the mugger has little to fear on that score. It has been noted that the courts have been unsympathetic to people who have taken reprisals into their own hands. We might expect the DA to support these procedures fully as an encouragement for the criminal (safe in the knowledge that the judiciary will deal harshly with anyone who attempts to usurp its authority as the sole arbiter of justice). The DA should perhaps have the foresight to proceed with caution in giving too much support to the attitude of the judiciary for as we discussed in chapter 2 a positive feedback loop which is unchecked will produce an untenable condition. If our DA is too successful in bolstering the criminals' advantages then the unrest that could be simmering within the civilised public could break out into drastic action.

It is clear that much of the public is dissatisfied with the level of protection that the courts provide.
If the vigilantes are to be punished by the courts for their actions in public then we must expect the reprisals to be conducted in secret. This is clearly a situation that is not conducive to moderate treatment of the criminal. If the judicial system does not provide a solution before the public's patience is exhausted, then we must expect other means to prevail. This does not mean the advocate has lost his influence for he can increase the potential for crime and social unrest by attempting to remove feedback altogether. Fertile ground, for this approach, lies in the gap between society and the no-hopers. It will be worthwhile examining this in more detail.

The DA should note the danger to his cause from a report in 1998. This referred to the mugging of the daughter of a barrister. The trauma affected her life so much that her father, who had been unaware how these crimes affected people, declared that he would be taking a much sterner view of mugging in the future. Our DA must be sure to repress this report and prevail upon the criminal to avoid people connected with the judiciary so that its members remain ignorant of the trauma inflicted on the victims.

The DA should be even more wary of a report [1] on a statement by Lord Justice Judge. Sir Igor Judge noted that:

> "*four out of five people thought that judges were out of touch and sentences were too lenient. However the (home office) report concluded that the public dissatisfaction was grounded largely on ignorance.*"

> "*Those who were most dissatisfied were most likely to overestimate the growth in crime and the degree to which crime is violent and underestimate the court's use of imprisonment and the clear-up rate*"

> "....many people believe that substantial numbers of rapists and robbers are not sent to prison. If they think that, it's not surprising that they believe that the sentences are too lenient. In fact, they are wrong – and that is because they have not been properly informed by the media".

> "..they (the media) do have a responsibility to inform the public what is actually happening".

The DA will doubtless have noted that society has a problem in deciding the punishments that are effective in deterring crime. The sanctions that society can bring to bear, to encourage good behaviour, are both positive and negative. In one case it is a reward, monetary or otherwise, for good behaviour. The alternative punishment for bad behaviour, however, breaks down if the "no hopers" have nothing to lose. It is one of the problems in a benevolent society that it provides a safety net below which people should not fall. Once they are at this level then there may be nothing to lose irrespective of their actions. In effect the result of opting out of society is to break the feedback loop. If nature abhors a vacuum and grasps at the first opportunity to fill it, then so too do people without direction respond to the influence of others. What was once a negative loop is likely to be replaced by a positive loop, where peers copy criminal behaviour with the subsequent instability that this implies.

Feedback and organised crime.

The DA would perhaps have little influence on organised crime, which have some of the attributes of a successful business. As it becomes more successful it makes more profits. In consequence it has more resources to plough into new technology to make the operation more efficient and effective. A criminal organisation is less likely to buy raw materials (unless it is in a trade such as drug trafficking) but it is likely to invest in capital goods, such as tools of the trade. As it becomes more wealthy these may encompass sophisticated electronics equipment and more efficient forms of transport. It has been reported that some of the drug cartels not only employ powerful speedboats but also helicopters and submarines!

A particular advantage that the criminal enjoys is the ability to choose the time and place of the next job. The difficulty of crime prevention is that it is necessary (unless there is prior intelligence) to monitor every possible location where a crime may be committed. Clearly the financial commitment is in favour of the criminal.

As the criminal organisation becomes rich it has the financial resources to bribe people in positions of power. This further increases the profitability of the organisation; a clear example of the positive loop in operation. When the resources of the organisation are greater than the resources the state can apply to policing the activity (as has happened in some of the smaller countries) then significant changes must be expected in the society.

We have observed, however, that all positive feedback loops either end in disaster, or they modify themselves so that they are self-limiting. The criminal organisation, which supplants the state, is as prone to such problems as the rest of us. It will be disadvantageous to reduce the wealth producing part of the population to the point where they have nothing to lose. Wealth has to be generated somewhere. There has to be the motivation to encourage the wealth producers to produce. Thus a once democratic society would, supposedly, be supplanted by a dictatorship in the shape of a drug baron or the Mafia. By that time the positive loop will have served its purpose. The parameters will then be modified to maintain the new status quo.

A look at the other side.

Having played the devil's advocate it is time to consider whether the feedback loop can provide counter measures. The problems appear to lie in two main categories. If we put organised crime in the first category, then the second relates to the sociological trends that are causing so much unrest.

The issues relating to organised crime are more clear cut. Crime has always been with us and doubtless always will be. The police have extensive resources and know-how to deal with the problem. Whereas the public may help the police by providing information it is unlikely that we can make a contribution to theory. It is nevertheless of interest whether feedback loops can operate in favour of the police. If there is are loops operating in favour of organised crime then can we see alternative ones that countermand that position? Are there any styles of crime prevention that slant the battle in favour of the authorities?

It is interesting to consider the ease with which a hooligan can sometimes upset a sophisticated organisation. A plan that relies on many interdependent procedures is vulnerable to damage at a point in its chain. The effect then proliferates throughout the organisation. Evidently it will be beneficial to find such a point in the chain of a criminal organisation. The more widespread a criminal organisation the more opportunity there should be to find a crack in the armour.

One method of finding such a crack is by the use of electronics to tag property covertly so that it can be traced. Some motor cars are tagged with a surveillance device. This enables the police to trace the whereabouts of a stolen car as it is moved through the criminal chain. By this means it is possible to round up many people in an organisation. Methods such as this, and the use of informants, are analogous to a positive loop. As more information becomes available so it opens up the opportunity to find more information.

We would hope that the advances in technology which favour both criminal and crime prevention authorities can be given an edge in favour of the authorities. One factor in their favour should be the advantages of being on the right side of the law; so that there are more people who will cooperate. Criminals are more vulnerable to a lapse in their own security than are the authorities.

In the second category the sociological trends typified by hooligans, muggers and the like have become more worrying. This is probably because they have more potential impact on everyday life. Drug addiction is blamed for much of the trend to criminality and it is a difficult problem to solve. There is evidently an additional trend that is being aggravated by the effect of the economy in reducing the opportunities for employment and perhaps social factors that are influential. It may be simply the natural swing of the pendulum, which causes the attitudes to oscillate backwards and forwards in reaction to excesses that have occurred in previous times? Has over-harsh treatment meted out by previous generations created a sense of guilt that influences attitudes? Where the positive feedback loop is seen to have effect, we should modify the situation. Either by cutting the loop altogether; changing the parameters of the loop; or alternatively endeavour to introduce feedback systems that provide rapid corrective action.

Immediacy of Feedback.

We have been told that punishment has little effect on crime since the criminal does not expect to get caught. Surveillance techniques, that use video cameras to record events in high-risk areas, seem to be the most effective deterrents. They may be offering a replacement for the religious influence on latent criminals who thought that all their actions were surveyed by the Almighty and a record kept until the day of judgement. It is interesting to note that there is no delay in the feedback. Both religion and surveillance have the benefit of immediacy in recording the wrongdoing. There is the further similarity that it is necessary for people to be aware of these influences if they are to be effective.

An unfortunate outcome may be the shifting of crime to areas where it is not deemed to be cost-effective to mount surveillance. The random distribution of surveillance devices may however cause sufficient doubt in the mind of the criminal to alleviate the vulnerability.

Immediate feedback is useful in identifying a fault before it assumes a degree that causes other influences to bear. Thus a wrong decision may be corrected relatively benignly if it is caught early but the consequences may be far reaching if a situation is allowed to continue until it has added momentum. One drug dealer on a housing estate should be removed before proliferation of the habit overwhelms the estate.

Catching a wrong decision early is also important in order for the facts to be readily ascertainable either before they have been lost in a tangle of detail or before e.g. the witnesses to a crime have forgotten the evidence.

We discuss in another chapter the analogy of the pendulum and its application to management where the corrective influence is proportional to the deviation from the desired norm. In this scenario the correction is a continuous process in which reward and punishment are different parts of the same scale. Whereas the legal process tends to be heavy handed in its approach we must look to the role of the social services to provide this more benevolent influence. This is, however, costly. It is clearly not feasible for a democratic government to influence every individual to behave according to society's values.

The important influence is participation in society with all that that implies in terms of peer pressure and the benefits that participation engenders. The peer group pressure must of course be of a suitable kind. In a society of no-hopers the peer pressure is likely to steer individuals in different directions. It is evident that reorganisation is long overdue. We need to give them a role that brings them within the rest of society's influence.

Power and Influence.

It is of concern that the actions of various establishments have not always appeared to be in the interests of the general public. The power of the media is one example. The influence of pressure groups is another.

Studies on the power of the group to influence its members are reported by Irving Janis [1] an American psychologist (see also the chapter on psychology). He has described many establishments' views as the result of groupthink, whereby a small group of like-minded individuals are recruited around an idea. They share feelings of moral superiority and a sense of mission. It is said that such a group masterminded the anti-corporal punishment legislation in the teeth of opposition from teachers and parents. Subsequently aiming to prevent parents having the right to smack their children. A small group working with glossy brochures, selective quotes and media personalities created the impression of a considerable force to convince professionals in the fields of child care, social work, fostering and child-minding. In contrast bouncers in pubs and nightclubs have the power to molest people and this has earned them the respect of the hooligan mob.

In regard to the media the copycat effect of the feedback loop is not the only issue caused by the publicity of antisocial behaviour. There is also the question of distortion when a single event is blown up out of proportion by a sensationalist newspaper implying that everyone is at risk. Thus the report of a rape or murder disseminated to a million people distorts the influence of the event. The number of people at risk, from the criminal involved, may be less than a 100. If a million people stop using footpaths or short cuts for fear of a repeat of the crime then an alternative problem has been created. Not only have a million people been put at unnecessary inconvenience but the diversion to walk over the public highway, or take the car, means that the chance of a traffic accident is undoubtedly greater than the chance of meeting the criminal in question. The number of older people who fear to go out at night is a measure of this affect.

In 2007 a headlines proclaimed that there were 1,500 deaths in the National Health Services due to mistakes by the medical services. A patient due for an operation the next week feared for her life and was afraid to have the operation. It was necessary to point out that out of the millions of operations performed every year the deaths represented less than one in a thousand. It would have been more responsible for the newspaper concerned to point out that it was an error rate of 0.1%, which is good and is not achieved by many professions.

The problems deriving from the stance of the media could be countered to some extent if publicity were given to the reality behind some of the reporting. Thus the public might take comfort if it considers the following truism: "The media thinks that news only qualifies as such if it is an unusual event". By that token the crimes that reach the headlines are unusual and therefore unlikely to happen to the public. It would be a public service if the media added a note indicating the probability of a reported event happening to the reader. It might help many more people to sleep peacefully at night.

It is tempting to blame the misrepresentation by the media, in making mountains out of molehills, as the main cause of our worry. Whereas the media may be guilty of causing a part of the problem, there is further evidence that a problem exists: namely the statistics published by the Home Office; the experiences of people known to us; and the increase in insurance premiums.

The interesting question is: where is the influence coming from? We have seen that there are feedback loops in operation but they do not exist as separate philosophical entities. They acquire substance because people with the appropriate power are influenced by the situation that causes the loop. We should note that not only are these people influenced by a situation; they also influence the situation themselves - a necessary condition for the loop to exist. These can be loops that exist outside our supposed democratic framework. They may account for the discrepancy between much of public opinion and some of the behaviour of the authorities. We have many candidates to choose from in our search for culprits. Some of the possibilities are:

Pressure groups, which concentrate on their own benefits to the detriment of the rest of society;

Advisers in the spheres of sociology and psychology who are pursuing a particular theory (we have discussed the problem of delay in feedback when corrective action is required and such spheres of endeavour are particularly subject to delay in the feedback loop);

Economic conditions, which are not based on realistic accounting - that is to say accounting which considers not only short-term financial considerations but also long-term effects, human rights and environmental issues.

Media influence which distorts the public perception of events.

We will be looking at these issues further in other parts of the book.

Summary.

1. Emphasis on the activities of anti-social groups can set a fashion that encourages further anti-social activity
2. The kudos received for anti-social behaviour needs to be replaced by motivation for more socially constructive activities.
3. A feedback loop should also be operating in favour of the police in acquiring information.
4. Immediacy of feedback is obtained by the use of video cameras to record wrongdoing.
5. The safety net provided by a civilised society nullifies the sanctions against the no-hopers.

6. The media has considerable influence on the behaviour of people.
7. Media reports on unusual events create an atmosphere of distrust with the courts.
8. Distortion in reporting creates unnecessary fear and counterproductive behaviour.

References:

[1] Rozenberg J., "Fighting to keep justice in the courts". DT 29/5/2001.
[2] Irving Janis, Groupthink, 2d ed., Houghton Mifflin, Boston, 1982

Chapter 8. Organisations and Social Relations

Clubs and societies.

I was fortunate, as a youngster, to belong to a very successful youth club. Its success became a criterion by which I judged other organisations and over a period of time I analysed the reasons for success and failure. There were of course various factors influencing the success of a club or society. It was clear that the leader of the first youth club I attended was born for the part. He was also attractive to the girls and many more went because of him. They in turn attracted a larger number of boys and a positive feedback loop was in operation.

The official leader is not necessarily the attraction, there are many occasions when the personality of one person will influence the attendance of a number of people and a loop is set in motion when it becomes the fashionable thing to do. The personality of one or more individuals may be important in the initial stages but the basic requirement is stated in the well-known phrase: "Nothing succeeds like success".

Each meeting of an organisation is an advertisement for the next one. If people expect the next meeting to be worth attending then you have the main ingredient for an expanding organisation. I am judging success, in these examples, by the numbers attending since it is in the nature of a youth club that a large and enthusiastic membership implies success. The feedback loop is based on the expectations of the membership and the likelihood that members will recommend the club to their friends.

Some years later, when I joined a young political organisation, I attended a social that had been organised by the committee. There were only twelve people present but the chairman was enthusiastically declaring it a successful evening. I thought it was anything but successful, eight of the twelve people attending were on the committee anyway. The next meeting was unlikely to be any better; no one knew when it would be. When it became my turn to be chairman I decided to plan events with previous lessons in mind. Every meeting was to be a good advertisement for the next one and members of the committee needed to believe that they were building a successful organisation. In addition there needed to be some regularity so that the next meeting could be advertised before people left. In this way the feedback loop could be made as efficient as possible. The methods worked and the attendance of twelve increased to over a hundred - the maximum number that could be squeezed into the premises.

The Ratchet effect.

I have mentioned that feedback loops can be stopped by external influences and it is in the nature of positive loops that events reach a magnitude that may cause problems. In the case of the youth club its success was such that it attracted the youth from far and wide - way beyond the bounds of the parish in which it was situated. The bubble was burst by the new curate who was not happy with the reputation that the club had attracted. It was closed and reorganised on more parochial lines. It was never the same again although it did regain some of its popularity when a more benevolent leader was appointed.

Some years later when I was married we went to live in a new housing complex; a delightful setting with its own mooring site by a river. Many of the neighbours had similar interests. It was natural that we should organise a party and, since every one enjoyed them, others also organised parties. Unfortunately a ratchet effect occurred in which people wanted to do slightly better than the previous event. It is of course a part of human nature that we have to do it at least as well as others. Since it is difficult to do it exactly the same then it has to be better. The parties became more lavish until one of the wealthier members went over the top and organised an event that no one else could equal. It meant that the loop was broken and that was the end of the parties. It is important to monitor feedback loops and consider whether they are arousing effects that will stall them.

Feedback effects are in operation in the Old Boy network and similar organisations that have a restrictive membership or elitist policy. Thus members of the in-group vote for people who are one of them and as the numbers increase so the number of acquaintances deemed suitable for membership increases. These kinds of groups usually survive since they limit their membership to a manageable figure and the loop does not go on increasing ad infinitum.

There are some points to be made in favour of such networks since they are likely to produce groups of people who can work well together. In particular the feeling of trust, that is often a feature of these groups, can allow organisational methods that are not crippled by security precautions.

Groups of this kind may be detrimental to society if they acquire the power to manipulate people or are able to create a monopoly in some field. Alternatively the inbreeding, which becomes a feature of such groups at management or government level, can limit their ability to govern in keeping with advances in other fields that a wider membership would be able to address. Some people argue that parts of the civil service are elitist and that the inbred effects cause policy decisions that are ignorant of the potential of science and technology. As late as the 1980's it was reported, Highfield [4], that a Treasury mandarin had implied (when addressing the Lords select committee) that there was no relationship between scientific research and the economy.

China has been cited as an example of the danger of an inbred administration. The Mandarin class, which governed China for centuries, admitted new recruits by examination that selected those candidates whose opinions were in accordance with the culture of the administration. A further factor in the decline of the Chinese during that period was the long period of peace that enabled China to be cut off from the rest of the world. It was not exposed to the advances being experienced by other countries. Especially those who were engaged in conflict that required them to obtain or develop the weapons and other machinery necessary to support a war effort.

The confidence loop.

I became aware of the effect of feedback loops in social relations when I was a teenager. One of the girls in our youth club was much sought after for, with her ready smile and shining eyes, she was considered the most attractive girl in the club. She, of course, had a boyfriend but her admirers were ready to take his place if they were to break up. In the course of time they did break up and it had a marked affect on her. She no longer smiled and her eyes no longer shone. In fact she seemed to be a changed person. This opinion was clearly shared by many others for fewer boys asked her to dance and she ceased to be sought after. The change continued, she became withdrawn and sullen but the most surprising difference in my view was that she ceased to be attractive. We wondered what we had seen in her.

It was some years before I understood what had happened. Her confidence had been subject to a positive feedback loop. After the break up with her boyfriend she had become less confident in herself. She was no longer vivacious, and the sparkle that had made her so attractive was no longer there. The attentions which had previously given her the poise and social presence were removed and with it the social magnetism which she had possessed. She was not in fact attractive and in a basic sense she had never been. It was simply that her personality had shone through. If you the reader are a young person, and unsure about your appeal, then perhaps this account will help you to understand what might be happening.

This question of self-confidence is of so much importance that it is worth investigating it further. You will observe in everyday life that there are confident people and worried people. The confident people stride ahead, are more successful and increase their confidence ready for the next task. They are the winners in a positive feedback loop, which reinforces their confidence just as the losers are in a similar one that takes them in the opposite direction. It could be argued that life is manifestly unfair. What is needed is that the confidence losers should be able to break out of their particular loop and achieve some corrective influence. Specifically they need to move into a correcting negative feedback mode so that they cease to be on a one way trip.

My comments have so far have painted a rather simple picture. Confidence is not, of course, an absolute guarantee of success and from time to time such people will fall flat on their face. When they become over-confident they are more prone to corrective action. Similarly, diffident people will have their successes, which helps them take a more positive attitude.

The young girl I described suffered more dramatically than most people did but the effect was perhaps more important for the teenage boy. The confidence required to initiate contact with the opposite sex was invariably acquired by trial and error, a difficult process if girls were looking for a self-confident mate. Some research into this topic has been reported by Knight [1] who observed: *"When you are single no one wants to know. Yet the minute you get a partner, the others come running. Ever wondered why?"*. The conclusion was that a quick way for women to identify a quality mate is to choose someone pre-filtered by someone else. If more women were attracted to a male then he probably had a good sense of humour, good social skills and possibly wealth. This *peer attention rating* (when choosing a mate) strongly influenced women, and also men but to a lesser extent.

Knight did not mention self-confidence though it is often necessary for good social skills and other attributes. Fortunately of course there are various factors at work but what is particularly required is a compensating loop so that as confidence is lost so the responses are such as to help restore it. Such a loop in this context could imply meeting a person of the opposite sex with maternal or paternal instincts who would be attracted to someone needing reassurance. An open loop response would be for such people to divert their attention from their fears by finding an alternative pursuit or perhaps paying more attention to other people's situations.

Public speaking.

Where else do we find confidence loops? A prime candidate must be in public speaking. The confident speaker gains the respect and attention of the audience and becomes more confident. Lack of confidence on the other hand leads to fear and embarrassment and the likelihood of forgotten lines - all destined to make matters worse. The novice, by contrast, is likely to panic and then go into a loop of increasing panic. An unkind audience might start heckling the speaker - especially at a political event. This is a situation in which the experienced speaker can gain the upper hand by a confident response. An example was John Ratcliffe who used to be a soap box speaker at Lincoln's Inn in London. His ability to quell a heckler was legendary. He would string out a heckler with a series of questions, which gradually became more difficult until the heckler became too embarrassed to continue. His continuing success gave him the confidence to continue the technique and be more successful. In contrast the confidence of the heckler was dissipated by failure to gain the upper hand. The confidence loop illustrated in figure 1. often affects people who have a fear of public speaking.

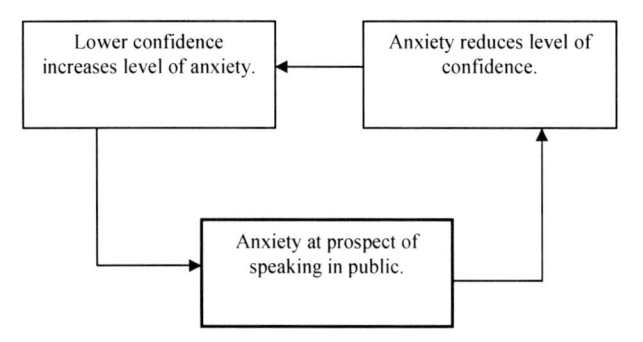

Figure 1. The confidence loop.

The quantity circulating around the loop is fear; the Scoldent list, illustrated in figure 2, might suggest the following:

Saturation:	Limit effect of audience.
Cut-off:	Read the speech.
Open-loop:	Separate speaker from audience.
Low gain:	Visual aids.
Delay in feedback:	Tape recording.
External force or influence:	Use a moderator to oversee meeting
Negative feedback loop:	Plant supporters in the audience.
Theme change.	Make it into an interview or discussion with audience.

1. Saturation of the fear/no-confidence loop will occur if there is a limit to the affect the audience will have on the speaker. This might arise by selecting a polite or friendly audience who encourages the speaker. Alternatively a public speaking class is likely to be composed of like-minded people who are sympathetic when it is the speaker's turn to stand in front of the audience. Maybe a stiff drink or tablets lower the level of anxiety to the point where it is not a problem then we can think of this as saturating the influence of fear.

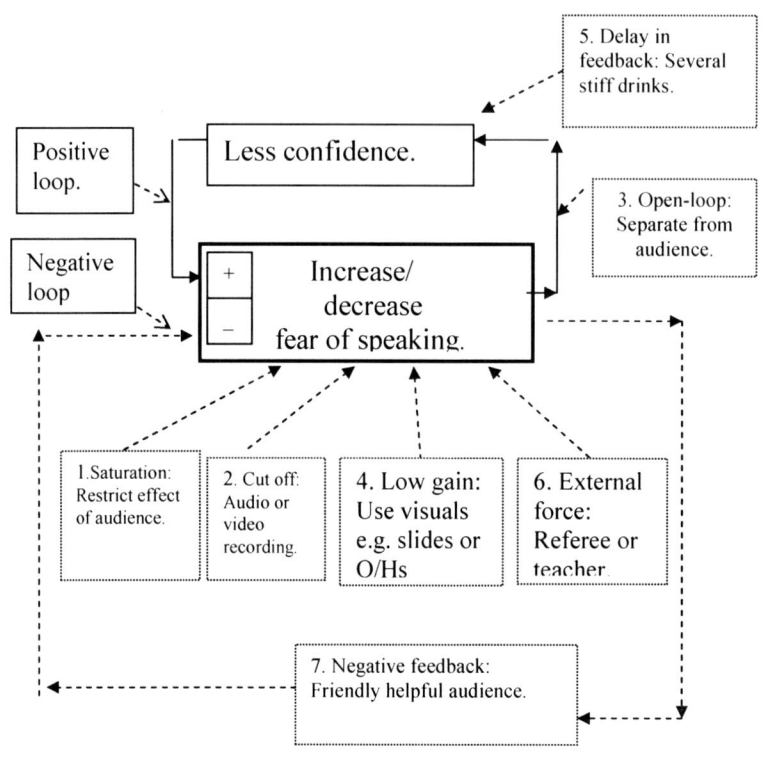

Figure 2. The application of the seven methods to control of fear

2. To cut off fear implies that you are not aware of the audience reaction. Concentrating on reading a speech is a way of ignoring the audience. It is not of course a good way of delivering a lecture but maybe better than becoming a nervous wreck. Alternatively a speech can be recorded on audio or videotape for playing at a later date. The opportunity to re-record the speech removes the fear of making an irretrievable blunder (perhaps replaced by the fear of having it recorded for posterity).

3. One way of opening the loop would be to sit the speaker in front of a microphone in a separate room and let them practice the speech without being aware when it is a live broadcast.

4. Low gain in the loop can be achieved by making the speaker less aware of the audience reaction. Slides or overhead projectors are a significant help here since the speaker can address the information on the screen. This information, in addition to helping the audience, also provides a prompt for the speaker and reduces the fear that the details of the presentation will be forgotten. Power point presentations are particularly useful. Low-gain will also be achieved in part by experience so that the fear factor is less pronounced and possibly by a small audience that can be dealt with on a one-to-one basis

5. Delay in the feedback implies that the speaker is slow to react to the audience response. A few stiff drinks beforehand might have this affect. Too many might make the speaker oblivious of the audience and have the same affect as cut-off.

6. An external force or influence implies a referee to see fair play. It might be the teacher at a public speaking class or an experienced chairman at a public meeting who keeps hecklers under control. Supporters in the audience can perform a similar role perhaps by laughing in the right places and by asking pre-prepared questions that the speaker is happy to answer. Alternatively the meeting might be reorganised as an interview in which the interviewer prompts the speaker with questions.

7. Negative feedback in this context is likely to be misconstrued if it thought of as unhelpful (as mentioned in chapter one it is important to distinguish between feedback and a feedback loop). A feedback loop of this kind will help abate the fear of the speaker and increase self-confidence. It implies a friendly audience who sense the insecurity of the speaker and help compensate by friendly responses and encouraging comments.

8. A change of system can be achieved by running the meeting as an interview. A good interviewer can remove the influence of the audience by causing the speaker to concentrate on the interview and be prompted in what to say next. The recording of the presentation mentioned under method 2, or publication of the material rather than a live presentation, are further possibilities.

Alternatively the confidence, which comes from an audience reacting well to your talk, can make you more relaxed and confident so that the audience is at ease with you and this too has a cumulative effect. Whether the situation will develop one way or another may depend on the first minute and the inexperienced speaker is on the proverbial knife-edge. I have found it important to know that I am well prepared and to have a definite purpose in making the speech. It is important that the purpose is not related to yourself. It is also advisable to have the safety net of some notes in case you need them.

Social interactions and partnerships.

A degree of feedback is inherent in the admonition to "do as you would be done by". This advice has been given in various forms. Jesus put it slightly differently "..whatsoever ye would that men should do to you , do ye even so to them" [2]. Confucius on the other hand put it in the negative when he wrote "Do not do to others what you would not want done to you" which is attributed to an old Chinese saying and is quoted in other religions. (G B Shaw [3] however, advised "Do not do unto others as you would expect they should do unto you, their tastes may not be the same." It is a quote that comes to mind whenever a smiling hostess offers me garlic bread).

It may be noted that these recommendations have the characteristic of a compensating loop since behaviour is chosen in the expectation that others will behave considerately towards us (there may be exceptions where the other is in a powerful position and need not worry about repercussions).
It is a different matter if it were rephrased as "Do unto others as they have done to you". Here we have the conditions for war that can escalate as each side perpetrates more revenge on the other so that a positive feedback loop is in being.

Young boys who hit other children and receive appropriate retribution no doubt discover such advice in the nursery. It becomes a negative feedback loop when successive assaults are made and the response assessed to find the limits that are acceptable. Such feedback becomes more limited, however, when polite society or political correctness restrains the response. The plain speaking adopted by some people has the advantage of a high gain loop.

In a continuing relationship the benefit of the feedback loop needs to be of the proportional kind exemplified in the pendulum. Here the force (or encouragement) to return to its centre increases with its distance from the centre. Members of a partnership, whether in a business or more personal relationship, do not want detailed rules and regulations that would constrain them. If successful they are likely to complement each other in their abilities and work together without too much friction. Thus if one partner is talkative then the other must be a good listener; if one is short tempered then the other must be tolerant and if one is domineering then the other must be submissive. It is of course necessary that partners are aware of the needs of each other and some feedback will be necessary. It seems likely that the analogy to the pendulum should be explored.

The principal here is that encouragement to maintain an acceptable stance should be proportional to the departure from that stance. If one partner is annoyed by another then some response should be made rather than bottling up the annoyance and saving it until there is an explosion. An analogy here is to a dam, which stops the flow of water until the pressure becomes so great that the dam breaks down. The quantity of water then released in a short time causes damage. A response does not mean a complaint every time the other does something slightly annoying. That is assuredly one way of introducing a straitjacket. There are more subtle and gentle ways of showing displeasure. In its most gentle form the partner may be hardly aware that feedback is there and if it can be made subliminal so much the better. The manager who doesn't smile at you as expected, or who does not say "Good morning", could be sending an important message.

Alternatively a positive loop can apply insofar as good attributes are to be encouraged and, as they happen, so more encouragement is applied. Reinforcement of this nature is likely to make a more stable relationship.

Gearing.

The responses in a partnership are clearly modified in consideration of a person's stake in it. A person will tend to behave with a view to the effect on their future liaison. The more separate a person is from a situation the more critical can be the comments without repercussions. It is a form of gearing in so far as a distanced person can risk a response that a person intimately involved in a relationship cannot risk. It is not the intention to introduce mother-in-law jokes but it is evident that problems have arisen in some families where the mother-in-law did not feel as restrained in her comments as would have been prudent if she were more intimately tied into the relationship.

Similarly a senior manager can be more critical of people than a colleague at the same level.

This notion of gearing should perhaps be compared with other situations where people pronounce on how others should conduct their lives even though they are ignorant of other people's situations and do not suffer the consequences. The chapter on "The Dangers of No Feedback" discusses this problem further.

Argument.

Disagreements can hopefully be resolved by negotiation. The alternative is a positive loop that leads to argument, which in turn can lead to violence. The quantity circulating around the loop is annoyance maybe anger. A Scoldent list for this situation might be:

Saturation:	Vocal limitation
Cut-off:	Move away and shut the door.
Open-loop:	No reply.
Low gain:	A 90% response.
Delay in feedback:	Count to 10 before replying.
External force or influence:	Adjudication.
Negative feedback loop:	A reasoned response.
Theme change.	Discussion, not argument.

Vocal limitation is an example of true saturation insofar as there is a limit in how loud people can shout. This is not particularly helpful in resolving an argument; it simply defines the maximum degree of hostility that can be reached. A sore throat, however, will cause saturation to be reached earlier and make the argument less intense. Cut-off is more effective if one party leaves the room and shuts the door since it gives a cooling off period that may end in a more reasonable discussion. Alternatively no reply means that there is nothing to circulate - provided the body language is not provocative.

John F Kennedy demonstrated low gain when, to prevent a dangerous confrontation spiralling out of control, he made a response that was 90% of that needed to confront the Russians. If both sides reduce their response to 90% then the gain of the loop is less than 1 and the regeneration subsides. The advice to count to 10 before responding to an argument has been handed down through the generations. A delay gives time for a reasoned response rather than provocative repartee.

When the argument cannot be resolved then it is time to bring in an external influence to adjudicate the differences, provided both sides agree to the choice of adjudicator. If a reasoned response has the effect of mollifying the opponent then anger is being reduced and perhaps argument changes to discussion; itself a change of theme giving a preferred mode of engagement.

Generation sequences.

"I'm not going to let my daughter behave the way I did when I was her age." The speaker was a mother who had been a teenager in the 1960's. Evidently the mother had lived life to the full and had become aware of the dangers and pitfalls. The daughter was to have a relatively sober upbringing without much of the excitement that the mother had enjoyed. It is an example of overshoot causing an excessive response in the reverse direction. The mature parent will adapt the response to lower the excess. An unintelligent response accentuates overshoot. Many people with a Victorian upbringing did not want their children to suffer the repressed upbringing that they had to endure. Accordingly their children enjoyed more freedom. When such children had an excess of freedom then it paved the way for the response of the mother quoted above. Every second generation would have an adventurous childhood and the alternate generations a repressed one. (There were other parents, of course, who had endured a very strict upbringing who then thought that what was appropriate for them was appropriate for their offspring also.)

Summary.

1. A positive loop of some kind is necessary for an organisation to expand.
2. Methods for limiting expansion are necessary at some stage.
3. Inward looking groups lose competitiveness.
4. Self-confidence is a function of feedback.
5. Social interaction is an essential negative feedback loop.
6. A 90% response may be necessary to prevent argument going out of control.
7. Parental experience may lead to disparate methods of upbringing in successive generations.

References.

[1] Knight J. "Move over Casanova", New Scientist, pp 30-33. 1.2.2000.
[2] The Bible, King James version, Matthew 7, 12
[3] Shaw G B, "Maxims for Revolutionists – The Golden Rule".

Chapter 9.   Feedback loops in Psychology.

Self-confidence.

One person is the life and soul of the party; another hides in the corner. One person always leads; another always follows. Why are some people so much more confident than others and is that confidence always justified? What are the mechanisms that give some people such an advantage?

It is evident that confidence breeds confidence. A person who succeeds at a task will become more confident and be more ready to tackle further tasks. It is more noticeable when the task concerns interaction with other people, especially if a measure of leadership is involved. In this case it is the person who is more responsive to a situation who is likely to be proactive and take the lead. Having taken this position the leader is likely to retain it when others are more hesitant in coming forward. Where people are equal in ability, a slight edge of greater confidence may be the deciding factor in determining the leader. This of course only applies if the leader succeeds in the task and thereby accumulates greater confidence and the support of followers - the necessary condition for this positive feedback loop. The converse is also a positive feedback loop in which the no-hopers generate greater degrees of no confidence, Figure 1.

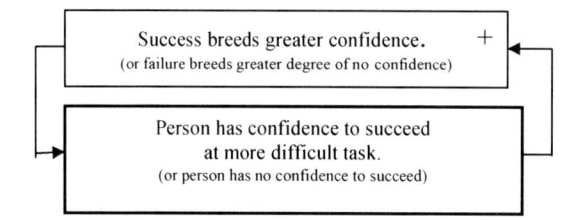

> Success breeds greater confidence.   +
> (or failure breeds greater degree of no confidence)
>
> Person has confidence to succeed
> at more difficult task.
> (or person has no confidence to succeed)

Figure 1. The increasing confidence (or no confidence) **loop.**

Over-confidence on the other hand is likely to lead to a downfall sooner or later. This will be a corrective action - the condition for a compensating negative feedback loop. Such a loop would tend to maintain the person in a stable position - being just able to succeed at a lesser task, Figure 2.

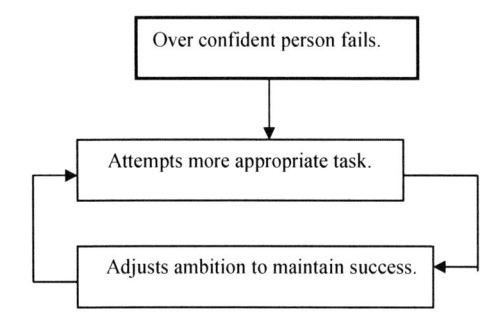

```
┌─────────────────────────────┐
│ Over confident person fails.│
└──────────────┬──────────────┘
               │
   ┌───────────▼─────────────────┐
┌──│ Attempts more appropriate task.│──┐
│  └─────────────────────────────┘  │
│  ┌─────────────────────────────┐  │
└─▶│ Adjusts ambition to maintain success.│◀─┘
   └─────────────────────────────┘
```

Figure 2. The compensating confidence loop.

The confidence loop is evident in children some of whom are out-shone by their contemporaries. The problem of siblings in a family is discussed in the chapter on education.

An unenviable task must be to teach rebellious children who do not wish to learn; especially when sanctions are inadequate to deal with miscreants. The problem is evidently not insoluble since whereas some teachers preside over a riot, there are others who manage to maintain such discipline that you could hear a pin drop. As before the side of the coin on which the teacher lands is probably decided in the first few minutes of the first class. The rebellious child who plays up the teacher with immunity encourages others who reinforce his confidence. If such a positive loop is in operation then the only solution is to break the loop. Either by the appearance of the headmaster who moves the situation into a new domain, by separating the children to prevent the reinforcement of others' behaviour or by the threat of punishment of sufficient deterrence which it is known will be carried out. A factor in the problem appears to be the absence of a self-correcting mechanism since the rules are made by people who are insulated from the task of enforcing them. If the authority had to cope with the effect of their ruling one suspects that the rules might be changed.

The feedback loop occurs in many other areas of psychology although its influence may not always be apparent. It is also an area where the difference between feedback and feedback loop is more likely to be confused. Reassurance from a mentor or peer group is important and often described as positive feedback, but it is not a feedback loop until the consequent alteration in a person's behaviour influences the further feedback that is received.

Crowd behaviour.

A familiar example of a positive loop occurs in crowd behaviour where a person encourages others to behave in a similar manner. If these in turn encourage the original person then a positive feedback loop is in operation. The extent of the behaviour is likely to increase until it is limited by circumstances such as the inability to shout, or applaud, louder. In the event that behaviour extends to a riot then the limit may be decided by the police. If it is a lynch mob then, the death of the victim may signal the limit.

The problem of crowd control might be analysed similarly. Open loop would be achieved by separating troublemakers by a partition or wall. Restriction on the number of people attending would keep the loop gain down and mild mannered people whose saturation level is below the level of violence would be a preferred audience. The external force would evidently be the police or stewards skilled in crowd control.

The calming influence of suitable music is known to help prevent panic and takes on the role of feedback. A change of system occurs, for example, if people watch a football match on television rather than in a stadium.

Crowd behaviour need not be aggressive. Subdued behaviour at a religious service, or orchestral concert, is also likely to be due to crowd influence. It will be seen in relatively mundane situations such as the laughter spreading around an audience which is likely to be greater if reinforced by many people. It appears that this behaviour does depend on a core of appropriate people in the audience. This no doubt explains why actors and humorists find some audiences active or dull depending on whether or not such a core is present.

The situation is illustrated in Figure 3 where the "adjacent person" box is replicated many times throughout the crowd and revisits the first person.

Similar effects are evidently at work at an auction if many people are caught up in the bidding fever. They pay more for a lot than they would if they were taking the time to make a rational decision. Indeed it can be observed that the bidding for second hand goods sometimes goes higher than the goods can be bought for in a shop, complete with guarantee.

```
┌─────────────────────────────┐
│  First person starts a      │
│  behaviour pattern.         │
└──────────────┬──────────────┘
               ▼
┌─────────────────────────────┐
│  Adjacent person takes up   │──┐
│→ behaviour and reinforces it.│  │
└─────────────────────────────┘  │
   ▲                              │
   └──────────────────────────────┘
```

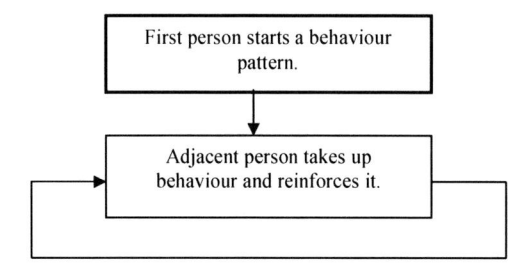

Figure 3. Reinforcement of Crowd Behaviour

A further example is the stock market. In a rising market many punters feel afraid of being left behind and go with the crowd, albeit often too late and near the peak of the market. Such behaviour pushes prices to a higher level than is prudent and other incautious investors may join the crowd.

Reinforcement

The topic of reinforcement has been considered extensively by psychologists e.g. Skinner [3]. Reinforcement occurs when a beneficial result occurs as the result of a change in behaviour so that the subject is motivated to repeat the behaviour and perhaps improve on it. In general it is not considered as a feedback loop but it becomes a loop if the subject builds on the benefit so as to repeat the actions for greater benefit.

For example, Walker [1] discusses the role of reinforcement in helping disabled people to succeed in recovering some of their faculties. It is important to provide external feedback in order for patients to be aware of the behaviour that improves the function required. Biofeedback is such a method of feedback to control biological functions and provide a degree of voluntary control over internal organs. It is discussed more fully in the chapter on medical issues. Daniels [2] has considered it in relation to management and draws attention to the relative benefits of positive and negative reinforcement. It should be noted that, in the following quotations, Daniels is referring to behaviour patterns at work and an *increase in behaviour* means *doing the job better*. He observes that:

> *"People do what they do because of what happens to them when they do it".*

> *"Positive reinforcement causes behaviour to increase because a desired meaningful consequence follows the behaviour."*
>
> *"Negative reinforcement causes behaviour to increase in order to escape or avoid some unpleasant consequence."*
>
> *"Negative reinforcement generates enough behaviour to escape or avoid punishment. The improvement is usually described as "Just enough to get by".*
>
> *"Positive reinforcement generates more behaviour than is minimally required - the only way for an organisation to maximise performance."*

Daniels first statement implies that people know what will happen when they perform an action. Clearly many actions will be on a trial and error basis and the actions modified in order to achieve the optimum.

The second and third statements raise an interesting comparison with feedback loops as shown in figures 4a b and c. Positive reinforcement generates a positive loop since praise causes performance to increase resulting in more praise. This then continues increasing until the performance is limited by other factors.

Negative reinforcement depends on criticism or sanctions to make the worker perform better in order to reach the minimum standard required for the job – a negative feedback loop. Looking at the analogy of a driving instructor teaching a pupil, the instruction to move the steering wheel becomes more urgent at the car is steered further off course. That is to say the urgency is proportional to the error in the position of the steering wheel. The error and consequent criticism cease when the steering is correct.

The performance of a worker performing a job is compared to the standard required. The difference is "the error" or the measure of the pressure to perform the job properly. Consequently the performance reaches a maximum when it reaches the standard required; namely the minimum that is acceptable.

The analogy here to positive and negative feedback loops is interesting. The negative reinforcement is analogous to the damped pendulum that has its stable position at the point of "just getting by". As with the pendulum the force or management pressure to perform is likely to be proportional to the departure from the norm. The pressure diminishes to zero when the norm is reached and there is no incentive to perform any better. The analogy might be taken further to compare the behaviour with the oscillation of the undamped pendulum. If the management is slow to take corrective action for under performance then the pressure to improve might be greater to encourage the worker to perform over the expected level only to return below the norm when management depart.

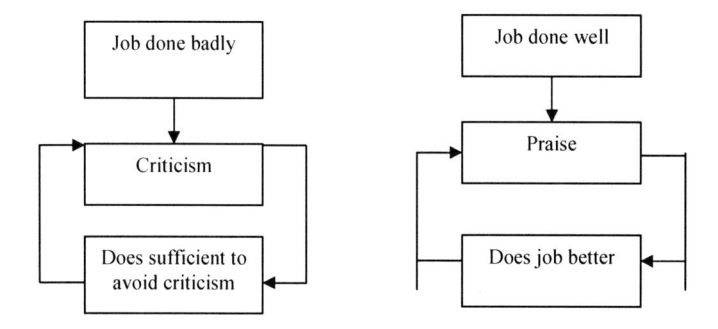

Figure 4a. Negative reinforcement   Figure 4b. Positive reinforcement

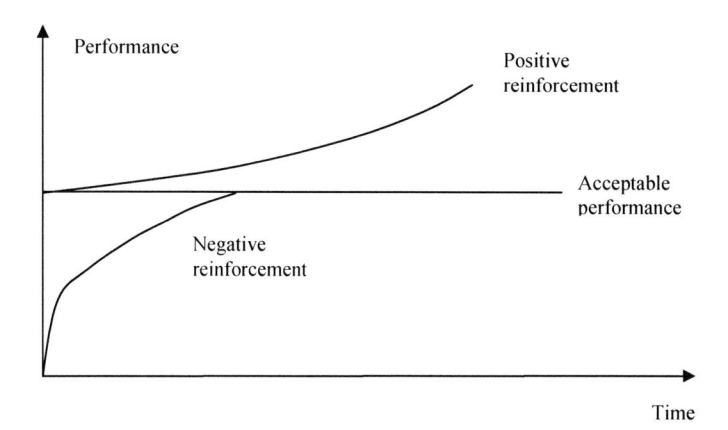

Figure 4c. Negative versus positive reinforcement.

The benefit of positive reinforcement implies that the spirit of the worker is so improved by the appreciation shown by management that he/she works better than required. If this then results in more pay and better conditions so that the improvement continues then the characteristic of the positive feedback loop will be seen as an increasing level of performance until limited by some external factor.

Daniels further notes that: "Doing nothing is doing something to performance" and is likely to lead to extinction; where extinction means the removal of incentive to maintain the current level of performance. He defines extinction technically as:

> *The withdrawal of positive reinforcement from behaviour. E.g. the performer does something and nothing happens. Extinction occurs when people say: "Nobody appreciates anything I do around here".*
> - their motivation becomes extinct.

At first sight this phenomenon is outside of the feedback experience but in fact is equivalent to a feedback loop with a gain of one, i.e. the quantity circulating around the loop remains the same and never increases. In the above case, management is not taking steps to contribute to gain around the loop. It is relevant when the losses in a system are taken into account. As discussed elsewhere in this book any business, or successful venture, requires a surplus in order to survive. This is necessary because in the real world there will be losses or costs to be covered. In the present context this implies that people feel the need to be appreciated and this is a "cost" (whether in time, counselling or money) that management must pay for.

Motivation.

Motivation of an employee and job satisfaction has been explored extensively by Skinner [3]. It has been reduced, he claims, by the separation of work from the outcome. Thus workers on a production line, making small widgets to fit into some larger machine, do not have this satisfaction. It is important to see the result: that their work has been worthwhile other than simply to make up the pay packet. This concept has similarity to the knowledge of results discussed by Daniel [2]. There it was necessary for the worker to be aware of the outcome of the work in order to benefit from reinforcement

This knowledge of results is important for generating a sense of responsibility, especially where due diligence is required on the job. It not only applies to someone who is producing equipment, it applies in many other areas such as examiners who check the output of a factory. Here the sense of responsibility is reduced if several examiners duplicate the checking procedures. If there is one examiner then he/she is solely responsible and will be blamed for failures. If there are several examiners then each may assume the others are checking sufficiently and so be less thorough in their actions. Not only is this a psychological issue it also applies to the equipment itself as discussed in the chapter on industry.

The feedback loop here is compensating for the extra checking applied to the job when the actions are considered more than necessary, as shown in figure 5. As more controls are applied there is a tendency to counteract the increased regulation and regress to the norm that is considered sufficient.

A similar behaviour occurs when safety measures are improved. A degree of danger or adventure is necessary for many people to feel satisfied. Whether this is to portray a macho image or simply because of the inconvenience of extra work necessary to comply. Thus when people use seat belts in a car they may drive faster and more closely to the car in front. The best way to keep people to a slower speed with ample distance behind the next car is to place them at the front of the car in a glass cage so they suffer first in the event of an accident. Others take up dangerous sports, perhaps in part to compensate for an unadventurous life in a regulated society.

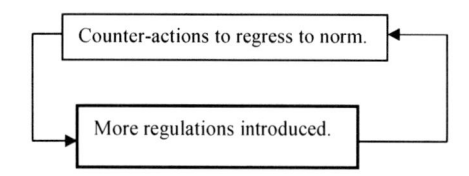

Figure 5. Compensation for excess regulation.

Chaos and development.

There has been much debate about whether a child's development is influenced more by family or by peers at school. Evidently there are elements of both though much depends on the group or gang the child joins at school.

There is probably a degree of chaos in the system. Chaos theory is often illustrated by the much-quoted butterfly. In this situation it is postulated that the flapping of a butterfly's wings in one part of the world could influence the beginnings of a weather pattern elsewhere. Chaos theory relates to systems where a minute difference in the initial conditions causes very large differences later. The chaotic aspect arises because it is usually impossible to recreate the initial conditions sufficiently exactly for the system to evolve in the same way. Consequently it is impossible to forecast the outcome.

An example could be a runaway bus, which careers down hill out of control and without a driver. Supposing the bus was not damaged; would it be possible to re-position the bus back in precisely in the same position for it to follow the same path? Any stones hit during the run would also be exactly repositioned. On the second occasion the temperature will be slightly different and consequently the tyre pressures will be different. They will bounce off a stone in a slightly different way and this slight diversion means that they will hit different stones subsequently. It is a positive feedback loop where the quantity fed back around the loop is diversion or difference from previous positions, Figure 6.

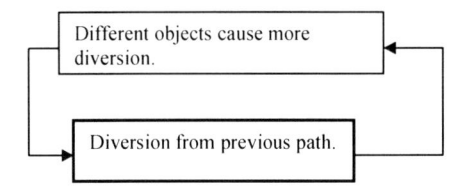

Figure 6. Amplification of change.

How much is the development of children dependent on their initial experience and how relevant is the opinion that declares a child's development is dependent on peer pressure alone? An important consideration must be the peer group that they join. It seems likely that parents, in their child's early development, influence this choice. Parents might reasonably expect that their offspring make a choice that is consistent with their child's upbringing. The most marked effect of peer group pressure is evident when parents choose a private school. The likelihood of peers meeting such parents' approval is doubtless increased.

Groupthink.

Irving Janus [4] has drawn attention to the behaviour of people in groups. He defines Groupthink as the behaviour of people when they are deeply involved in a cohesive group. The pressure on individual members to conform to the views of the majority stifles alternative opinion. Various examples have been given of the errors in decision making that have resulted from the behaviour, primarily because with alternative opinion stifled the full picture is not assessed.

Conditions that induce Groupthink are: a highly cohesive group; isolation from contrary opinions and direction by a leader whose opinions are known.

The problems that arise are:
- discussion is limited to only a few alternatives;
- the solution most favoured is never reassessed to check on potential problems;
- expert opinion is not sought;
- the group is so confident of its ideas it does not plan for contingencies.

The place of a feedback loop is apparent in the pressures applied to dissenting members. As more members agree with the leader the pressure to conform to the opinions of other members increases. In addition to the issues being discussed there may be a fear of being left out in the cold rather that sharing in the warmth of a collective opinion. A danger is that these groups become over-confident in their opinions, since their voting becomes unanimous. This particularly applies when a moral issue is addressed and the group feels justified in manoeuvring to get their way irrespective of the opinion of others who may be adversely affected. The motivation gives them the power to be effective in getting their own way. Such people, it has been claimed, have been responsible for introducing legislation that is contrary to the opinion of a democratic majority.

The increase in understanding.

The value of knowledge helping to increase knowledge occurs in several situations. A positive loop operates when we are solving a crossword puzzle or reading a signpost. As more words are solved in a crossword so more help is provided by giving the letters needed in the further words.

A signpost seen from a distance may be too indistinct to read. As we approach some letters become visible to provide clues to the words, then one of the words can be recognised and this helps decide on the remainder. Once we have been close enough to read the message the familiarity will enable us to identify the words on the signpost from a greater distance than previously. As we move further away our awareness of the words contained enable us to discern which sign post we are looking at; until eventually the outline is too vague to be meaningful.

Memory is a further example of loop benefit. As more features of an event are recalled further memories are triggered often leading to the wanted item. This feature taught in memory classes helps recall by associating the thing to be remembered with other features. This triggers the path to the appropriate area of the brain.

Visual phenomena are not the only ones to benefit from looping. Conversations with people who have a different accent may be difficult and a learning period may be required in order to understand the full conversation. As more words are understood so it becomes possible to comprehend more of the conversation. Telephone answering services often present this problem. The problem is unfortunately compounded when the caller is referred to another line to be subjected to a different accent. The value of the loop is lost when it is necessary to start the learning again.

Observations on alcoholism.

It was mentioned in chapter one that a positive feedback loop that runs out of control is likely to be a disaster. It may be a disaster for the people concerned but it is also a time for reflection on why the situation has reached such an extreme position and whether a change of procedures is necessary. A business in the throes of bankruptcy is the victim of a vicious loop of increasing losses due to perhaps to the non-viability of the business. The business may then be taken over and reorganised in a manner which is profitable and a benefit to the community.

Bateson [8] discusses this situation in psychology and its role in providing a technique to change the mindset of patients. The therapy works by taking them to an extreme position. If the discomfort or consequences are sufficiently severe they can alter the outlook of patients and encourage them to mend their ways.

He gives as an example of the problem faced by alcoholics in controlling their addiction. A positive loop is assumed insofar as one drink generates an irrepressible desire for another. It is the conflict arising when the alcoholic believes he is cured that causes so much grief. If the alcoholic believes he is cured then he believes that he has the self-control to refuse another drink. The only way to test the cure is to start drinking and stop when commanded to do so. This procedure for the alcoholic results in failure. The only way to combat this is to realise that he does not have the self-control to take only one drink and it is necessary to abstain.

The equivalent to a positive loop running out of control and hitting the end-stop is referred to as "hitting bottom". Alcoholics' Anonymous attaches much importance to hitting bottom if the victim is to be cured. An alcoholic who has not reached this state is regarded as a poor prospect for their help. There is the consideration that a person may hit bottom several times before really hitting bottom. At that stage *"their despair is adequate"* and they admit that they *"are powerless over alcohol - that their lives have become unmanageable"*. They have undergone a spiritual experience. *"The myth of self-power is thereby broken by the demonstration of a greater power."*

Bateson observes that:
> *"Problems of this general type are frequent in psychiatry and can perhaps only be resolved by a model in which .... the organism's discomfort activates a positive feedback loop to increase the behaviour which preceded the discomfort.....and might increase the discomfort to some threshold at which change would become possible."*

He further observes that a positive feedback loop is often provided by the therapist who pushes the patient in the direction of his symptoms - a technique which has been called the therapeutic double bind.
> *"An example of this technique (is) where the Alcoholics Anonymous tutor challenges the alcoholic to go and do some 'controlled drinking' in order to discover that he has no control."*

In a similar way a parallel was drawn with the experience of Perceval [9] (a psychotic) who was driven by his belief in mythical voices which chastised him for his behaviour. A devout catholic, he was in thrall to his voices (which he believed came from the Holy Spirit). The voices were reproaching him for his attitudes of mockery and blasphemy. In order to redeem himself he should perform an action which would break this neck. He imagined that if he performed the action "in the power of the Holy Spirit no harm would result". His might break his neck and die but would be raised again immediately.

In spite of his fears for his salvation, he did not give entire credit to the voices:

> *"I perished from an habitual error of mind, common to many behaviours, and particularly to our brethren the Roman Catholics, that of fearing to doubt, & of taking the guilt of doubt upon my conscience; the consequence of this is want of candour and of real sincerity; because we force ourselves to say we believe what we do not believe, because we think doubt sinful. Whereas we cannot control our doubts, which can only be corrected by information. To reject persuasion wilfully is one crime; but to declare wilfully that we believe what we doubt, or presumptuously that our doubts are wilful, is another".*

The loop in this case occurred because, as he revisited his doubts, his feeling of sinfulness accumulated to the point where only a drastic action would atone for his attitude. Percival survived because he realised in time that his beliefs had reached the limit of credibility - the bottom described by Bates in respect of Alcoholics Anonymous. On realising this he was able to analyse his condition and cure his own psychosis.

Summary.

1. Self-confidence is a feedback issue.
2. Crowd behaviour is subject to positive loops of both vicious and virtuous kinds.
3. Positive reinforcement yields better performance than criticism.
4. Motivation and responsibility go hand in hand.
5. Chaotic development is highly dependent on the initial situation.
6. Groupthink is a potential danger to society.
7. Understanding helps further understanding.
8. It is necessary to reach the limits of credibility to cure some conditions.

References.

1. Walker S, "Learning and reinforcement", Methuen 1975.
2. Daniels A, "Bringing out the best in people." April 2000
3. Skinner B F.,
4. Janus I., Groupthink
5. Maslow AH - ""The farther reaches of human nature" - Penguin
6. Robertson R. and Combs A, (Ed.),"Chaos theory in Psychology and the Life Sciences".
7. Young TR, "Chaos Theory and Social Dynamics" - in Robertson & Combs.
8. Bateson G, "Steps to an ecology of the mind"
9. Perceval J, & Bateson G (Ed.), "Perceval's narrative; A patient's account of his Psychosis 1830-32."

Chapter 10.   Sociology.

Living with Change.

As discussed in other chapters it is important that there is not too much delay in the negative feedback loop required to compensate for departures from optimum. It otherwise causes oscillations, or at worst takes on the characteristics of a positive loop and exacerbates the condition. The feedback is only useful if it arrives in time to be effective. If, however, a situation changes very rapidly (i.e. the goal posts change) then a system may never have time to reach an optimum condition. This problem can occur whether it is a human, social or physical system.

We live in an age of rapid change, as people who have a computer will testify. One of the problems with owning a computer is that systems keep changing. It is no longer feasible to learn a system and then sit back and reap the benefit. New systems are developed every two years or so and it becomes necessary to learn the updates, not to mention paying more money in order to be compatible with other products that come on to the market and require an updated system.

A further problem is the enormous number of features that are provided. Not only are there many features that the average user will never use but they are hidden behind drop-down lists leading to further sub-lists that may lead to even more. It is a different world to the place many were brought into, when features were displayed for all to see and could be selected without the need to remember where they were. It is common these days for children to be more adept at handling new technology than their parents. A possible outcome is less respect for older people and a degree of self-confidence in the young that is not backed by experience. The ramifications of computer systems of course extend far beyond the computer interface. It has in many ways introduced more efficient systems (for those who understand them) but for others they introduce a challenge and perhaps mystery that is hard to comprehend.

The problem of rapid change has been addressed by Alvin Toffler [1]. The rate of change has, he believes, caused people to feel less secure. There is no longer the firm foundation on which to build their lives and they are continually having to adapt to new people, new situations and new places.

Vickers [2] has observed that:

"Men are adaptable, they can learn to live even in harsh and hostile environments - so long as the environment remains constant enough to give

them time to learn......... If they form a habit of adapting by constantly changing that to which they are trying to adapt, they build uncertainty into the very structure of their lives."

Adaptation can only be achieved when there is feedback from the goal to be aimed at. It is inevitable that people will take time and this delay would normally be expected to cause overshoot as people try to compensate for being late in adapting their behaviour. If the goal posts are continually being moved, however, then the required behaviour is less predictable and people are less certain where they stand. Vickers has noted that some people will opt out of the race. In this event the feedback loop will be cut and have no effect.

It may be that people do not choose to opt out but are forced to if new technology causes an increase in unemployment. The importance of finding a solution to this problem is going to increase as new technology continues to provide better ways of performing tasks at present performed by people. In the first place we have a feedback loop whereby the unemployed degenerate to the point where they become less eligible for employment. They eventually become unemployable by normal democratic means. If they now see themselves separated from traditional society then society's sanctions for good behaviour lose effect and the result is that we have a break in the feedback loop of society's influence on the individual.

If the loop is cut due to the rate of change problem, so that people cannot keep up, then it may also be cut for other influences of society. The person, in effect, opts out of society, its benefits and sanctions for good behaviour. The problem of people opting out of society also occurs with other causes. Its dangers are discussed later in this chapter and in the one on crime.

Compensating factors.

The concerns of Toffler and Vickers may be valid but we should also consider whether there is any compensating loop in operation. People learn to cope with increasing complexity by encapsulating collections of actions in modules or words that represent the total capability. The situation is well illustrated in electronics systems that have evolved from relatively simple circuits to highly complex modules. Thus the electronics engineer in the 1950s would design circuits using single components such as valves or transistors and resistors etc. Then in the 1960s it was possible to buy modules that performed the actions of several such circuits in one package. Later the microchip was developed that could hold thousands of transistors and be endowed with a capability that could only be defined in terms of the overall specification, be it a computer, television set or mobile phone. It was not feasible for anyone but the original designer to understand the detail of how it operated internally.

In many realms of academia, concepts are developed that are described by a single word to represent a complex line of reasoning. It is not feasible to describe the concept in detail every time it is referred to in other contexts. To do so would mire a discussion in treacle of detail that limits comprehension. A psychiatrist in conversation with a colleague might refer to a particular type of complex knowing that the colleague understands the details relating to that complex. A chemistry student who has learned about the Bauer process can similarly enter into discussion with a chemist knowing that the term has been adequately described.
At a simple level the memory of a number sequence such as 1,7,4,5,3,2,6,4 is more easily remembered if the numbers are encapsulated in double digits as: 17, 45, 32, 64.

These are ways that we cope with increasing complexity. To be sure there is the painful process of learning the meaning of some words, but once learnt they provide a shorthand way of coping with advances.

Further friction arises between people, who see the potential of the progress of science and technology, and others who try to opt out and deny that there are important changes taking place. The latter feel at risk from a change in the environment and endeavour to maintain the status quo. The reluctance of older people, to recognise the implications of new methods, weakens their influence and in consequence the wisdom of age, manifested as the feedback of past experience, is lost. The problem is greater the more powerful a position the person is in. The rise of the whiz kid in the seventies and eighties was a consequence of frustration with shortsighted management. In fact the young people, who were promoted on the basis of enthusiasm and drive, often created chaos due to lack of experience and a more careful selection procedure has resulted - the feedback of experience to generate a better solution.

Feedback comes in a variety of forms. It does not just mean by word of mouth or the written word. One of the biggest dangers to society at present is the gap between society and the no-hopers. The sanctions that society can bring to bear to encourage good behaviour are both positive and negative. In one case it is a reward, monetary or otherwise, for good behaviour. The alternative punishment for bad behaviour, however, breaks down if the no-hopers have nothing to lose. It is one of the problems when a benevolent society provides a safety net below which people should not fall. Once they are at this level then there may be nothing for them to lose irrespective of their actions. In effect the result of opting out of society is to break the feedback loop. The loop should be seen as a continuous process in which reward and punishment are different parts of the same scale. The important influence is participation in society with all that that implies in terms of peer pressure and the benefits that participation engenders. The peer group pressure needs to be the right kind, i.e. worthwhile peers who conform to society's principles.

Several speakers at the British Association Conference 1999 [4] considered the problem of uncertainty and the feelings of insecurity that stem from it. It was declared that a happy society is associated with self-effectiveness; that is in being effective in determining one's own fate. On this basis the freedom that democracy permits should make the occupants happy compared with totalitarian regimes; but Lane noted that "*Anxiety undermines the positive hedonistic gain of the market experience*". Banman put it slightly differently when he said: "*Insecurity is the fly in the ointment of personal freedom*".

Toffler argues that by bringing together people who are sharing, or are about to share, a common adaptive experience, they are helped to cope with it. 'A man required to adapt to a new life situation loses some of his basis for self-esteem. He begins to doubt his own abilities. If he is brought together with others who are moving through the same experience, people he can identify with and respect, then he is strengthened. The members of the group come to share, even if briefly, some sense of identity. They see their problems more objectively. They trade useful ideas and insights. Most importantly, they suggest future alternatives for one another.

The aspiration for riches.

The adage that wealth alone does not make for happiness is well known, although it might make unhappiness more pleasant. Since, however, so many people strive to earn more money then you would expect some degree of increase in happiness to occur. It is not unusual to find people in relatively poor circumstances who appear happier than wealthier apparently successful people. The strain of maintaining the success, and coping with the demands that go with it, evidently mars the happiness that might be expected to result from all the effort made. The problem is compounded by consequent familiarity with increased living standards and the increase in expectations that go with it, not to mention the greater the fall consequent on failure

The problem of raising the material standard of living is that it soon becomes accepted as normal. It is particularly true of children born into the culture of modern conveniences that they accept it as the norm. It is as if there is a ratchet that clicks up the expectations as each increase in the standard of living arrives. A feedback loop can be visualised as shown in figure 1.

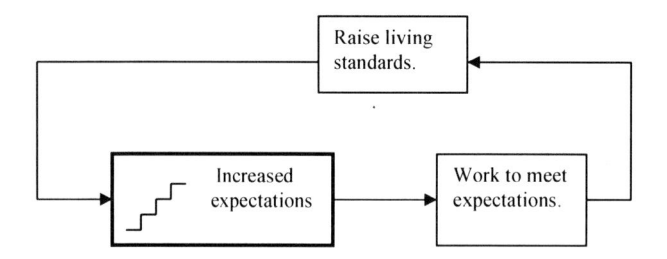

```
┌─────────────────── Raise living ◄──────────────────┐
│                    standards.                       │
│                                                     │
│              Increased          Work to meet        │
└──────────►  expectations  ────► expectations. ──────┘
```

Figure 1. The ratchet effect of increasing expectation.

Such increasing standards carry a price; life becomes more complex. There are more cares and worries to cope with. Not only are there more things to go wrong there is also the task of keeping up appearances and responding to the expectations of peers to conform to increasing standards. These expectations form a positive loop symptomatic of crowd behaviour where every participant adds to the influence.

This increase in the pace of modern life has been blamed for creating misunderstanding between different generations. Whilst this has always been so, insofar as a younger generation have different priorities to their parents, the situation is, no doubt, aggravated by the rapid advances in technology. Many older people are unable, or unwilling, to understand the implications of modern equipment and how to use it. The gap in understanding does not make for good communication although there is evidence that young members of the family are respected for their ability to cope with the new video recorder or personal computer more quickly than their parents.

Crowd behaviour.

A riot may be the first thought that comes to mind when considering the effect of a vicious loop on a crowd, but the effect can be manifested in many ways. It has been touched on in the chapters on psychology and the media. The importance of the media in accentuating a trend has been noted in copycat behaviour with fashion, either in form of dress or in other behaviour. Whether the media influence is good depends on the people influenced. It may be important for industry wishing to advertise products and enjoy the benefits of mass production. Users may benefit by conforming and becoming accepted as one of the crowd. Alternatively those who cannot afford to buy the trendy products may feel more deprived than if the advertising were less obvious. Others will feel that they deserve more and that their rights are being negated. It is not surprising if a degree of social unrest is a consequence.

The media is not the only channel for encouraging conformity to fashion. Gladwell [3] draws attention to the "tipping point", which he defines as when a trend in fashion takes off. The tipping point can be considered as the threshold above which a positive feedback loop becomes active. Gladwell suggests that there are people who are connectors. These are people who strike up acquaintances easily and so have many connections to get things done. A consequence of this is that an idea can be communicated across a nation by as few as 5-6 people if they are connectors who know many other people. If they in turn have sufficient contacts they can influence a large number of people. He gives as an example Paul Revere famous for his midnight ride from Charlestown to Lexington Massachusetts in 1775 to warn of the approach of the British troops from Boston. He and his contacts were able to rally a considerable force to oppose the invasion. In modern times people in the media are evidently good connectors with help from the technology for television, radio and newsprint.

Adherence to fashion is largely by information, perhaps by word of mouth or by observation. There are other less obvious influences at work for example in crowd behaviour. Here the influence may be subliminal, depend on the expressions on peoples' faces or the noise they are generating. It is a clear example of a positive loop since the influence of people, when taken up by a crowd, will return to them and reinforce their attitude. The influence does not have to be rowdyism. It may be the quiet that a respectful audience expects, and the hush (or tut-tutting) that descends over the audience is the influence that is perpetuated.

Pressures to conform may be small in big cities where there is a degree of anonymity but much stronger in village life where everyone and their activities are known to each other. The effect must be even greater when people are imprisoned together. The influence of the prison system has long been criticised for the opportunity it offers to the seasoned criminal to influence the younger offender. There is a positive feedback loop in the situation where attendance at a prison influences the offender to learn from other prisoners new techniques for committing crime. The likelihood of an offender committing a more daring crime and receiving more prison sentences may be increased as more prison sentences are served.

Crowd behaviour in the modern world must include contacts on the Internet by email, which by its very nature can be multiplied to reach ever more people. Many instances are recorded where the crowds joining in demonstrations have been increased significantly by the spread of information and influence over the Internet.

Social Stability.

The rules governing society are many and varied. The law, being a relatively blunt instrument, is ineffectual in the normal run of life where social conventions are more prevalent than criminal activity. There is of course a feedback loop in action but it may be implemented in subtle ways that are not obvious to a bystander. They are nevertheless very evident to those schooled in the "correct" behaviour for the particular sect of society in which they are living.

Such loops only operate if people have something to lose by not behaving "correctly". This issue becomes important when people have been deprived of so much that they have nothing to lose. There are people who would be fed better in prison than in every day life, consequently there may be no incentive to behave and prison may be less of a sanction for good behaviour than for others of a more fortunate position. It is often necessary for children to join gang for their own protection and going to prison may be considered a badge of honour by a gang of delinquents.

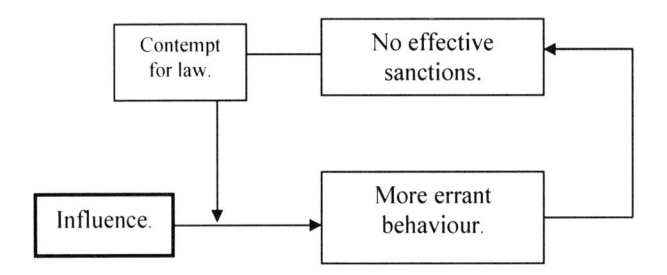

Figure 2.   Sanctions versus influence

A similar problem arises when people are below the poverty level and then become subject to the poverty trap, which gives no incentive to work. When there is a safety net below which people are not allowed to fall then sanctions in a humane society may have no effect. It is necessary for sanctions to overcome a detrimental influence.

Swing of pendulum to liberalism.

Numerous articles and reports have been published concerning the problems arising from an increasingly liberal attitude. On the one hand it was shown that it was financially beneficial to be a lone parent, rather than a married couple, with two children. One parent families have been cited in the problem of perpetuating the cycle of deprivation in which children of one parent families are more likely to become single parents. There is a danger that taxation to pay for the welfare will rise to unacceptable levels.

Bailey [7], commenting on how Britain's inner city young are being failed, gives a devastating critique of the problems arising from the liberal attitude to the welfare state and its role in removing any sense of responsibility in children. He sees too many children who are socially repressed and criminally inclined and whose behaviour has a disproportionate effect on other children. He thinks society seems to be encouraging more single parents:

> "..any young girl living in the inner city will be clued up on how the system works. They won't be too careful about not becoming parents, in some cases they will deliberately become pregnant, as they know that if they do they will get a flat. Only later do they realise the loneliness and sheer work involved in bringing up a child on their own"

- an example of the feedback coming too late to be effective.

He observes that it is the same with benefits.

> "These people are not stupid, if the state offers them money for doing something then they will do it. It is financially beneficial for married couples to present themselves as single parents, why have the father move in if it means they get less from the government."

Bailey's criticisms are important because he is matched to these people from a communications point of view. In his youth work he can do things statuary organisations cannot do because he understands the local people. He speaks the same language and understands issues from their point of view. The situation requires compensating feedback by developing peer groups to interact with young offenders.

It has been argued that people should not be motivated to become dependent on the state, not only to prevent them becoming a burden on the rest of the population, but also for their own self-esteem. This is especially true where a feedback loop causes yet more dependence. As more people are known to receive beneficial treatment so the message spreads. The greater the benefit, the higher the loop gain and the greater the abuse. Money thus deployed could otherwise be used to house more people, shorten waiting lists at hospitals or improve the pensions of people who have been contributing to retirement schemes during their working lives.

There is a trend for many people to believe in their right to welfare and ignore the fact that others have to work to provide that welfare. This separateness from reality might well be termed the new reality that will be tolerated provided the nation remains sufficiently wealthy and the system does not break down. Institutions are in place to protect most people from the unthinking behaviour that might evolve and these provide a form of feedback that keeps matters under control but only so long as the institution keeps in touch. Problems arise when the people running the institutions become insulated from the general population who are funding their work.

Minorities in a democracy.

A possible problem in a democracy is that minority interests are ignored or voted against, since by their very nature they may not command a majority vote. Such situations are not uncommon and usually result in pressure groups whose enthusiasm for their cause outweighs their small numbers. The silent majority, content with their lot does not wake up to the influence of a minority group until it has established a power base to work from. The influence is not so much a vote by numbers as a vote by a quantity that is numbers multiplied by enthusiasm. This influence is perhaps a safety valve that is important in maintaining a stable society. The importance of the safety valve is noted by the phrase "The dominance of least stable subsystem". This is the power of some minority groups to wreak havoc on the whole. Modern society being composed of complex systems, that are often centrally controlled, is vulnerable to isolated attacks by agitators who feel their rights are being infringed.

A better solution and one that gives immediate feedback is to employ an ombudsman and bring minorities into the consultation process and listen to the grievances of the people concerned. As Toffler has noted:

"The best way to deal with angry or recalcitrant minorities is to open the system, bringing them into it as full partners, permitting them to participate in social goal-setting, rather than attempting to ostracise or isolate them. Red China locked out of the United Nations and the larger international community is far more likely to destabilise the world than one laced into the system."

The older generation, excluded from the modern world by the incomprehensibility of advancing technology, may also cease to communicate and society will lose their experience for the common good. Whilst they are unlikely to become physically aggressive they are becoming a dominant economic influence, but their increasing numbers, influential at the ballot, will become less well informed.

Vicarious existence.

There is a trend for people to lead ever more a vicarious existence that shields them from the realities of life and obscures the feedback that real experience provides. Thus television provides a substitute for real life experiences and crowds watch football matches rather than playing the game themselves and experiencing first hand the consequences of errant behaviour. The future virtual reality is likely to be even more enticing and provide a powerful substitute for living. By virtual reality I mean the systems that will become available in 10 to 20 years when computing power and speed is sufficient to provide a virtual environment that cannot be distinguished from the real world. I do not mean the current systems that are being marketed under that name and used as arcade games. Aircraft simulators for training airline pilots have reached an impressive state of capability but they are too expensive for the ordinary individual to contemplate.

One of the consequences of people leading a vicarious existence in preference to an active life is the lack of feedback. It is important that their own decisions affect the outcome of a situation and provide lessons on the advantages or dangers of their mode of behaviour. The watching mentality that continuous television encourages has been apparent in the ghoul like attitudes of people who congregate around the scene of an accident, often hampering the rescue services.

Vicarious existence takes on a more ominous role when war is involved as observed by an editorial in Electronics Weekly [5].

> "......*Cold blooded and ruthless decisions taken on the battle field during the Gulf war and in the boardrooms around the world affect the lives of real people. Yet you would not believe it from the way decision-makers talk. The ability of computers to handle huge volumes of information is part of the problem allowing decision makers to retrieve abstract numbers to be analysed coldly and anonymously divorced from any worries about what the numbers actually mean, about the people hidden from them behind the faceless computer screen. Modern communications and jet travel put real physical*

distance between those that give the orders and those who feel what they mean. You cannot see the misery that unemployment brings on the printout of a spread sheet program. You can't see the blood of the injured and of the dead on the radar screen."

In a sense most people are leading a life detached from reality since a modern civilised society provides for the wants of a population without the need to concern themselves how their benefits are derived. Thus food is provided ready packed in hygienic containers in a form that is not recognisable compared with the original. Someone else killed the chickens or butchered a cow for the meat, or braved the weather to catch fish and gut them. Similarly transport is (much of the time) provided in a clean and efficient manner. Someone else in a remote factory had the task of assembling the components and welding them together to provide the car, bus or train. We only see the padded seat, a clean window and a polished exterior. It is unusual these days to look under the car bonnet to check on water and oil, let alone maintain the engine. This separateness from the basic requirements of living is of course a triumph of science, engineering and the logistics of business management. It is also supported by a nation's social capital discussed by Dasgupta [6] where national institutions administer the rules that regulate the interactions between people, industry and commerce, and people develop trusting relationships that benefit all parties.

Nevertheless whilst social capital is considered to be beneficial there are instances where institutions are storing up trouble in the years to come. Like the capital invested in a company it can be misused. The disciplined management required to build up a company in the first place may give way, as it prospered, to more relaxed behaviour that would be incompatible with building a fledgling company, and which if taken to excess, would cause the company's decline. The analogy between a company and a nation lies in misusing capital in ways that are not to a nation's benefit. Social benefits, that undermine a persons motivation to be self-supporting, fall into this category.

There is some similarity between a nation's activities and a business that prospers by the efforts of its founders. Eventually the business is sufficiently successful that the workers do not need to work as hard as they did when building up the business. Such an attitude is understandable and appropriate when the people responsible for its success take the decisions - since they are the ones who know the procedures necessary for survival.

An alternative scenario could be envisaged where outsiders take over the company and decide that the profits should not be fed back into the company. Instead they are used to fund others who make no contribution to the wealth but who it is deemed should be supported because they are unable or unwilling to make a living for themselves.

In a nation the analogy is not quite precise since those who deem that the unwilling should be supported, no matter what their attitude, are not outsiders but part of the nation affected. There are people who feel guilty of the standard of living that they enjoy if they have not contributed much to its increase. Our current wealth owes much to the toil of our forbears. Many people feel it is their duty to distribute not only this inherited wealth but also that generated by other people. The attitude is tolerated so long as the nation can support the process that enhances the nation's wealth. On the other hand if it amounts to haemorrhage of wealth that is needed to support the generating process then another feedback loop of damaging proportions will arise.

There is a duty to maintain the system that created the benefits that enable the largesse to be so distributed. The social capital is damaged when the institutions used to administrate the nation's welfare are used to distort this wealth producing process. Such social capital includes the willingness of the public to contribute to worthy causes and tolerate a degree of dependency for disadvantaged people - Figure 3. The lesson of positive loops is that the system will eventually be out of control and when the goodwill is exhausted then the system will change and some form of social revolution is to be expected.

Warren Buffett and Social Capital.

The aforementioned examples raise the question of whether the nation's capital is being invested wisely. This capital means not only the financial capital but also the social capital mentioned in the chapter on economics. Social capital comprises the institutions and way of life developed over many years of a nation's development. It consists of the beneficial ways of doing things as determined by professional institutions that can be trusted by the users. It also comprises the trust that develops between people who have to work together and rely on each other's integrity.

Warren Buffett's philosophy is outlined in [8]. It is based on the most beneficial investment of capital, specifically that the managers of the capital should act as if they are the owner's of the capital. They should invest it where it will do the most good and realise the greatest return. This philosophy is claimed to have produced a compound rate of return of 25% per annum for 37 years. This considerable performance is an example of a positive feedback loop with a loop gain of 25%. It is due in no small part to the honesty and openness of Warren Buffett. He is careful to select managers with integrity who share his view of how capital should be invested. The turnover in his investors is a mere 3% - an indication of the trust they place in him - even when he makes mistakes.

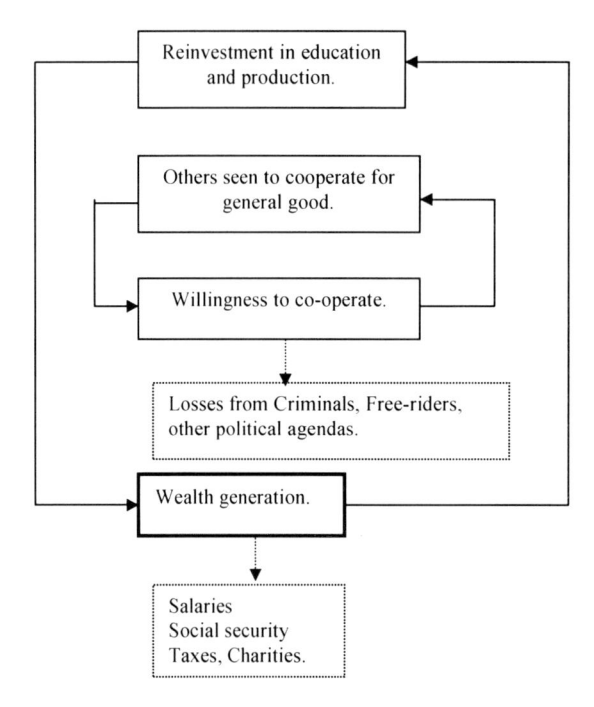

```
┌─────────────────────────────┐
│  Reinvestment in education  │◄──────┐
│  and production.            │       │
└─────────────────────────────┘       │
         ▲                            │
         │                            │
┌─────────────────────────────┐       │
│  Others seen to cooperate for│      │
│  general good.              │◄──┐   │
└─────────────────────────────┘   │   │
         │                        │   │
         ▼                        │   │
┌─────────────────────────────┐   │   │
│  Willingness to co-operate. │───┘   │
└─────────────────────────────┘       │
         ┊                            │
         ▼                            │
┌─────────────────────────────┐       │
│  Losses from Criminals,     │       │
│  Free-riders, other         │       │
│  political agendas.         │       │
└─────────────────────────────┘       │
                                      │
┌─────────────────────────────┐       │
│  Wealth generation.         │───────┘
└─────────────────────────────┘
         ┊
         ▼
┌─────────────────────────────┐
│  Salaries                   │
│  Social security            │
│  Taxes, Charities.          │
└─────────────────────────────┘
```

Figure 3. Utilisation of financial and social capital.

With this philosophy in mind the question is: can it be applied to social capital? The further question then is: is our social capital being misapplied?

The situation is different from the Buffett situation since the owners of the social capital are the general public and they do not have much choice over the managers employed to utilise it. The ballot box is one method but rather too ill defined and infrequent to be as useful compared with an investor in a business, who can walk away at a moment's notice.

Some of the managers of this social capital are parts of the civil service, and the county and town councils. They may have their own political agenda.

Various articles have noted the problems arising when donations of tax payers money are used irresponsibly. Such uses include:

> Funding a drug habit that furthers drug dependency;
> maintaining an unemployment culture;
> single parenthood that encourages single parenthood in the succeeding generation;
> children of unemployed parents becoming themselves unemployed.

These situations are fertile ground for feedback loops. An aspect of social capital is that people are prepared to contribute to worthy causes and pay their taxes provided that they believe everyone else is doing so. If too many others are getting a free ride then it reduces the willingness of otherwise honest people to pay their dues.

In many cases the media distorts the true picture and gives erroneous feedback. Advertisements often aim to increase feelings of deprivation and raise expectations too high. This may lead to belief in deserving more rights. However advertisements that show wealth enjoyed by others do not show the work and preparation that is needed to generate that wealth. A true picture might remove some of the jealousy from discontented people, and consequently one ingredient of social unrest, to help stabilise society,

Summary.

1. The increasing rate of change of environment is causing problems.
2. Methods of compensating for increased complexity are being developed.
3. The ratchet effect increases expectation.
4. Crowd behaviour is subject to positive feedback loops.
5. Social pressures are important for stability in society.
6. The pendulum may swing between repression and liberalism.
7. Power in a democracy is a function of enthusiasm as well as numbers.
8. A vicarious existence lacks the feedback necessary for learning.
9. Social capital is enhanced by mutual trust.

References:

[1] Toffler, Alvin, "Future Shock."
[2] Vickers, Sir Geoffrey, "Human systems are different".
[3] Gladwell, Malcolm, "The Tipping Point".
[4] British Association for the Advancement of Science - 1999.
[5] Electronics Weekly editorial,
[6] Dasgupta, Partha, "Social Capital and Economic Performance". Royal Institution meeting, London 2004.
[7] Bailey S, "No Man's Land", Centre for Policy studies, 2005.
[8] O'Loughlin J., "The Real Warren Buffett", Nicholas Brealey Publishing 2004.

Chapter 11.   Education.

There are so many ramifications to education that every aspect of the feedback loop is to be expected; whether this is in respect of changes to the curriculum, the maintenance of discipline in schools, the positive loop of privilege or the saturation attendant upon rapid advances in technology.

The pendulum of curriculum in the UK.

The latter half of the 20th century saw a determined effort to change the way of teaching from rote learning to a more creative form. It was envisaged that freedom of expression would enhance the creative instincts in children. These, it had been argued, had been stifled in the past.

Education is a prime candidate for the delayed assessment problem. New methods of teaching can affect a generation of children and the results not be apparent until they are tested against the needs of commerce and industry, or by the requirements of universities. Complaints from university tutors observed that some students could not write a grammatical sentence and that the standard of mathematics was inadequate for university entrance. There is no doubt that the methods of teaching, suffered by a generation of school children during the earlier part of the 20th century, needed improvement. Many children of that era perhaps became sociologists and educationalists with a mission to improve the methods and curriculum.

Some of the critics of the former era declared that rote learning stifled the creativity of children and that free expression was to be encouraged. These critics seem justified but not to the extent of abolishing one form of learning in favour of another before the outcome could be assessed. The property of the pendulum - that the further it swings one way the further it will swing in the other- is relevant. The pendulum can, however, be damped (as discussed in chapter 2) so as to prevent the swing from continuing. This could occur due to a bureaucracy that responds so slowly that all the recommended changes are not implemented. It would be preferable for the swing to be reduced by opposing forces that respond quickly and limit the changes to a more prudent level. Thus some degree of rote learning might be retained for knowledge that is essential as a building block for subsequent education but without the pedantry typical of the earlier generation. If it is necessary to modify a curriculum or method then a gentle touch of the tiller is clearly more in order than a swing to the other side. The alternative is to generate another extreme position in which opponents are roused to greater counter measures than are appropriate and the system will never settle at a sensible level.

The curriculum not only suffers from the problem of assessment over a generation but has the further difficulty that society evolves during that time and the requirements of education are likely to change to a point not envisaged when the curriculum was set. As late as 1980 many in the teaching profession did not consider computing to be a useful subject and it was several years before it became a part of the curriculum.

The pendulum of discipline.

The change in quality of university candidates is due to more than one factor. It is evident that the larger university intake organised in modern times will encompass students with lesser qualifications than previously when only those in the top stream would have been considered for a place. Another factor must be the efficiency with which the teaching profession can tutor their pupils. Teaching, for many in the UK has become a fraught profession in which it is often difficult to maintain discipline. Many teachers in the state sector have left to pursue other careers that are more rewarding and do not carry the risks that have become too common in many schools. Such a situation would appear to be the result of inadequate feedback, to those in authority, of the problems being experienced by the teaching profession. A situation noted in chapter 6 resulting from the insularity of authorities that are not sensitive to the problems of those whom they regulate.

The precise nature of this authority is not so easy to define. It appears to be a combination of direction from the Education authority, legislators and the courts, and parents of troublesome children who disrupt classes. Two possible lines of thought present themselves. Firstly a check on whether this is an example of the pendulum recovering from an extreme position in former times and secondly to consider the means of acquainting the authorities with the problems they are causing

It is not feasible for legislators, the judiciary and parents to gain first hand experience of teaching an unruly class, although the reports in the national press should go some way to spreading light on the problems. Representation on those bodies from the teaching profession (at a level that has sufficient clout to influence the cause of events) may be one outcome. Alternatively, and perhaps additionally, the responsibility for quelling unruly behaviour should rest with the authorities who set the regulations, rather than with the teachers. Should the teacher be responsible for discipline in addition to the task of teaching?

> *The Plowden Report [2] noted that in place of traditional forms of discipline there is a deep understanding of children and careful*

> *planning. Two basic assumptions are that children respond in kind to courteous and considerate treatment by adults and they will work with concentration and diligence at tasks which are suited to their abilities. It further observed that neither assumption is true for all children, or for any child all of the time, but true enough for a working basis.*

These comments may be true for a majority of children but there have been sufficient reports of problems on discipline, and consequent devastation of the teaching environment, that complacency is not appropriate. Under the pseudonym of Jude Graham [8] a teacher from New Zealand declared that in six weeks at a British school she had more abuse hurled at her than she had encountered in 25 years back in New Zealand. This experience was not unique to her but was also suffered by other teachers at the school. Bad parenting was considered the most likely explanation. One staff member was quoted as saying:

"Most of these children come from one parent homes where there is no control or discipline. All mothers want is a bit of peace and quiet and they don't care what the kids do."

A factor in this equation is the feedback loop resulting from the perceived advantage of living in a good educational area. As Hutton [9] observes:
"...Opted-out schools in well-to-do areas perform well in the league tables, attract more pupils and thus more funding and expand further; comprehensives in more down-at-heal areas find themselves with less money and fewer facilities .... good teachers are harder to find. Inevitably they gravitate to schools with fewer educational and social problems; and schools in poorer areas with greater problems find it hard to afford the pay premiums required to compensate for the additional stress on their staff. Toffler [6] has noted:

> *"Today it is not uncommon, even in grammar schools, for a child to be taught one subject by two or three different teachers in the course of one year. With teacher loyalty to the school so low, the loyalty of children cannot be summoned either. If a high proportion of teachers are preparing to move on to a better job, a better district, there will be less care, concern and commitment on their part."*

In the light of these (and other reports) it seems that the Plowden report has a degree of complacency. It is much easier to destroy than to build, and only a small minority of disruptive children is required to cause havoc. Bantock [3] argues that

> *" the teacher represents an authority by virtue of his appointment, experience, legal responsibilities and being answerable to the*

community for his behaviour. "Power is an inescapable element in adult life, with which we all at some time have to come to terms. He deprecates the insincerity, which hides the true situation and prepares a child for a fictitious world. There is the need to learn respect for the idea of authority as a necessary element in the proper functioning of the community".

Perhaps teachers are authority figures who are overruled by a higher authority (or a more distant one). If this distant authority does not receive feedback on the consequences of its decisions then there is the potential for a situation to go out of control. A factor in this equation is the legislation on human rights that creates contention between the rights of different people. The rights of one unruly pupil appear to take precedence over the rights of a whole class whose learning is disrupted. Disruptive pupils can be the engine of a positive loop if other pupils are encouraged to also misbehave.

E C Wragg [1] observes that within school, teachers are inescapably members of a social and management structure, and in schools judged to be better, teachers felt more involved in decision making. They have to react to perhaps a 1000 interpersonal transactions in a day. Most teachers took action before disruption escalated, using a high degree of vigilance and nipping disruption in the bud. The demands of one pupil can, however, consume much of a teacher's time and it is often a matter of coping or using containing strategies rather than altering behaviour,

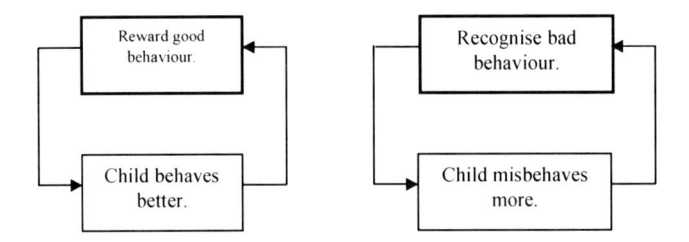

Figure 1. The positive loop of reinforcement.

B F Skinner [4] promoted the theory that we learn best when positive behaviour is reinforced, often by the reward of recognition. Children who seek attention and are told off are encouraged to misbehave further to attract more attention. It is important to ignore bad behaviour so as not to reinforce it, but to recognise and reinforce approved behaviour.

There is evidently a problem when behaviour is so bad that it cannot be ignored. In these circumstances sanctions are evidently necessary and this is an area where teachers appear to be emasculated.

The inequality of human rights.

If a teacher is denied the use of effective sanctions then evidently some support is needed to assist in the control of unruly pupils. An emergency button to call for assistance may be one option; the all-seeing-eye of CCTV could be another since bad behaviour could be recorded as evidence to present to difficult parents; particularly the ones who aggravate the problem by the rights they demand for their children. Such a system need not act as a big brother monitoring the teacher's performance since the recording could be directed at the class and the sound muted unless required for evidence.

In earlier times there is no doubt that, on occasions, methods of corporal punishment were abused and instances of teachers with sadistic tendencies could be found. Did present day legislators suffer in this way? The aim to correct an over-harsh environment in previous years is to be seen in the restrictions placed on current teachers. There are sufficient reports of trouble in the classroom to imply that the pendulum has swung too far and the revision to sanctions for bad behaviour is overdone. Whatever authority is responsible for determining these sanctions, it is too far removed from the outcome.

The bill of human rights is evidently one factor in the equation. It must recognise the rights of everyone involved in a dispute. There is the problem of measurement. In physics the contributions of different parts of a system can be precisely measured. In sociology the measurement is anything but precise. How is the relative hurt due to sanctions experienced by disruptive pupils to be measured against the hurt suffered by the teacher and the rest of the class of willing pupils whose educational prospects can be seriously hampered? There have been many reports in the press of the harm suffered by teachers who have been suspended from work due to alleged misbehaviour that has not been substantiated. The damage to the teacher appears out of all proportion to the comparatively slight discomfort suffered by the pupil.

It is to be expected that situations such as these will cause teachers to leave in greater numbers. A consequence, of their leaving the profession, is larger classes for those remaining. A larger class is fertile ground for greater behaviour problems and the basis for a positive loop accelerating out of control as shown in figure 2.

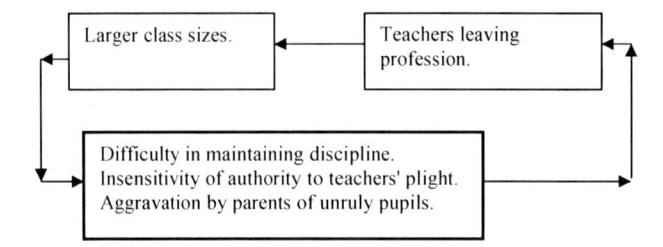

```
┌─────────────────────┐      ┌─────────────────────┐
│ Larger class sizes. │◄─────│ Teachers leaving    │◄───┐
└─────────────────────┘      │ profession.         │    │
   │                         └─────────────────────┘    │
   │   ┌──────────────────────────────────────────┐     │
   │   │ Difficulty in maintaining discipline.    │     │
   └──►│ Insensitivity of authority to teachers' plight.├────┘
       │ Aggravation by parents of unruly pupils. │
       └──────────────────────────────────────────┘
```

Figure 2. The result of insensitive authority.

An attempt to analyse some of the problems is shown in Figure 3 with a view to assessing corrective measures. The figure represents an aspect of the education system in which disruption by unruly pupils is the engine of the loop. The feedback loop is now the crowd effect on other pupils who copy and add to the disruption; the output of the system is chaos. Applying the Scoldent list to this situation would suggest the following:

1. Saturation would imply finding a means of limiting the effect of the pupil.
2. Cut-off will be achieved by removing the pupil from the class.
3. Open-loop requires that the influence on other pupils be removed, for example by screening them or teaching via a television link with earphones.
4. Low gain in this context means reducing the energy applied by the pupil to the disruption - perhaps by sedating him or using one of the drugs to prevent hyper-activity.
5. Delay: Diverting the attention of the disruptive pupils into something more interesting to them might delay the aggression. A scheme whereby pupils agree to communicate their aggressiveness to an intermediary would achieve a delay and slow the effect of the influence.
6. The external force could be an emergency button for support, possibly with a CCTV monitor.
7. Negative feedback would occur if the disruptive pupils were made aware of the effect of their actions - possibly by the other students who wished to study. Assessment of the pupil's problem, and diverting the pupil's energy into other pursuits could be a remedy.
8. Theme change: Time to rethink the legislation. There reports [10] of success by instilling more discipline and pride in the school.

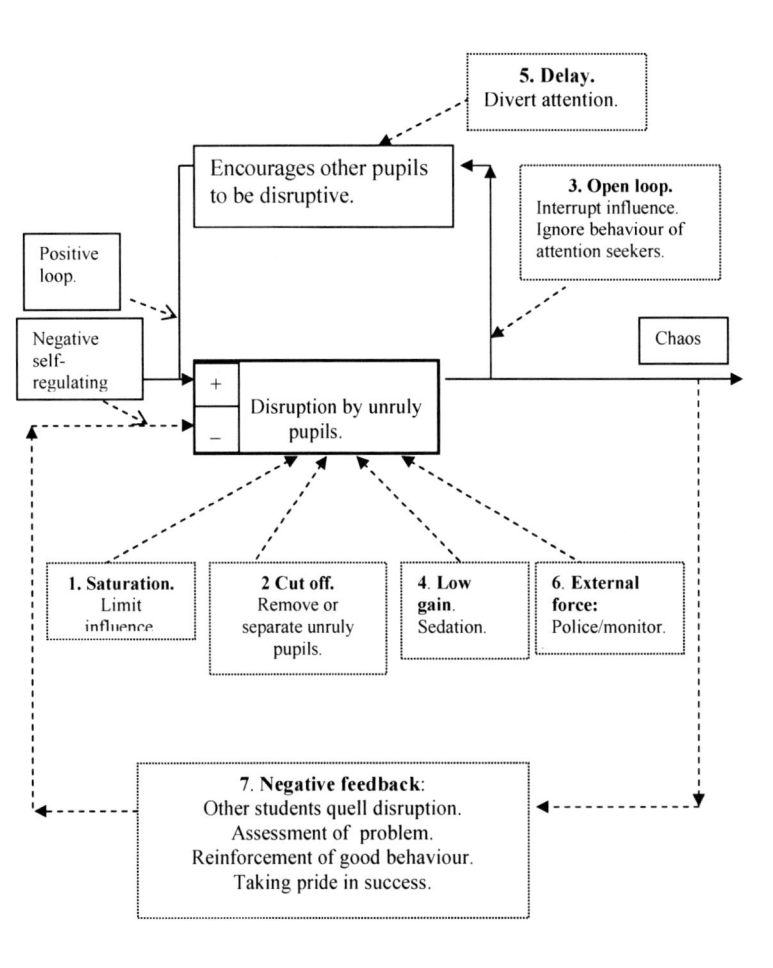

Figure 3. The disruption loop and factors to reduce the effect.

Higher education.

One of the evolving problems in higher education is the imbalance in numbers of candidates for some of the university faculties. The trend to sociological and business studies has its counterpart in the demise of the physical sciences. A shortfall, for example, in physicists and engineers manifests itself as a shortfall in physics teachers, particularly so if industry takes the first bite of the cherry. There is a degree of gearing here since if industry monopolises the take-up then even fewer are left for teaching than if the distribution were in proportion to those graduating. A positive loop is again in evidence since fewer physics teachers implies fewer students are prepared for that field of endeavour. The tendency for less qualified teachers to fill the posts is not one that will enthuse students.

The trend is one that has far reaching implications for the nation. It is important for scientists to communicate with the general public at a time when the march of technology is ever increasing. The larger number of graduates in sociology and media studies means that people who do not have scientific training dominate the media. Amongst television producers it is difficult to find someone with a scientific background - even though they might be producing programmes on scientific subjects. Their understanding of engineering is particularly fraught. For example a media session at the British Association for the Advancement of Science was addressed by a television producer who declared that she was planning a programme on "the lever" as an example of engineering. Such attitudes do not reflect the intellectual level required and spell disaster for encouraging students with the required abilities in physics and mathematics to study engineering at university.

The pendulum of requirement.

Delay in a negative feedback loop as noted previously causes oscillation as the system moves to either side of its neutral or preferred position like the pendulum. It is likely then that procedures, which do not reveal their outcome until many years later, will exhibit this oscillation over this period of years.

The flow of candidates into certain professions showed this behaviour. When solicitors were in short supply, parents recommended their children to study law. Many years later when all those children qualified, the profession was over staffed and many would-be solicitors sought jobs elsewhere. Accordingly the then abundance of solicitors encourages the choice of an alternative profession. There is then a shortage of solicitors and the pendulum swings back to complete its cycle over a time period of several years. At the time of writing Business and Finance courses are a popular choice and no doubt commerce will become overpopulated with graduates in this sphere. The salaries caused by the shortage of skills in computing will cause a trend to over-population in this field. A potential shortage will be aggravated by the rapid changes in technology occurring in the foreseeable future which will require more informed staff.

The obvious counter to this problem is to anticipate the trend and go against the crowd. Thus a sage's advice to a young man was to choose the profession that is over crowded now. Evidently there would still be a problem if the advice were spread too widely.

The Private School and unequal opportunities.

There has been much debate and criticism of the benefits received by pupils in private education. If learning aids learning, it is evident that an important loop is in operation and it is one that will accentuate inequality. Whether or not attempts should be made to reduce the effect of this loop is subject to debate. When a nation is in competition with other nations then it must nurture its brightest talent to research and organise the nation's needs adequately. Maximisation of ability (and in consequence accentuation of inequality) in these circumstances is clearly important. This trend is increased when children are screened according to ability and further increased when a bright child is awarded a scholarship giving access to tuition at a more advanced level. A reasoned line of argument could make the case that everyone should be educated to the maximum of their ability; subject, of course, to the problem of paying for it. Doubtless Aldous Huxley [5] would have argued the need for the less able to fill routine jobs, and that they should be prepared for this by their education.

Attempts to counteract the inequality come in different ways by, for example, schools that are not streamed. When pupils of mixed ability are taught in the same class, the less able children receive more of the teachers' time. If the able spend more time without instruction then the degree of inequality will tend to be reduced. It might be considered that there is an analogy here to the inverse tournament referred to in chapter 4.

An alternative method of boosting the chances of the less able child occurs when parents pay for private education. Whereas not all independent schools provide as good an education as the state schools, there are complaints that the wealthy give undue advantage to their children by paying for more intensive tuition. If the independent sector is able to give more attention to the less able pupil then a reduction in inequality is expected. Criticism of a self-perpetuating elite (itself a loop phenomenon) is understandable when the pupil is also capable. In principle this complaint should also be directed at parents who give their children extra tuition either by helping with the homework or by paying for extra lessons. It is clear that parental support can make a great deal of difference to the child's performance. Evidently the aims of the parents and the benefits to the nation may not always be compatible. The nation benefits more by placing students in university places and in jobs according to their innate ability rather than by exam results that have been elevated by extra resources.

There have, however, been reports of universities making allowances when selecting underprivileged candidates so as to counteract the influence of wealth alone - a manifestation of a negative loop. It is evidently more difficult to assess the appropriate allowances when the advantages incurred by the pupil derive from home background rather than type of schooling. The principle extends to counteracting the influence of a school with a poor academic record. Candidates who succeed in spite of the disadvantage are likely to be of inherently greater merit and their entry to higher education should benefit the nation.

The issue of private education includes an element of fashion, which as discussed in chapters 7 and 15 is subject to a positive loop. Its influence on parents, augmented by reports of some inadequate schools in the state sector, has caused an increase in the number of parents willing to pay extra for education. (The inadequate private school seems to have escaped the same publicity.)

It is not the purpose of this book to comment on the moral issues of buying a place on the escalator of private education but simply to observe that it is a social phenomenon that affects a proportion of the population. If money is limited then there maybe a conflict between funding gifted children who will otherwise be held back, and funding less able children who would benefit from education in another type of institution. In the former case the inequality between the children is accentuated. In the latter case the difference is reduced to some extent.

Education and accelerating change.

Sir Geoffrey Vickers [7] observes:
"The rate of change increases at an accelerating speed without a corresponding acceleration in the rate at which further response can be made; and this brings us nearer the threshold beyond which control is lost".

The rate of change of technology has far reaching implications both for education and culture, and for the ability of many to keep up with the consequences. Inequality in awareness will be a factor that divides society into a new category of haves and have-nots; and a new category of underclass drawn from people who cannot cope with the new technologies.

Computing is one such category. Not only does it require much effort to comprehend the instruction manuals; the mode of operation is different to instruments used by previous generations. Thus switches and knobs from which to choose an activity were all visible at once. A computer on the other hand presents only a limited view of the options available and it is necessary to remember which drop-down list contains the necessary action.
This problem arises because there are so many facilities provided by a computer system that there is not room enough to make all options visible at the same time. It nevertheless causes difficulties for people weaned on a parallel interface.

A loop now operates as shown in figure 4. People who receive adequate education in Information Technology have access to more facilities, especially on the Internet, that provide cheaper and more services. Whether booking a holiday or buying equipment at lower cost they have more disposable income left over to buy more resources and perhaps online tuition.

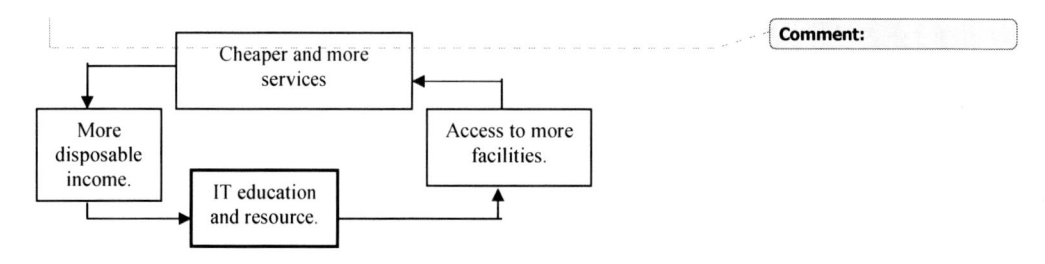

Figure 4. Advantages of Information Technology.

Various writers have commented on the exponential expansion in technology and invention that has occurred during the last century. Toffler [6] worries about the ability of people to cope with the information overload.
"No previous generation has been exposed to one tenth of the amount of vicarious experiences we lavish on ourselves and our children. What happens to emotional development as the ratio of vicarious experience to real experience rises?"

A greater divergence between young and old is likely and this can only accentuate the problem in figure 4.

The issue of vicarious experiences raises a new problem. Many computer games do not represent reality. Children need to experience reality to comprehend the results of their behaviour. The feedback received from the real world teaches them the consequences of their actions so that they learn the dangers of behaving inappropriately. This compensating negative feedback helps the child to adjust to the world. Whilst most children will not believe that the more extravagant behaviour exhibited by the icons in computer games will represent reality, nevertheless the time spent in vicarious activities is a source of disinformation. It is not only computer games that limit their experiences of reality. The nanny state is also playing a role in not exposing children to potential dangers from which to learn safe behaviour.

Summary.

1. Changes in education suffer from excessive delay in the feedback necessary to assess the outcome.
2. An excessive swing has occurred from an authoritarian regime to a liberal one.
3. There has been insufficient feedback of the problems caused by legislation.
4. A lack of incentive is steering students away from more difficult subjects
5. Candidates for certain professions oscillate between abundance and scarcity.
6. Education is a basis for positive loops that accentuate inequality.
7. Such loops are necessary to nurture a nation's brightest talent to compete internationally.
8. The complexity of modern technology accentuates the diversity of benefits.
9. There is a danger that the vicarious experience of virtual reality will over-ride the feedback from real life.

References.

[1] Wragg E C, "Primary Teaching Skills" 1993.
[2] The Plowden Report, 1967.
[3] Bantock G., "Freedom and Authority in Education"
[4] Skinner B F (1954)
[5] Huxley A., "Brave New World".

[6] Toffler A., "Future Shock". Pan books 1971.
[7] Vickers G, "Value systems and Social Progress". 2001.
[8] Graham J, "Bullied out of Britain". 2002
[9] Hutton W, "The State We're In". Vintage books 1996.
[10] Stanford P – Interview with Martin Tissot.

Chapter 12.   Companies

Profit or loss?

A commercial company is a complex business. It is necessary for it to generate enough profit to compensate for the expenses incurred and still feed back enough into the business to generate at least as much profit the next time round. A positive loop may be beneficial by increasing benefit or detrimental by accelerating failure. The quantity in the feedback loop represents the profit (or loss), which is fed back into the business in order to sustain and hopefully increase the business. Thus a village baker sells loaves of bread to buy flour. If he is successful he is able to buy more flour than previously and thereby sell more loaves to achieve extra profit. In this case the influence fed back is the ability to buy flour; as long as this increases the business expands - subject to all other factors being favourable.

Eventually he saturates his market and his business has reached its maximum. At this stage the loop gain is unity and the feedback no longer operates to increase the business because sales are held constant by the market restraints. It could still operate to decrease the business if other factors change, causing the loop gain to reduce to less than one. Suppose a new manager takes over and siphons off so much profit that the baker has to buy less flour. Fewer loaves are baked and the profit is less and the business cycle declines. Under these circumstances it will continue to decline until the manager has a change of heart, or is replaced or the business goes bankrupt. It will be remembered that this is the same positive feedback loop. It is the change in profit (or loss) being fed back that alters the outcome. In both cases the change in profit is accentuating itself. It will be seen that there is a threshold of income above which the business will prosper and below which the business will decline. This simple example is unlikely to occur since it will be complicated by the sale of cakes, by competition from other shops in the high street and hopefully by a manager who is more astute than this one.

Start-up companies.

The Start-up Company can be a particularly fragile example. It is analogous to the ball on top of a cylindrical mound. A slight nudge can start the ball down one side of the cylinder, which represents profit. Alternatively it could fall to the side representing loss. The nudge will be a combination of the finance required to keep the company afloat until it is profitable and the expertise required to perform the tasks on hand. An under-capitalised company will be ineffective when compared to a company with the resources necessary to fund efficient methods and equipment. Too much funding by way of loans, however, may not only be expensive but may also generate too relaxed a style of management which will not auger well for future success.

The Start-up has little in the way of reserves save for the commitment of staff who are likely to have shares in the company and willing to dedicate much time and effort for its success. This provides resilience to cope with problems. A small staffing is also compatible with good communications and each can assess the contributions and capabilities of each other. The entrepreneurial style of management will in time change to a more routine style. In the early days the founders will know all the staff and be able to influence them directly. They will get to know the problems first hand and be able to deal with them with little delay. The management of a large firm in contrast, delegates these tasks and in particular delegates the choice of staff to others. The hiring of more people and especially the selection of the best people is a costly overhead. The commitment of new staff is likely to be less than that of the founders and significant effort will be expended in keeping each member usefully employed. These costs together with many others represent a large drop in the gain of the feedback loop of the system which is the company. The feedback will consist not only of money from profits but also knowledge derived from the experience of running the business.

In the larger company this feedback loop may be further removed. The capabilities and problems are slower to be addressed and the efficiency of the work force is reduced. This problem was illustrated in the report [1] on the decline of Marks and Spencer Ltd. It was noted that senior management did not receive from middle management, in sufficient time, the warning signals of the dwindling popularity of its merchandise. This problem is due to the delay consequent on accountability, as noted in the chapter on employment.

If the losses are serious enough to threaten failure then the business may have to rely on extra efforts by dedicated staff or by an understanding Venture Capitalist who extends the terms of the funding. The larger company on the other hand usually has reserves to tide it over a lossy period and some resilience in costs for services that are less necessary in the short term.

When seeking funding for a new company a plan will have to be made that assesses the costs of development, manufacture, marketing and sales. Figure 1 (scenario A) is typical of a presentation made to a Venture Capitalist to justify investment. It is, however, dependent on forecasts being met and in particular on sales income being received on time. Initially the company goes into debt before a product is available for sale. The maximum negative cash flow occurs when sales income equals outgoings and thereafter increasing sales income exceeds the company's costs (under scenario A) until the loans can be repaid and dividends paid to equity investors.

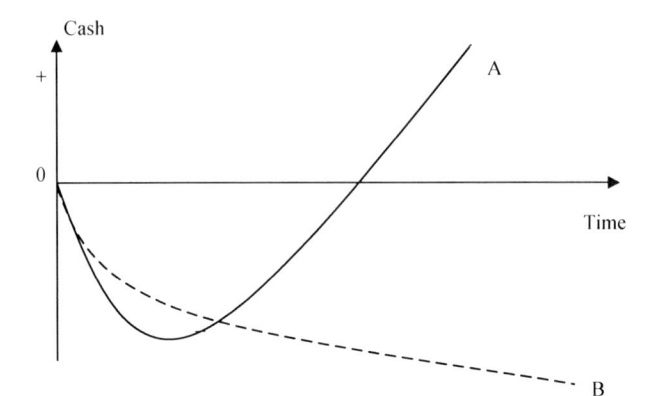

Figure 1. Cash flow issues.

Typically there will be many unknowns, and problems in development and manufacture will delay the contribution from sales. Such a delay can have a crucial influence on the success of the company. Since a start-up is a high-risk situation the cost of loans will be expensive; the interest payable is cumulative and adds to the outstanding capital to be repaid. A point can be reached (scenario B) where the cost of loans exceeds the likely sales income and the business ceases to be viable. The business is subject to a positive feedback loop that can act either to the benefit or failure of the company depending on which side of the threshold or "hill" the company is situated. In systems terms it is analogous to the starving chicken referred to in chapter 1 where the robust chicken secures an ample share of food but the starving one is too weak to fight its way to an adequate share.

To take the analogy further a young chicken must be strong to secure enough food to make itself stronger. A start-up company must be invested with enough capital to cover the costs before income is generated. A loss making business will lose capital at an increasing rate as the interest payments to cover increasing debts reduce the company's assets to the point that it is not viable. A classical detrimental positive feedback loop. The successful business of course benefits from income exceeding costs sufficiently to cover the credit required to fund increased sales. Available cash will be reduced by the delay between paying for the raw materials and labour, and selling the product. The delay in receiving payment for sales further reduces the cash available for investment. These together introduce a delay into the loop, which, in effect, reduces the gain. Whereas this is true of manufacturing, some retailers sell their wares before they pay for them so that sales improve their cash flow position. Such retailers shift the credit burden to the producers.

Investment or subsidy.

The financing of development and manufacture are but two of the issues facing management. The generation of sufficient sales income to pay for the outgoings depends on adequate marketing. Not only is it necessary to bring the product to the notice of potential customers but it must be priced at a level that is both attractive to customers and sufficient to cover costs. Here is another example of the starving chicken syndrome; a positive loop can appear in two guises.

A fledgling bus company illustrates the principle. It must price its fares so that sufficient customers use the service to pay the running costs. Management seeks to maximise revenue. There will be an optimum price. If the price is increased then fewer people choose to use the service and if the price is further increased, in an attempt to regain the loss in revenue, then the result is even fewer customers. A situation known to the economist as the law of diminishing returns. Alternatively if the price had been reduced to attract more customers then the increase in customers may not compensate for the lower fare. In this example the marketing people will be acting in a negative feedback loop. In order to find the optimum fare it is necessary to vary it above and below the optimum in order to assess where the maximum revenue lies. A decrease in revenue indicates an error in their judgement so they must retrace their steps to minimise the error.

It is possible that even when services or products are pitched at the optimum price, to maximise revenue, the business is not viable - Figure 2. In these circumstances there are often other factors to be considered: such as social or economic benefit from other activities. The service might be subsidised by a council as a benefit to local residents; or a supermarket might subsidise transport to its out of town store in order to benefit financially from increased sales. The graph of income versus fares changes is then as shown in figure 3.

A thriving company depends on its shareholders and the banks to provide the capital necessary for expansion. Some companies, such as those in the

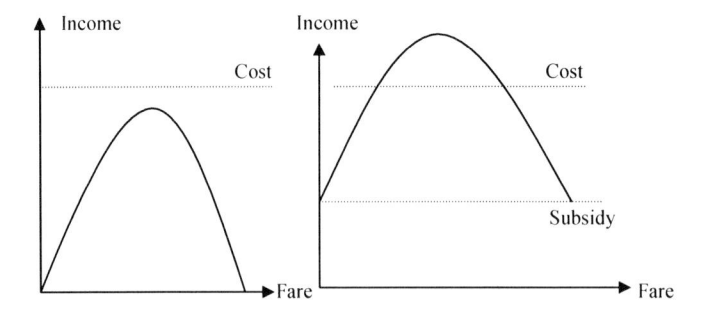

Figure 2. **Figure 3.**

Information Technology industry, may be sufficiently profitable to fund their own expansion. A company must make the most of its resources by negotiating finance to benefit from the economy of scale. A loan provides a form of financial gearing that increases the effect resulting from the management and expertise of the company. Gearing can give greater gain in the loop and acts as a multiplier of profits or losses.

Other positive loops will manifest themselves as a company increases in size. Just as technology feeds on itself so the skills and ideas of a larger staff will feed upon each other to produce better ideas and methods. Good staff morale can also generate a positive loop. Expertise encourages the arrival of more expertise whether in the prime technology or in supporting skills. The pool of talent that is generated is available to the companies in the neighbourhood and movement between companies spreads the expertise upon which each can build. A not dissimilar effect has occurred in university industrial parks where legal and financial expertise is also available as required. The needs of small companies have been identified and the experience is available to support all the companies in the park.

It is evident that the rate of expansion of a business is a function of the loop gain. If the money fed back into resources is doubled then (all other things being proportional) the output of the business will double. Whereas this is a simplified picture of a complex system in which it could be hard to assess accurately the contributions and costs of each resource, nevertheless the overall picture holds true. All costs and inefficiencies (including the treacle of bureaucracy) reduce the gain of the loop. The positive loop is expected to produce useful output and a proportion of the output is expected to be fed back around the loop of a company to help it grow. Where the output is money (representing profit from sales) some of it will be used to pay dividends and interest on bank loans.

The example of the baker can be measured from day to day but a company of any size must be measured over a period, which is long enough for all the contributions from the fixed, and variable costs to be identified. Typically this will be over a year but a company conducting significant Research and Development would have to be measured over a longer period. Pharmaceutical companies are particularly prone to the problem, which is accentuated by an extensive period of evaluating a drug for safety. Oil exploration, also, is a long-term enterprise.

Forecasting the market.

A change in circumstances arising from a change in the market or competition may cause a profitable company to drop to the level where the business fails. For the high technology companies the profit used to buy flour becomes, in the longer term, the proportion of profit fed back and used to pay for research and development.
The positive loop described above is necessary for a system to survive and overcome setbacks but a negative compensating feedback loop incorporating market information is also required to help steer the right path in the economy. The market provides the information for management to make corrections to the business. This may be in respect of the quantity of sales, type of product or the need to redesign.

At a time of rapid change in technology much of the money fed back will be ineffective unless channelled into the right prospect. Choosing the prospect that is appropriate for the expertise of the company, and will at the same time meet the future market demand, is a challenging one for scientific and engineering management. It is especially difficult when competing against the cultural advantages enjoyed by overseas nations – both in terms of their attitudes to industry, and long term finance without the need for short-term profit. The overall picture as might be expected is a complicated one in which many influences contribute to success and failure.

A scoldent list of factors that cause failure in industry might be:

Saturation:	Of supply line.
Cut-off:	Of supplies
Open-loop:	No reinvestment.
Low gain:	Internal expenses
Delay in feedback:	Late payment
External force or influence:	Change in market
Negative feedback loop:	Competition

1. *Saturation* of the supply chain, for necessary components, limits production and consequent profits.
2. *Cut-off* of supplies may be due to bankruptcy of supplier or failure to pay invoices
3. *Open loop* could be due to no profits being fed back because of business climate, mismanagement or because customers are over-stocked.
4. *Low gain* in the loop (due to taxation, bureaucracy and inefficiency) reduces wealth generation.
5. *Delay* in money fed back due to late payment on sales reduces available cash flow for purchase of materials.
6. *External factors* such as a change in the market due to fashion or new inventions, cause reduction in sales and may require redesign of the product.
7. *Negative feedback* occurs when competitors see a successful business and are tempted into the same market.

Figure 4 shows the above factors diagrammatically. Items 1, 2, 4 and 6 reduce the effectiveness of the wealth producer. Items 3 and 5 oppose the feedback of profit around the loop. Item 7 shows competition that increases with sales.

Much has been said about the influence of the financial community in demanding a fast turn around in investment. Whilst this may keep the management on its toes there are conflicting aspects. In the one case as outlined above, there is the requirement to anticipate the market and technological trends and this becomes more difficult as the development cycle lengthens. One the other hand it is important for a company to make significant investment in time and money for research in order to achieve a lead over its competitors. There are always certain developments which will stand a company in good stead whatever the market decides. It is usually of merit to make a product that performs faster, more accurately or more efficiently. Even so the whims of the market may not be entirely predictable.

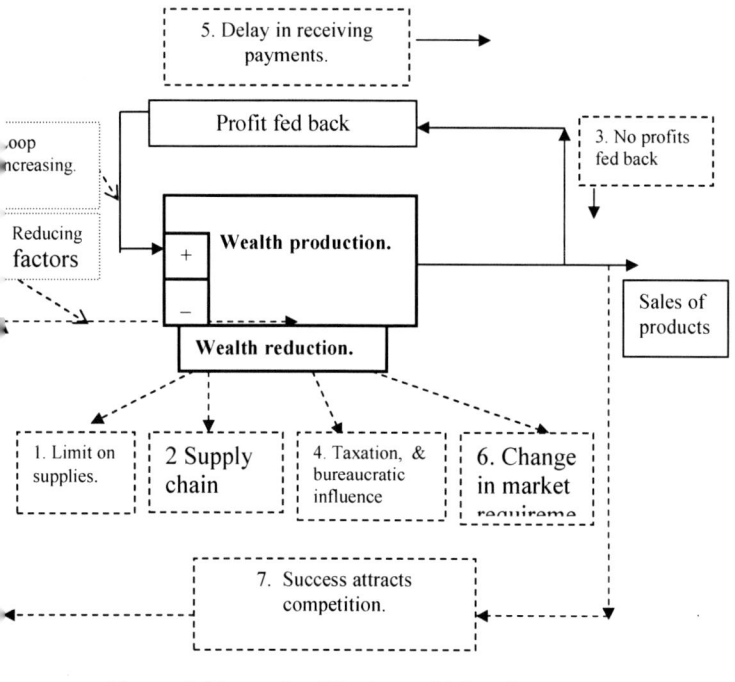

Figure 4. Example of factors which reduce company efficiency.

Summary.

1. Positive feedback loops in various forms are essential for an expanding company.
2. The start up company requires impetus, by way of finance or expertise, to be in the right mode of looping.
3. Delay in feedback to senior management is a cause of company failure.
4. Maximum sales performance depends on optimising conflicting requirements.

5. Continuing feedback from market performance is essential to steer the company strategy.
6. Market forecasts during a period of rapid change may mean leap-frogging the competition.

References.

BBC2 Money Programme, October 2000

Chapter 13.   Employment.

"The rise in the total of those employed is governed by Parkinson's Law and would be much the same whether the volume of work were to increase, diminish or disappear altogether"
- C Northcote Parkinson 1909-1993.

Management.

If we walk into a well run company we will find the staff going about their daily work with an air of competence and, as likely as not, with contentment. The Personnel Department will have done their share in choosing people who are compatible with the aims of the management. They in turn will have installed a set of incentives to ensure that the staff behaves in a manner considered to be in the best interests of the company. I use the term "best interests" in its enlightened sense to include staff welfare on the basis that discontented staff are not as beneficial to the employer.

How does an employer choose so many potentially disparate people who can work in harmony? People are not the same and will not do a particular form of work in an identical manner (unless e.g. controlling machinery). Placing people in a form of organisational straitjacket is a short route to discontentment. Offering a degree of flexibility to staff enables them to feel more responsible for success and is beneficial for morale. The staff may also find more efficient ways of performing a job.

It is useful to make an analogy with the pendulum. One of its properties mentioned in chapter one is that the influence, which causes it to return to its stable position, increases as the departure from the midpoint increases. The analogy with management is that the influence on an employee, by way of benefits or potential sanctions, also increases as the employee departs from the preferred mode of operation. This influence does not prevent a degree of flexibility in the operation caused, for example, by the Monday morning feeling or by domestic problems.

Practised managers control staff in subtle ways so that they may be unaware of any overt influence. It may be the absence of a smile rather than a reprimand; it may be a reference to how well others are settling in and coping with the work or perhaps an enquiry into the employee's health. The salary review time is too late in the year for the effective manager to take action.

Even if the analogy to the pendulum is taken it is important to bear in mind the example of the learner car driver. The experienced managers can steer their departments with a barely perceptible touch of the steering wheel. A new manager, in part due to inexperience and in part due to not having developed sensitive antennae, is likely to apply the influence later and with more force. The greater the force the greater the swing in the other direction and less even the path of the organisation. The analogy in management, to the drunken driver, is hopefully rare and no more likely to get through the promotion ladder.

A positive loop is also in operation with the effective manager. Maslow [1] and others have drawn attention to the benefit of positive reinforcement in contrast to the detrimental effect of criticism. Praise improves work and therefore generates more praise. Criticism creates the potential for more criticism.

If an employee can do the job adequately then the effective manager will allow more freedom to do job. The manager's confidence in giving a subordinate more responsibility is likely to make the subordinate more responsible and the loop increases until reaching a level of maximum competence.

Delay of accountability.

Managers in most situations can monitor progress and influence trends quickly before a problem arises. This is particularly true in the small business where everyone is in close contact. As the business expands and employs more people so the line of influence is carried through more layers of influence, which delay the impact of planning. By the time the chain of influence has reached board level the delay may be 3 months, rising to a year or more for the shareholders.

Accountability is necessarily a response to the past. It is the substitute for direct control by the employment of someone to do their best under the threat of sanctions if they fail or do not perform adequately. The retrospective sanctions thus imply delay in the feedback loop. The preferred route must be to employ someone who benefits directly by the actions taken and in accordance with the goals that are set. One way is to employ someone who has the expertise and also a share in the profits enjoyed by following the optimum path.

Parkinson's law.

This discussion would not be complete without reference to Parkinson's law [1]. Its basic form "Work expands so as to fill the time available for its completion" hides some interesting derivations. "Work" does not imply useful work. Its alternative theme as a rising pyramid derives from two statements: (1) An official wants to multiply subordinates, not rivals; (2) Officials make work for each other. The result is a positive loop that increases the workforce to a surprising degree.

Parkinson argues that a manager who considers himself overworked has three options. Firstly to resign, secondly to share the work with a colleague or thirdly to demand two subordinates. Option 1 loses his pension and option 2 introduces a rival for future promotion. Option 3 however increases his prestige and if he divides the work of his two subordinates into two categories he will be secure because he will be the only person who understands both. In the course of time one of the subordinates will seek assistance and the same options will apply. In the cause of equality the second subordinate also acquires two assistants. The manager's workload now consists of co-ordinating the extra staff and seven people are doing the work that one did before - Figure 1. Parkinson's amusing presentation softens some pertinent facts that were an embarrassment to many in management.

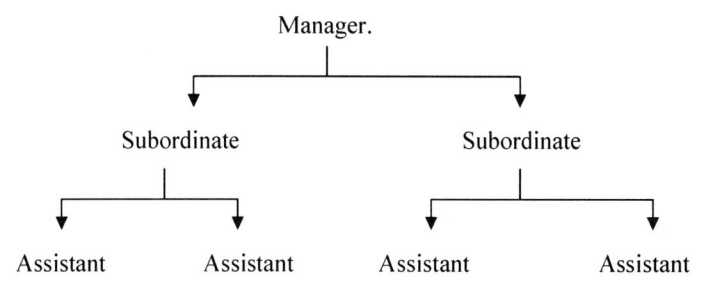

Figure 1. Parkinson's laws,

Government.

The role of government in supporting employment is less immediate than that of the employer. It is, nevertheless, one of the trials of the politician that government is blamed for unemployment when it rises above acceptable levels. Government is relatively ponderous but the delays in reacting to a situation may not be its fault. Even with computers to help in processing the data, with which to decide policy, there is a significant delay in collecting the data. It is not possible to know where the economy is at a given moment.

By the time the data is analysed it may be so out of date that consequent actions have a perverse effect. This is sometimes referred to as the "notorious touch on the tiller". In that case the helmsman is steering from a different position in the economy to the one he thought he was. If out of date data indicates a recession when in fact the economy has started to recover, then a decrease in interest rate intended to halt recession may overheat the economic recovery. Conversely an increase in interest rate to limit inflation can push the economy towards recession if applied after the economy has changed and lead to greater unemployment.

Rate of change

A greater cause of delay, in response to adverse situations, is the inertia exhibited by many people. They are often fully occupied with detail and consequently do not take notice of other situations until they have reached the level of a problem: an example of an intellectual straitjacket for which a solution is greater flexibility and responsibility in achieving the company's goals.

The Trade Union movement in the past has often been inflexible. The time to respond to necessary changes has sometimes been many years. When a company has lost its competitive edge the results are damaging to both the employers and staff in the long run.

It has been noted (Toffler) that the increasing rate of change caused by new technology causes more and more people to be out of touch with modern developments. In consequence fewer people are in a position to evaluate current circumstances. The young are more willing to accept new situations as though they have always been there. In contrast the older generation, knowing that such situations may not stand the test of time, are slower to give approval. If the older generation are less in touch with modern technology then the younger people will evaluate the results of change; but both experience and understanding are necessary for the evaluation. Otherwise it is likely that trends will be more far reaching before detrimental effects are assessed. The market feedback is likely to be a factor in determining which staff play which role within the company. This will be a delayed loop and some companies will fall behind if inertia prevents fast enough change.

The question then arises as to who should be employed to evaluate new technology. Much of the technology that has revolutionised the turn of the century has originated in Asian countries. One reason for this may be the culture where a top down approach is replaced by a lateral organisation. In one of the most successful companies it was reported that the job of management was to supply the services needed by the engineers. The company planning is the responsibility of the engineers since they are the people who are in touch with the technology & its potential, and who are aware of its problems. Management is there to provide the resources required and no doubt to act as moderators with the benefit of experience of matters outside the realm of the technology.

Matching of employer and employee.

Perfect matching of an employee to a job is difficult. Three of the problems that arise are:
1. There are costs involved for both employer and employee in changing jobs.
2. Subsidies and taxation distort the corrective action of a feedback loop.
3. A government-enforced minimum wage breaks the loop action.

In a free economy the employer is able to offer a wage that reflects the value of work to be performed by an employee. Similarly a person is free to bid for a job at a certain wage in the expectation of contributing sufficient value to a company to justify the wage. A feedback loop is in operation. In the event that an employee does not contribute the value expected then there is the option of dismissal or payment of a lower wage. If the value of the employee's contribution exceeds the wage, there is then the option of demanding a higher wage or seeking a higher paid job elsewhere. The corrective action of the loop tends to maintain a fairly constant rate of pay for similar jobs. The loop does not operate perfectly for two reasons. Firstly the change in wage may not reflect the cost of obtaining the change. Secondly the influence of government may interfere with the operation of a corrective loop.

An employee dissatisfied with the wage or salary received must weigh up the prospects of another job with higher pay versus the cost and upheaval that the change may entail. The cost of change must be added to the present (inadequate) salary before negotiating an increase in salary. This implies the worker will continue in an underpaid job longer than if there were no penalties in moving. The result may be a dissatisfied worker who does not perform at full potential and becomes frustrated. In these circumstances his attention may be diverted to unprofitable activities such as chatting with colleagues who are then also diverted from their work.

Alternatively an employer, who is dissatisfied with a worker, must evaluate the cost of obtaining and training a successor. In this case the wage paid may initially exceed the value of the contribution. Not only does the employer have to pay the cost of recruitment and training but also the new employee may be seeking compensation for the cost of change (such as moving house and travel) on top of salary paid. The effect of these changes is to cause a delay in the feedback loop and the payment oscillates about a figure that represents the value of the contribution.

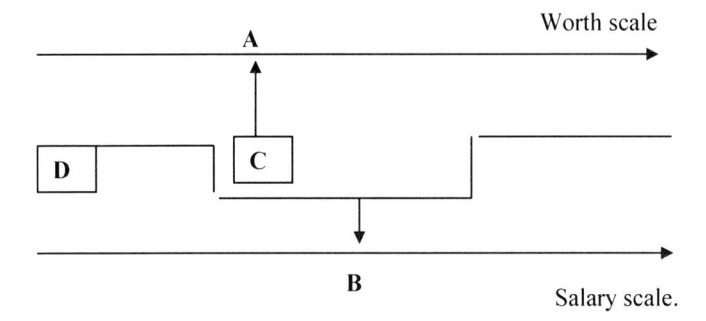

Figure 2. Slop in the system.

The mismatch is illustrated in figure 2 where pointer A can move along a scale representing the worth of the employee to the company. The pointer A is attached to a box C that can move a device D, left or right, once it makes contact. The amount C can move before D moves represents the slop in the system. The device D is attached to a pointer on the salary scale that determines the earnings of the employee. Initially the new recruit is paid rate B, which is higher than his worth. Pointer A moves to the right as the recruit gains experience and starts contributing to the success of the company. When A and B coincide the employee's earnings are appropriate for the contribution made. The box attached to the pointer must move further to the right before it connects with the block attached to point B. B now lags behind A, reflecting the cost of moving to a new job. There are of course many companies that review salaries earlier to maintain contented employees.

Decline of employment in manufacturing.

One of the issues concerning the UK is the decline of the manufacturing industry and consequent decline in the employment that the industry provides. There are several factors at work such as the competition from people in developing countries where wages are lower and possibly where governments subsidise their own industry with grants. A further factor must be the change in cultural attitudes in England in contrast to the attitudes at the time of the industrial revolution.

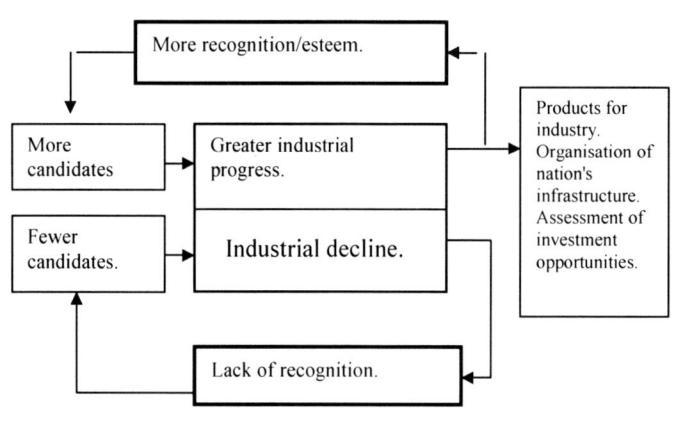

Figure 3. Some factors in industrial decline.

It is common to hear complaints that science research in the UK is exploited overseas. If the science is of merit, then it should enable advanced systems and equipment to be manufactured. This, however, requires a sufficient engineering resource for the planning and design. This resource is compromised when so many university students opt for less intellectually demanding courses.

An additional factor is the limited prestige attached to the profession. The situation was noted by a New Scientist editorial, which asked: what is unique about British society that it holds the engineer in less esteem than any other society in the world? The problem is unlikely to be resolved while the person who services the washing machine is confused with engineering graduates who in the present day need to be of the calibre to compete internationally. A further consequence is an insufficient pool of people with the expertise to evaluate organisational problems. Engineering expertise is also a necessary ingredient for investment by merchant banks in industry - figure 3.

Loop distortion.

There is distortion in the feedback loop for organising employment when lower paid workers are subsidised by the state especially since the subsidy is removed as the earnings are increased. Not only is it necessary for an employee be matched to the job, it is also necessary that an improvement in performance is represented by an equivalent increase in earnings. Removal of subsidies is equivalent to taxation at a higher rate than the rest of the population.

More serious are breaks in the loop caused by the State. Thus the minimum wage removes elasticity in the contribution/compensation equation. If a person's contribution does not justify the minimum wage then it ceases to be economic to employ that person. Alternatively the person is subsidised by the other workers, the shareholders or the taxpayer. In order for the feedback to be viable the equity of the employee/employer contribution/compensation must not be damaged by interference. In order for the loop to again operate, the minimum wage must be subsidised by the State.

This burden of subsidy may be disguised by a government by creating unnecessary jobs in order to reduce the unemployment figures. There is evidently benefit in keeping up the morale of people who would otherwise be out of work. Such a workforce provides a pool of capability when useful jobs arise. The worker is, however, in competition with new technology whereby machinery is introduced which performs certain tasks more economically. In purely financial terms it benefits the employer to make a worker redundant when machines, or imports, cost less than the worker's contribution. If the true costs of making a worker redundant (i.e. the national cost of social security payments for no work) were taken into account then the financial incentive to reduce a work force would await greater savings from machinery and imports. The effect of this break in the feedback loop, in national terms, is that the taxpayer shoulders a greater burden of paying for the subsistence of more unemployed. It appears feasible to develop a system whereby the threshold of the minimum wage is removed and these concepts are discussed in greater detail in the appendix to this chapter.

The importance of finding a solution to the unemployment problem is going to increase as new technology continues to provide better ways of performing tasks at present performed by people. There has already been much discussion of the problems to be created by an underclass, which is alienated from society. In the first place we have a positive loop whereby the unemployed degenerate to the point where they become less eligible for employment. They eventually become unemployable by normal democratic means. If they now see themselves separated from traditional society then society's sanctions for good behaviour lose effect and the result is that we have a break in the feedback loop of society's influence on the individual.

Summary.

1. The experienced manager acts quickly and subtly.
2. Positive reinforcement is beneficial
3. Accountability is a delayed negative feedback loop.
4. Parkinson's law continues to apply.
5. Delay in the provision of data can cause errors in judgement.
6. Rate of change has increased to the point where management may find it difficult to assess priorities.
7. Perfect matching of employer and employee benefits is difficult.
8. The decline in manufacturing facilities in the West raises potential problems for the future.
9. The benefits of employment are distorted by the methods of subsidy.
10. A national wage offers a method of realistic accounting.

References.

[1] Maslow J, "Positive reinforcement".
[2] C. Northcote Parkinson. "Parkinson's Law", pub. John Murray 1958.
[3] Grover D, " Optimising Employment in the Microelectronics Age.
...."Computer Weekly 1979, Computer Age 1980.

Appendix.

The following article was published in Computer Weekly and Computer Age when there was much concern that new technology would threaten jobs. It is perhaps even more relevant now that there is a problem in funding pensions.

Optimising Employment in the Microelectronics Age.
- Derrick Grover

The current debate on the effect of Microelectronics on employment is being carried on amidst a number of trends that indicate the need to review our system of employment, its incentives and security measures. Microelectronics technology is not of itself creating the problem, it is accentuating an existing problem through improvements in efficiency that will aggravate the trend.

As fewer people are needed to produce the basic necessities in the way of goods and services, so more of the remaining population will be employed in work of more limited benefit for which limited funds will be available. Insufficient funds, in fact, to compete with the existing threshold produced by unemployment pay. Basic remedies are necessary to give incentives for the able to work efficiently while maintaining a basic minimum living standard for the less able - in a way which does not impair the necessary feedback that is provided by a free market. Measures, which have been introduced, carry anomalies that cause deterioration in the economy and reduce the living standards of those they were designed to protect. The answer must lie in separating the measures designed to protect the unfortunate from those measures necessary for an efficient and strong economy. In the present confusion the drive for national wealth is enervated by legislation for the needy to the detriment of all.

An important anomaly occurs in the method of paying social security benefits. Others have pointed out that legal minimums for wages have always been one of the surest methods of depriving the marginally employable of their jobs. The social security system benefit is, in effect, in competition with the employer; and, by competing for the attention of the marginally employable, it sets a de facto minimum wage. The taxpayer provides a substitute for earnings, while the employer seeks to replace staff with capital equipment if the earnings are too high. The pending microelectronics revolution is destined to cause many of the employed to be replaced by capital equipment if the existing legislation continues. At least one enlightened Union leader has drawn attention to our plight if advancing technology causes unemployment at a level where the economy can no longer support subsistence payments.

Let us first make the assumption that unemployed people should be paid a subsistence allowance sufficient for them to survive with a measure of dignity. We are then faced with the reality that the saving in national terms resulting from making a person unemployed is not the salary and overheads at present borne by the employer, but the difference between these and the unemployment subsistence allowance. The employer, however, will act as though the full salary is saved in the short term, since the true effect is at least one step removed and only apparent in the longer term.

Industry, as the producer of wealth, ultimately pays for the unemployment subsistence. This fact should be recognised in accounting procedures when assessing the merits of labour versus capital equipment. In order for accounting procedures to be realistic and helpful in assessing an organisation's plans, they must truly reflect the value of various contributing factors; such as work performed by an employee undistorted by social benefits. Looked at from a systems design viewpoint, the greatest efficiency (i.e. the maximum economy of effort or maximum transfer of benefit) will occur when the needs of the receiver are matched by the capabilities of the donor.
The employee, whose capabilities exactly match the requirements of a job, will perform that job more efficiently than anyone else; this supposing psychological and external factors to be constant while the comparison is made. It will be noted that the match is a two-way requirement. A person should be capable of doing his job; and the job should provide employee fulfilment; but a person who is overqualified would have spare capacity which would give rise to frustration, and the job would return a lower rate of pay than his capabilities would warrant.

It should be the aim of employment to achieve this match. The match is most likely to be achieved when the employer can pay an employee a wage that truly reflects the contribution made for the company's benefit. The fault in the present system is that below a certain threshold, defined by unemployment benefits, the employer cannot pay a rate which is matched to the job with the result that people, who might otherwise have performed useful work, are unemployed.

Let us now consider the objectives of our system:
- Payment of a subsistence allowance in accordance with public opinion.
- A free market to decide the goods and services required.
- A match between employer and employee for their mutual benefit.

The third objective will only be met, in the case of the lowest paid workers, by nullifying the effect of the threshold. Two ways to overcome the problem are apparent. The first is to remove the threshold, which implies the unacceptable stopping of unemployment pay. The second is to raise the level of the environment to that of the threshold so that a step ceases to exist. This second solution introduces the interesting possibility of paying a basic national wage to both the unemployed (in place of unemployment pay) and the employed, with the employer supplementing this by a smaller salary, such that the employed person receives a total net payment similar to the present. On average, the employer's expenditure would be the same, since higher taxes would pay the basic national wage allowance.

The important difference compared to the present is that the incremental cost of employing someone is less and it can be, in proportion, to the benefit of the employer, rather than taking the larger step over the threshold at present determined by the social security payments. It would not then be beneficial to replace people with capital equipment until the equipment realised greater savings. It would not stop the progress to be expected from investing in more efficient techniques; it would simply delay those investments until they were economically feasible when taking account of the realistic costs of making people unemployed. Accordingly, unemployment with its effects on morale would be less, and greater mobility of employment would be likely since the incremental cost to a company of increasing its staff would be lower. In this respect, the system would be preferable to a system of employment protection and redundancy payments, which inhibit the employment of new staff. The benefit of the system in increasing employment of the lower paid workers will also extend to the extra management and professional staff necessary for administration. The nation will benefit since the employment of people, otherwise paid to be unemployed, would increase the services and goods available to all.

The minimum salary paid by the employer would necessarily cover the extra costs of working, such as those for fares and meals, plus an incentive factor. The employer in these circumstances would not only be industry and commerce, but would include those people who are unable at present to pay for such services as, for example, home decoration, window cleaning and many other jobs which could be undertaken by people who are otherwise on subsistence, and who are suffering its attendant demoralisation. If the present trend continues, then the burden of supporting the unemployed and underemployed will prevent the majority of people from enjoying the smallest of services.

It has been argued that if labour is comparatively cheap then the employer may not invest in the latest equipment, which could be detrimental to the national long-term interest. The date at which an employer invests in superior equipment should be dictated by the interests of the company; since, if it is in the company's interest, then the national interest, being that of a collection of companies, also benefits.

Investment in new equipment will not, of course, be determined by the short-term view. It will depend upon benefits both in the present and in the future, bearing in mind the need to gain experience of new techniques to be competitive - especially against overseas companies. It is the job of management to draw up this equation so that the long term investment in equipment marries with the short-term interest in a manner which is of most benefit to the company.

Opinions on how to equate the short term and long term interests will no doubt differ, but the realistic assessment of the opportune time for investment will not be endangered by introducing marginal costing for labour, provided the marginal costing is itself realistic and not disguised by hidden subsidies.

It is important to distinguish between a subsidy, which is a pecuniary aid aimed at selected recipients in order to soften the natural market discipline, and a basic national wage which performs the role of "underpinning" the employment system to provide a foundation on which to build in accordance with the nation's conscience. In the latter case the free market discipline continues to apply in order to judge what products and services the consumer really wants.

In the case of a subsidy, there is the implication that it is an activity which is not wanted by the recipient, due perhaps to inadequacies in management and labour relations, or to the type of goods and services being produced. It will be distinguished from the capital investment necessary to carry a new industry through an initial growth phase until it reaches a mature position, where it becomes self-supporting in order to repay the initial investment. An investment of this nature is accordingly entered into with the anticipated market as a guiding factor. It is perhaps fitting, at a time when the small business is being encouraged, to consider the benefit of lower incremental labour costs in a start-up situation. The true effect on the new company will be influenced by the tax system which, it is clear, could be modified to make or mar an entrepreneur's prospects. But whether such modifications would be considered a subsidy, or the nation's investment in future business prospects, is debatable.

The method of taxation required to provide for a Basic National Wage needs careful consideration. Taxation of an employer in proportion to the number of staff will nullify the effect of the scheme, and a negative income tax scheme appears to have similar problems. The Swedish experiment is a different concept. Taxation based on turnover or capital equipment may cause multinational companies, for example, to invest elsewhere. A consumer tax similar to VAT appears to spread the burden appropriately without countering the advantages of the system.

It is optimistic to suppose that we can effectively control a system as complex as a national economy better than the naturally occurring forces of a free market. In the event that we wish to safeguard the population from being exploited by the unscrupulous, these safeguards should be simple and capable of being implemented without damaging the free market forces. The introduction of controls and subsidies has the effect of disguising reality and, although this may confuse the critics, it is to the disadvantage of the country as a whole.

A basic national wage for all would control the distribution of a portion of the national wealth for an adequate living standard. The wealth remaining after this distribution could be subjected to the discipline of the free market which, coupled with realistic accounting, would maximise the utilisation of our resources in human beings and equipment.

Editor's Note: It is interesting to observe, in connection with Derrick Grover's comment on fewer people affording services such as home decorating, that a parallel or "black" economy flourishes in the UK. There's always a man who knows a man who, unburdened by the tax inspector can sell or do things cheaper, I am no economist, but perhaps the author's suggestions could lead to a reabsorption of this economy, giving increased tax revenues or the same level of revenue with an attendant opportunity to further cut taxes, for everyone.

Chapter 14. Economics

The Free Market.

"Let the price of a commodity rise and no rational household will buy more of it." Adam Smith. *

"It ain't necessarily so." Gershwin

One of the tenets of economics is that a free market has self-regulating forces that maintain its stability. The Free Market forces stabilise prices because the incentive to buy is reduced if the price is too high and the price becomes a function of people's willingness to buy as Adam Smith noted.

Evidently there is a negative feedback loop in operation. The reluctance to buy, or opposition to purchasing, increases as the price increases as shown in Figure 1. If the marketing manager's aim is to maintain sales at a constant level then the decrease in sales will initiate a reduction in price in an endeavour to maintain sales volume.

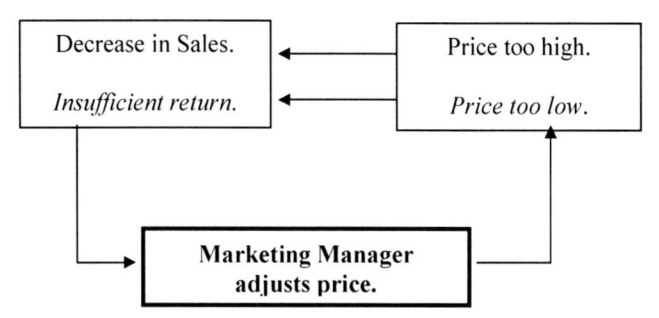

Figure 1. Effect of price change.

The aim of the marketing manager, however, is to establish a price that maximises profit. How is the price decided in the first place? If it is a new product then the price will be compared to other products that perform similar functions. If it is something that is completely new or does something never before achieved then the manufacturer (or producer of some exotic food) is dependent on adventurous individuals who are willing to pay the price for the experience. If priced too low then, whereas more people may buy it, the overall profit (after deducting cost of manufacture and sales) may be insufficient. As the price is increased fewer people will buy the product but the total profit will increase until a point is reached where the decline in sales is enough to counteract the benefit of the price increase. This is the point of diminishing returns; it determines the optimum pricing for the product for the producer's benefit as illustrated in Figure 2. Marketing aims to keep the price at a level corresponding to the peak in the total profit curve.

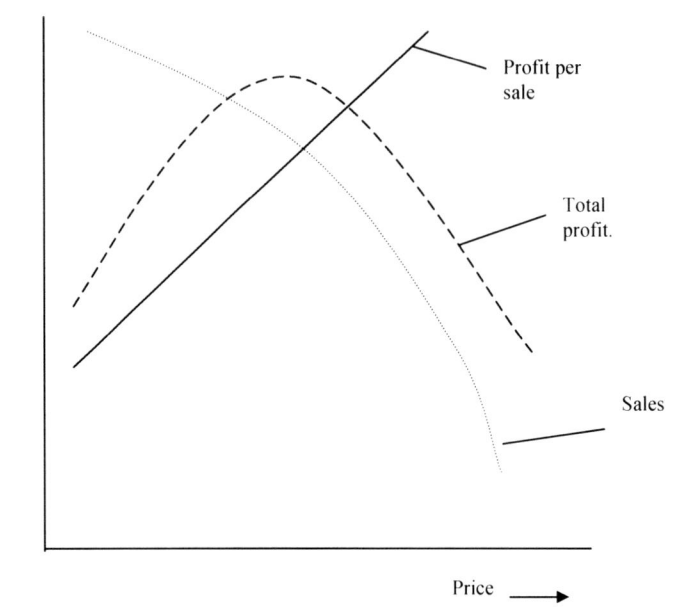

Figure 2. Diminishing returns.

When considering Adam Smith's declaration we might be tempted to observe that there are certain luxury goods that attract more buyers if the price is increased. Whether this is a difference between actual value and perceived value depends on your point of view. The perceived value can be enhanced by the exclusivity that a high price engenders; whether in watches, perfume or luxury cars. Adam Smith's view still applies if the value of the item is considered to include the psychological component of social status. The perceived values of shares in the Stock Market are often different from their actual value, especially during the latter stages of a bull or bear market.

The above example does of course ignore other factors that have to be taken into account when assessing strategy. The figures will be complicated by the change in unit costs with volume of manufacture. Mass production to minimise the manufacturing costs is likely to alter the scenario significantly. Competition from other producers and the cost/benefit of advertising are further issues. The generation of market-pull by social campaigners, or government strategy, represents an external force that may further alter the scenario.

Monopoly.

The converse of the free market with its self-regulating loop is of course the positive loop leading to a monopoly. Two aspects of monopoly suggest themselves. Firstly the tendency for a successful company to be able to afford to buy large quantities of raw materials at a lower price than other companies. The loop, as shown in Figure 3, occurs as the successful company grows richer and is able to afford raw materials at a lower price. It spreads fixed costs such as management over larger sales volumes - eventually becoming able to buy up other companies in its field in order to stifle

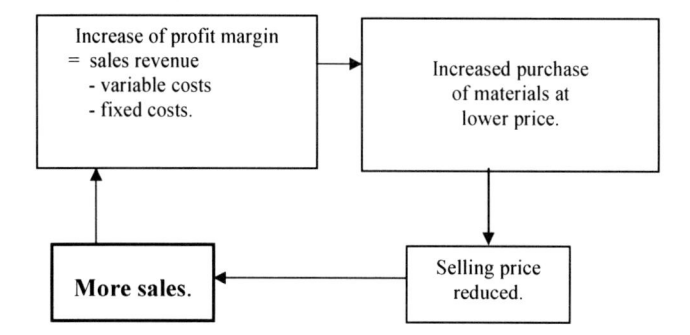

```
┌─────────────────────────┐      ┌─────────────────────┐
│ Increase of profit margin│      │                     │
│   = sales revenue       │─────▶│ Increased purchase  │
│     - variable costs    │      │   of materials at   │
│     - fixed costs.      │      │     lower price.    │
└─────────────────────────┘      └─────────────────────┘
            ▲                               │
            │                               ▼
┌─────────────────────────┐      ┌─────────────────────┐
│      More sales.        │◀─────│   Selling price     │
│                         │      │      reduced.       │
└─────────────────────────┘      └─────────────────────┘
```

Figure 3. Evolving monopoly.

competition. The second aspect arises from the first insofar as the company is able to corner the market in a raw material; especially something that may be in short supply. An example is land in an important area.

What methods can be used to make the loop less efficient and counter the tendency to become a monopoly? (The suggestions made below from the scoldent list are to explore possibilities and do not necessarily make sense in the real world)

1. **Saturation**. One way of limiting a monopoly would be to restrict the rate of supply of raw material or service. Thus whereas OPEC has success in controlling the oil industry, a method based on saturation to restrict the rate of growth of an oil company could be by limiting the diameter of its oil pipelines or the size of the oil tankers it can use to transport the oil.

2. **Cut-off**. This implies stopping the growth of a company entirely when it reaches a predetermined size. A property company that is restricted in the quantity of real estate it can own will fall into this category. A community that wishes to protect itself from being monopolised might lay down regulations of this kind.

3. **Open loop**. In the context of a business an open loop occurs when none of the profits from the business can be ploughed back into the company. It implies the company has ceased trading possibly because it is in breach of regulations and has been issued with an order by the courts.

4. **Low gain**. Low gain is assuredly the result of inefficiency either by managerial incompetence or due to a stifling bureaucracy. High taxation also will reduce the profits ploughed back into the business and accordingly reduce its gain.

5. **Delay in feedback** implies a slow turnaround of the funds generated from the business and might result from similar factors that influence the low gain example mentioned above.

6. **External force or influence**. The most influential force restricting a monopoly is government legislation to specifically monitor emerging monopolies, especially monopolies generated by taking over competitors.

7. **Negative feedback**. We are looking here for a mechanism that responds to the threat of monopoly and increases its opposition in proportion to the threat. It is the nature of the potential monopoly that it is able to provide goods and services at a lower price than the competition. It is perhaps unlikely that customers (of a potential monopoly) will purchase their goods and services elsewhere in order to bolster up the competition. It may be a different matter with the traders who lose their negotiating position if the monopoly becomes their sole customer. It could be in their long-term interest to restrict the goods and services they provide to a single customer, such as farmers providing a supermarket with vegetables. On the other side of the coin, traders do not want

to have only one source of goods and materials. It may be better to purchase from several suppliers at a higher price rather than be at the mercy of a monopoly. There are also examples of enlightened customers who (rather than buying at a supermarket) support their local shops to prevent them going out of business.

8. **Theme change.** This may mean changing from a democratic society to a form of dictatorship. Alternatively changing the mode of business to a bartering system in which it is more difficult to create a monopoly.

State Control.

The dangers of no feedback are mentioned elsewhere (chapter 6). State control runs a risk of ignoring important feedback issues or at least of distorting them. Even if the controllers are benevolent and understanding, there is the problem of legislating to anticipate future trends and particularly of the change in trends resulting from new laws. The problem of interpreting feedback may be due to political leanings but more likely due to being overwhelmed by the conflicting information available. There is the further factor of delay in the feedback, which as has been observed elsewhere accounts for the difficulty of controlling the economy to keep it from boom and bust cycles.

The free market calls upon the collective opinion of the population in assessing the feedback. Local variations - important to the people in the locality - are incorporated into the market model; it is not feasible for the state to cater for the smaller details. Attempts at such detail would assuredly generate an unwieldy bureaucracy for which the costs are likely to outweigh any benefits that might accrue. Legislation that puts behaviour in a straitjacket will inevitably cause loss of efficiency.

It is the presence of many small feedback loops at interpersonal and inter-business relationships that make a free market model more efficient. Slight adjustments in behaviour are often called for to optimise a situation for individual or joint benefit.

Credit and Money Supply.

The supply of credit in effect introduces delay into the loop of supply and demand, and is a factor in the cycle of boom and bust. Where a user is constrained in purchasing power by the need to pay debts out of immediate resources the feedback is immediate. The supply of credit, however, not only delays the fateful day of repayment it also introduces gearing into a person's finances. Whether this gearing is used to purchase more shares in the stock market, start on expanded business ventures or purchase a more expensive house the outcome is similar. A downturn in the economy has a more adverse effect. The problems of negative equity in the housing market in the 1990s and 2007-8 were amplified by the provision of excess credit when the opinion on the economy was optimistic.

The problem of excess credit is aggravated by the attitude of banks that call in loans to businesses when they are inadequately covered. If this results in the sale of assets when the market is low then a positive loop is present, the drop in market values is compounded; unemployment increases, people are unable or unwilling to spend money on goods and the downturn in the economy accelerates Figure 4. At some point confidence in the market returns, banks are willing to supply more credit and the familiar cyclic phenomenon in the market recurs.

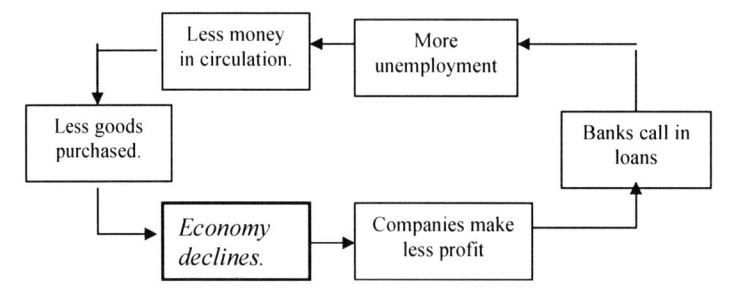

Figure 4. Accentuation of economic decline.

Methods for tackling the boom and bust in the economy differ from those for the positive loop since in this case the problem is a negative loop with excessive delay in the feedback. This is analogous to the notional Very Rich Man (described in chapter 2) who invested in the stock market at the wrong times. In this case the supply of credit is out of phase with the needs of the market. Correction would require the banks to increase credit during a recession and decrease it when the economy is buoyant. Overall correction of this kind is expected of a state bank.

It is of course easy to sit back in an armchair and criticise but it must be recognised that banks have a duty to remain solvent (the collapse of this duty during the financial crisis of 2009-10 is considered in chapter 16). C Wood [3] mentions the insolvent thrifts (US building societies) that lend money on long term and receive in short term. If short-term rates are high then they must embark on riskier lending to get a high return. A positive loop occurs where the losses cause the making of risky loans, which in turn can deliver greater losses.)

Negative feedback that is so delayed that it is completely out of phase acts in a similar way to a positive loop but the correcting methods have to be applied differently. The most important issue is that the delay must be reduced in order to apply the correcting mechanisms in time. If it is not possible to remove delay sufficiently then the instability can be reduced by methods that in effect reduce the loop gain. These are 1, 2, 4, 6 and 8 in the scoldent list. Items 3 and 5 are counter-productive. Whether item 7 - negative feedback - is relevant depends on how it is defined and there is a danger of making the description confusing. It might be considered as a second order effect that influences other factors in the system. The relevance of these methods to an economy, in which the stability controls are delayed, might be as follows:

1. **Saturation** of the money supply by limiting the rate at which money (& credit) can be drawn from the banks in a time of boom, & limiting the rate that banks can withdraw money in a time of bust.

2. **Cut-off** implies that the supply of money or credit will stop when a predetermined ceiling is reached. Conversely the provision of a safety net for the unemployed falls into this category during a recession. Analogous to the cutting off of the supply of money when the economy is overheating there is the notion of cutting off the trend to penury during a recession. In this context penury is negative wealth and, from the point of view of the feedback loop, both penury and wealth are treated similarly.

3. **Open loop** methods are not relevant here.

4. **Low gain** implies making the engine of the loop less efficient. It is sometimes difficult to decide what this engine consists of but in this case it is likely to be the tools for supplying credit. If the driving force of an economic boom is the money supply then an increase in the rate of interest, or an inefficient banking system that cannot supply the money or credit demanded by the users, might be a notional solution to an economy that is overheating. Alternatively the gain of any system is reduced if there is leakage in the output. Taxation of the movement of money would cause such leakage; this leakage is unavailable for feedback and consequently less loop gain is available.

5. **Reducing the delay** in the system is the most fundamental of the requirements since it is the excessive delay before the birds comes home to

roost that is the basic problem. Delay in feedback needs to be reduced in order that corrective action is taken before there is time for the system to spiral out of control. The problem here lies in the difficulty in getting up-to-date information in time to be effective. On a national scale the time for data to be collected and assessed may be many months. In the case of company accounts, and data about the industrial and commercial arm of the economy, the audited data is likely to be more than a year out of date.

Insofar as delay in response is due to extended credit then the scale of the problem may not be realised before bankruptcies become excessive. This implies that credit should be limited and the payback period should be short compared to the economic cycle. There is, however, the alternative scenario that if credit is extended indefinitely then the borrower is able to ride out the economic cycles and recover in times of relative security. Evidently the credit should be for covering existing debt and not for the purpose of increasing indebtedness.

6. **The external force** or influence is by its nature independent of the loop, and any action that appears to be beneficial is a candidate for repair. Government intervention may be needed to prevent a crisis. The control of interest rates has some effect in limiting the extreme swings in the economy. Insofar as the yield on the stock market bears a relation to the interest rates obtainable on money deposits, the bank rate has some influence on the price of shares. If the interest obtainable on deposits is high then the price of shares must go down to give a yield that compares favourably with other returns. Conversely at the bottom of a bear market the yield on shares may look more attractive than the interest on deposits. The optimism/pessimism prevailing in a bull/bear markets may nevertheless be an overriding factor in deciding how the market will perform.

The downside may be that by removing the market forces the benefit of the free market is lost; if not now, then possibly some time in the future. The external nature of the influence implies that some parameters of the system are distorted from the values they want to be at in a free market and they will attempt to recover with a vengeance when a free system is restored (analogous to a pendulum swinging further from equilibrium).

7. **The use of negative feedback** in a negative feedback loop only makes sense when the delay in the basic loop has become great enough to change the phase to the point where the influence fed back is an aggravating action rather than a corrective one. Accordingly methods which enhance the beneficial influences in proportion to the scale of the potential instability should be useful. A complex system will have many loops and if one loop is not manageable then another may be.

The intervention described in paragraph 6 above is an example of negative feedback where the government is part of the loop. With computers controlling much of the financial sphere it is conceivable that the rate of interest or money supply is automatically adjusted to counteract excessive trends in the financial markets. The effectiveness of this approach could be undermined by the psychological boost that a high interest rate would give to the bullish investors since the introduction of such a rate implies an expectation of a higher index in share prices. Similarly the lowering of interest rates in a bear market is a sign of pessimism on the prospects of the economy.

In a system with excessive delays in corrective action it would be useful to predict the likely outcome based on present information. There is an analogy here to the delay in response of an oil tanker to steering. In that case it is possible to model the performance of the tanker by programming a computer to assess the effect of moving the tiller - in association with tidal and wind influences. Accordingly the exact movement required of the tiller can be defined. Modelling the economy has been attempted but it is more complex with possible unexpected influences arising to upset the prediction.

As K E Boulding [1] has noted, progressive taxation has some effect in helping to limit the rise of a heated economy. Insofar as a higher income becomes subject to a greater rate of tax then the tax is deflationary and acts as negative feedback to limit the excursion of inflation. It is the non-linearity of the rate that causes this effect. A constant rate of tax would devour a constant proportion of income and the greater apparent contribution to the taxman would simply reflect the lower value of money arising from inflation.

Supposing round numbers for the rates of tax as: 10%, 20% & 40% then as the economy increases some people move over the next threshold and increase their tax rate from 10% to 20%, or from 20% to 40 %. Government has the option of making the thresholds real by increasing them in line with inflation or holding them constant to give a deflationary influence.

Butterfly economics.

Conventional thinking supports the view that the free market will tend to give the consumer the best value obtainable insofar as competition reduces prices to a level that is economic by allowing efficient producers enough income to justify further production.
This belief is criticised by Ormerad [2] in his book "Butterfly economics". The discussion follows on from the often quoted butterfly, which, it is conjectured might possibly alter the weather on the other side of the world by the beat of its

wings. This notional manifestation of chaos theory is based on the outcome of situations where minute differences at the start of the situation can increase to enormous differences by altering the initial conditions of powerful forces. Such situations arise when very high gain positive loops are active.

Ormerod observes the behaviour of an ant colony. A pioneering ant explores the environment to discover a source of food. On returning to the colony his discoveries are conveyed to the others who follow his path to the jam or honey in the pantry. As more ants follow the path so the word spreads and yet more ants follow the track to the honey and the familiar sight of a trail through the kitchen is seen - a classic positive loop. The loop will be expected to go on increasing until the supply of ants, honey or other sweet stuff is exhausted. Ormerod noticed however that every so often a rogue ant does not follow its colleagues but goes off alone and sometimes finds another supply. When the rogue ant finds gold in the form of another pot of honey then another gold rush is started, which may distract from the first one. It does not mean that the second honeypot is better than the first, it is the crowd behaviour of an army of ants that is more influential. This, Ormerad conjectures, happens in the economy so that different projects arise spontaneously in competition with each other.

Like the honey pot it is not always the best product that is successful in the market. It is the combination of the product capabilities, social influence and the environment in which it is situated that is important. The oft-quoted example of the Betamax video standard versus VHS illustrates the issue. The quality of Betamax was better than VHS but marketing and social influences became more important as more people responded to the advertising and comments of friends who had already bought VHS recorders. Greater sales of VHS tapes and recorders meant that more products to this standard would emerge to support the standard and it became advantageous to conform to VHS as illustrated in Figure 5. It is an example where the action of a positive loop on a small beginning causes the trend to be magnified to the exclusion of other factors.

A similar situation has occurred with personal computers. The PC compatible machines running Windows operating systems have dominated the market because so much software has been designed to be compatible with the PC that newcomers are swayed into adopting them. In this case, however, Apple Mac still survives, largely because it has certain advantages in graphics and interactivity together with a dedicated following.

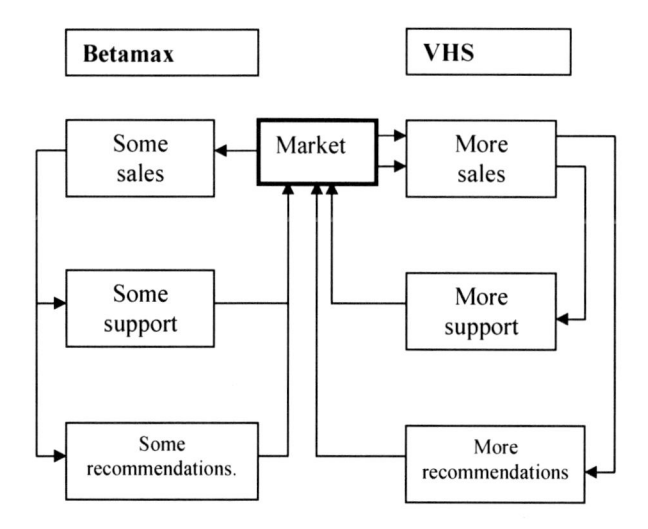

Figure 5. Effect of positive loop on market.

Well-established products may be in an unassailable position. The Qwerty keyboard was designed to be inefficient so that typists would not press keys in such rapid succession that the mechanical arms holding the typeface would be in contention. So many people have trained with the Qwerty keyboard layout that, even if a more efficient design were introduced, there is little prospect that a change in layout would be successful in the market place.

The problem of rising costs.

David Wise [4] in his address to the British Association for the Advancement of Science observed that governments have made promises that cannot be kept since financial commitments made in the past cannot be sustained. A major factor causing the problem is the rise in health care costs consequent on the advances in medical science, which are more expensive. Another factor is the rise in longevity and the need to fund adequate pensions. These are factors that were not considered when the investment required for an adequate pension was calculated at the start of the career of today's pensioners – an example of very delayed feedback. Their life expectancy has increased by many years and this places an unexpected burden on the pension funds. The increase in life expectancy has not been matched by a similar increase in good health; in spite of the increase in cost of health care due to advances in medicine. In consequence pensioners will need health care for a longer period than previous generations.

Wise introduces the concept of good and bad money. "Good money" is money that people would spend on health care if they were spending their own money. When health care is provided free however, then people will accept any treatment provided it does not harm them. The money spent in excess of the care actually needed is "Bad money". Unless there is feedback to make people more accountable for the costs, the funding of bad money is expected to cause insolvency in health care systems, in all countries, as costs increase further.

On the way to insolvency will be the inconvenience for patients such as waiting for a long time to get an appointment or travelling long distances because the required facilities are limited to fewer hospitals.

The challenge will be how to utilise high technology in an efficient manner and discourage its use when it is not effective. As noted in the chapter on legal issues there is a positive loop in regard to medical costs when litigation is rife. The effect in the USA is that medical practitioners use more treatment than necessary in case they are sued for neglect, and perhaps send a patient to a hospital rather than be treat them locally. Often, it is reported, the extra treatment may be detrimental for the patient but nevertheless ensures that there can be no grounds for the accusation that insufficient treatment was applied.

The problems arising from litigation are less amenable to correction by loop techniques. The law tends to be outside of the loop's influence and is too inflexible to adapt to the common good without new legislation to correct the problems that arise.

It is necessary that a controlling loop be introduced in order to keep expenditure to the minimum necessary for patient health. If people have to make a contribution to their treatment it will help ensure that "bad money" is not spent on unnecessary treatment. If it is not made then the contribution will be in the costs of waiting times and travel.

Pension and Social Security issues.

The basic problem facing the administration is the delay in accountability whereby negative feedback loops apply corrective action; either by revealing the likely outcome of the present behaviour or by way of sanctions for over-optimism. Thus contracts for pensions based on final salaries, or inflation proofed pensions agreed when the future trends were not known, are problems of delayed feedback. In the private sector there are more likely to be drastic sanctions such as bankruptcy of the employer if the outcome is not viable. In the public sector the only sanction may arise from the general population objecting to large pensions being paid out of taxation.

An interesting trend is shown in [4] where the number of people in early retirement is plotted against age for several countries. Those countries that have more benevolent social security provisions apparently have a greater number of people unable to work because of inability. Thus in Japan 80% of men aged 60 to 64 remained in employment, it was below 50% for most EU countries and dropped to 20 % for Italy.

A further comparison of retirement ages for several countries shows that about 50% of Japanese remain employed at the age of 70, and 20% for the USA whereas less than 5% of EU inhabitants remain employed.

The proportion of men collecting disability benefits is a further illustration of the effect of lenient social security legislation. In the UK 30-35% of men aged 60 to 65 were claiming disability benefits, about 25% in the Netherlands but only 5-10% for countries such as Spain and the USA.

It has been noted that many social security programmes are generous and become too costly as the population ages. Social Security systems typically encourage retirement by reducing the benefit from working after pensionable age; this encourages older employees to leave the labour force early and magnify the financial burden. The penalty is in effect a higher level of taxation. Thus if 50% of earned income is deducted from a state pension then with a standard rate of taxation of 20% the total burden is a 70% tax on extra income earned - Figure 6. The effect is to reduce the net income to 30% of the benefit that would be enjoyed by moonlighting unburdened by the tax inspector.

The number of retired people is likely to become larger than the fraction of the population that is in the labour force and paying for the benefits - particularly since they are financed on a pay-as-you-go basis. Social benefit discourages work when people who do continue working after retirement are penalised by the withdrawal of benefits they would otherwise receive.
Ref [5] refers to the concept of actuarial fairness. A person retiring later should receive an annual pension that increases for each year that retirement is delayed. Whilst the length of time a pension will be drawn is unknown the pension will nevertheless be drawn for a shorter time. It is not only fair that the total compensation in respect of contributions should be similar, it gives a greater incentive to continue working, Figure 7.

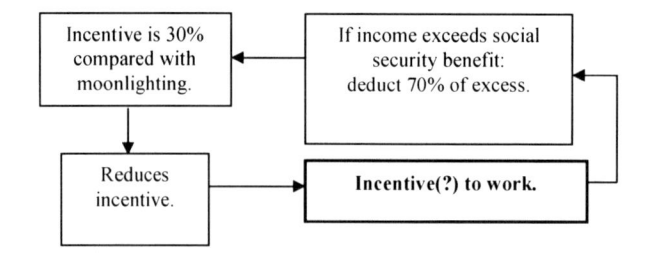

```
┌─────────────────┐      ┌──────────────────┐
│ Incentive is 30%│◄─────│If income exceeds │
│ compared with   │      │ social security  │◄──┐
│ moonlighting.   │      │ benefit: deduct  │   │
└────────┬────────┘      │ 70% of excess.   │   │
         │               └──────────────────┘   │
         ▼                                      │
┌─────────────────┐      ┌──────────────────┐   │
│    Reduces      │─────►│ Incentive(?) to  │───┘
│    incentive.   │      │     work.        │
└─────────────────┘      └──────────────────┘
```

Figure 6. Burden of Social Security Adjustment.

In addition to the shorter time for drawing a pension there is the question of the value of money drawn at different times. Thus money drawn a year later is worth less not only because of inflation but also because if received a year earlier it could have accumulated interest at perhaps 5%. The value of payments can be calculated according to when they are drawn and are

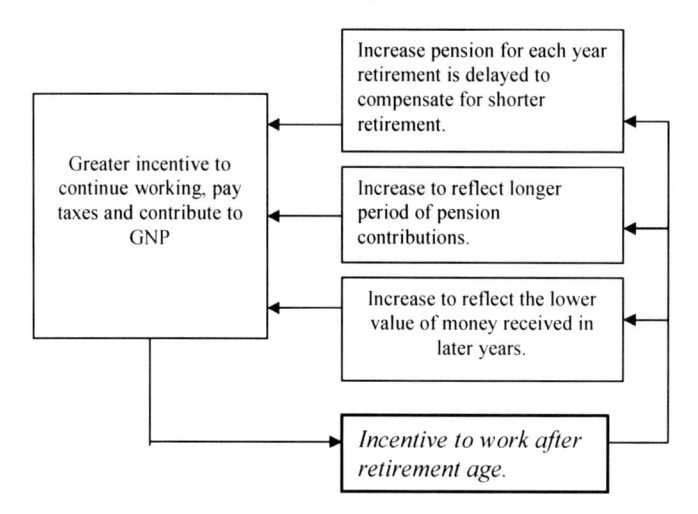

```
                        ┌───────────────────────┐
                        │ Increase pension for  │
                        │ each year retirement  │
                   ┌────│ is delayed to         │◄──┐
                   │    │ compensate for        │   │
                   │    │ shorter retirement.   │   │
┌──────────────┐   │    └───────────────────────┘   │
│ Greater      │   │    ┌───────────────────────┐   │
│ incentive to │   │    │ Increase to reflect   │   │
│ continue     │◄──┼────│ longer period of      │◄──┤
│ working, pay │   │    │ pension contributions.│   │
│ taxes and    │   │    └───────────────────────┘   │
│ contribute   │   │    ┌───────────────────────┐   │
│ to GNP       │◄──┘    │ Increase to reflect   │   │
│              │◄───────│ the lower value of    │◄──┤
└──────┬───────┘        │ money received in     │   │
       │                │ later years.          │   │
       │                └───────────────────────┘   │
       │                ┌───────────────────────┐   │
       └───────────────►│ *Incentive to work*   │───┘
                        │ *after retirement age.│
                        └───────────────────────┘
```

Figure 7. An alternative scenario to encourage work.

expressed as net present value. This value should be positive if extra years are worked. It is increased by 6.7% per year in USA but in most EU countries the accrual is negative - an actuarially unfair system.

If social security provisions encourage people to retire early then this adds to the problems of pensions for an ageing population. Since they have to be paid for by the younger working force the question arises as to what outcome is likely if the system is not sustainable. A rebellion against people over a certain age might occur. Whereas this may conflict with concern for loved parents there will be others for whom family life has not been so beneficial and whose regard for older people is lacking. It only requires a small number of people to create significant problems in a community.

Summary.

1. The price of a product is determined by two opposing negative feedback loops. i. Customer resistance to higher prices.
    ii. Company resistance to lower prices.
2. An unchecked positive loop leads to a monopoly.
3. State control is often associated with inadequate feedback.
4. Credit introduces delay in the loop that would otherwise constrain excess borrowing.
5. The quality of a product is not necessarily the criterion for market domination if fashion intervenes.
6. The delay between the signing of pensions contracts and their fulfilment prevented feedback on the consequences of increased life expectancy.
7. People need to be made more accountable for health care costs to prevent insolvency of the service.
8. A social benefit culture that discourages work will damage the economy.

References.

[1] Boulding K E, "Business and Economic Systems".
[2] Ormerod P, "Butterfly Economics".
[3] Wood, Christopher, "Boom or bust".
[4] Wise D A, "Facing the Age Wave and Economic Policy", British Association Festival of Science, 2004.
[5] Gruber J and Wise D A, "Social Security Programs and Retirement around the World." CUP, 2004.

Chapter 15.   Industry.

Capital risk.

The differences in attitudes of providers of capital are often cited as the reason for the different industrial performance in various countries. Hutton [1] has observed the UK problem of a rentier society that is anxious to get a quick return on capital invested. 75-80% of the funding in the UK is from pension funds and institutions that will transfer their money elsewhere if performance is not considered adequate. A Company dependent on this finance is less able to invest in long term research and development. Financial systems tend to respond quickly to changes in influence. The comparative ease with which money can be transferred allows a financial system to react to changes in circumstances very quickly. Systems that require the manufacture and movement of hardware are, by comparison, slow to respond.

Such companies were at a disadvantage compared, for example, to companies in Japan, which enjoyed government funding for research into silicon technology. It contributed much to the evolution of its semiconductor industry. Silicon technology has led the way not only to the microelectronics industry but also to displays for television and the computing industry where for a while they developed an essentially monopolistic situation, which made it difficult for other nations to compete.

Forecasting trends.

A factor in industrial performance is the ability to forecast the trends in a technology, both in terms of what the market will require and in identifying the technical breakthroughs that make new systems possible. We see here the potential for a delayed negative feedback loop with the inherent problems that accompany it. The delay being due to market data not being available in time to steer the company's planning. In this case it may be argued that the data may be uptodate but it is the need to plan forwards which creates the disparity between the data and the needs of the company. In other words the data that is required is that which will be available in a few years time when the product is introduced to the market. Thus if a company wrongly forecasts a trend in the market, either due to changes in fashion or due to the new developments (which a changing technology makes possible) then several years of research and development may be wasted. It is a situation where the basic loop has to be controlled by intelligent input in order to anticipate changes.

Whatever the problems experienced by individual companies there are overall problems arising from the march of technology to ever more capability. Advances are being made faster and faster. The computer can be used to design faster computers and the fall out from this loop is also greater and more complex capability in other spheres of endeavour. Equipment may become out of date before it has paid for itself; it is sometimes out of date by the time it has been developed ready for manufacture.

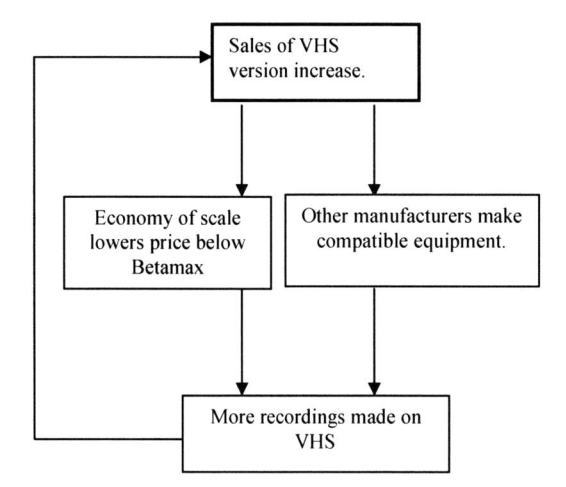

```
         ┌─────────────────┐
    ┌───▶│ Sales of VHS    │
    │    │ version increase.│
    │    └─────────────────┘
    │         │       │
    │         ▼       ▼
    │  ┌──────────┐ ┌──────────────────┐
    │  │Economy of│ │Other manufacturers│
    │  │scale     │ │make compatible    │
    │  │lowers    │ │equipment.         │
    │  │price     │ └──────────────────┘
    │  │below     │        │
    │  │Betamax   │        │
    │  └──────────┘        │
    │         │            │
    │         ▼            ▼
    │    ┌──────────────────────┐
    └────│ More recordings made │
         │ on VHS               │
         └──────────────────────┘
```

Figure 1. Effect of market lead on uptake of technology.

Companies must leap frog each other to remain competitive and this presents an important feedback problem. If anticipating the market for the next product is difficult, anticipating the market for the product after the next increases the chance of error significantly. The market may establish a fashion for a particular product, not because it is the best but because it sells in such numbers that it sets the standard for a particular operation.
Perfectly good products have floundered in the market place. The promotion of a competitive product may be sufficient to set the standard of use in the population or set the style expected by the market. The successful product is over the hill and into a positive loop where take-up by a majority of the population sets the standard. The much-quoted example is the Betamax versus VHS videotape standard. Whereas Betamax gave better quality, the VHS

standard sold larger numbers initially and other manufacturers were forced to be compatible. This positive loop is shown in figure 1.

Cultural differences.

While the attitudes of financial institutions is a factor it is not the only one. The phenomenal rise in the economy of Japan and SE Asia compared with the demise of many engineering industries in the UK has also been influenced by cultural attitudes.
This was recognised by New Scientist magazine [2], which asked: What is unique about British society that causes it to underrate its engineers compared to other nations?

It is evident that a feedback loop has been in operation in which many people with a degree in engineering took up the profession for the interest and challenge in designing and developing new ideas, rather than the higher salaries and social prestige that drive other professions, Figure 2. There was, however, a price to be paid for this situation manifested in such issues as the low uptake of engineering courses at universities; low uptake of UK inventions and an inability of merchant banks to assess new technology. Many British Engineers have been more dedicated to the intellectual challenge rather than commercial aspects and financial gain. Accordingly they were less likely to influence management and the banking community than their opposite numbers in, for example, the USA.

The American engineer enjoys higher prestige and receives a higher salary. The higher reward goes hand in hand with the expectation of greater achievement in so far as results are expected more quickly. The pressure to achieve results encourages a design engineer to licence in new inventions in contrast to those motivated by the challenge of finding their own solution. (It should, however, be noted in passing that a less pressured atmosphere often results in more profound solutions that take time to evolve.)

A further consequence is that engineers, who are commercially orientated, gain more experience of the financial world, Figure 3. People with the breadth to assess both the technological and commercial aspects of proposals are needed by Venture Capitalists and Merchant Banks. This influence feeds back into the engineering profession.

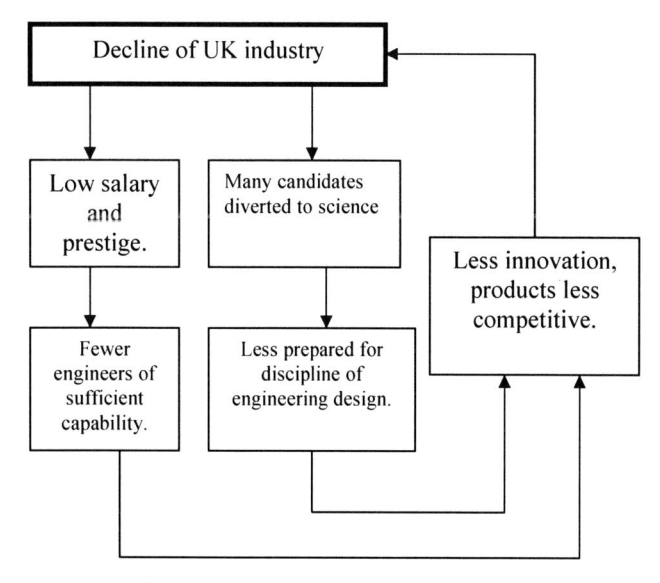

```
┌─────────────────────────────┐
│   Decline of UK industry    │◄──────┐
└─────────────────────────────┘       │
      │           │                   │
      ▼           ▼                   │
┌──────────┐ ┌──────────────┐  ┌──────────────┐
│Low salary│ │Many candidates│ │Less innovation,│
│   and    │ │diverted to    │ │products less  │
│prestige. │ │science        │ │competitive.   │
└──────────┘ └──────────────┘  └──────────────┘
      │           │                   ▲    ▲
      ▼           ▼                   │    │
┌──────────┐ ┌──────────────┐         │    │
│  Fewer   │ │Less prepared │─────────┘    │
│engineers │ │for discipline│              │
│of suffi- │ │of engineering│              │
│cient     │ │design.       │              │
│capability│ │              │              │
└──────────┘ └──────────────┘              │
      │                                    │
      └────────────────────────────────────┘
```

Figure 2. Factors in decline in UK industry.

Evolving Industry.

The transition from a start up company to an established business requires a change in the style of management. In a company of few people, feedback to management is direct; the staff are familiar with each other and they were probably chosen from candidates whose capabilities were already known to the management. This provides an efficient negative feedback loop in which action can be taken quickly by the management to correct errors or diversions in behaviour. As discussed in earlier chapters it is beneficial if the delay in feedback is short so that errors can be addressed quickly. In the larger company this feedback loop is at least once removed. The capabilities and problems are slower to be addressed and the efficiency of the work force is reduced. This, however, should be compensated for by the economies of scale.

The sequence of events that must occur, before a high technology product reaches the market, will sensibly start with a discussion between the marketing director, sales director and research director. If the company is market led then it is the marketing director who will float the ideas for new products that will

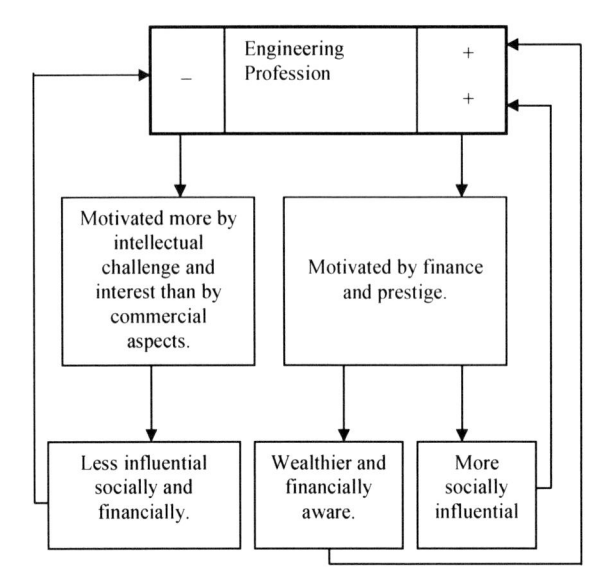

Figure 3. Cultural influence on industry.

be needed in 2 to 3 years time. The feedback for marketing
will come in part from the experience of the sales force and also from the department's surveillance of the movements in the areas of interest. The requests for a product must be assessed by the director of research and the chief engineer. The first to assess that the company either has, or in due time will have, the expertise in science and technology to meet the requirements. Secondly the Chief Engineer must assess that the company can utilise the science with efficiency and economy to make a product at a price that is competitive. Advantage will go to the company that achieves the best performance price ratio.

The risk is clearly greater for the small company. Whereas the small company can often change course and reorganise more quickly it does not have the resources to finance a failure and it is likely to be more dependent on one product. The larger companies will usually have several products in development at one time. This is partly to offset the risk of failure if the technology is not forthcoming and partly to be able to adjust to the market's demands if the marketing department guesses are erroneous.

Market forces do not always provide the influence necessary to keep a company competitive. British industry after the Second World War was able to market its goods to the former empire. This market was in some ways protected from the degree of competition suffered by other nations. Accordingly it was not necessary for the British industry to be ruthlessly competitive and it was not geared to cope with the more efficient competition when its protected market disappeared.

China had a long period of peace that enabled the Chinese to be cut off from the rest of the world. It was not exposed to the advances being experienced by other countries. Especially those who were engaged in conflict that required them to obtain or develop the weapons and other machinery necessary to support a war effort.

It has been suggested also that China has also been the victim of a protected culture and has been cited as an example of the danger of an inbred administration. The Mandarin class, which governed China for centuries, admitted new recruits by examination that selected those whose opinions were in accordance with the culture of the administration. By stifling new ideas they restricted innovation. A further factor lay in the difficulty of preparing the type for printing. Such printing as there was emphasized the traditional thinking. In the West printing was a major factor in the exchange of information resulting in more efficient processes leading to the industrial revolution.

Another factor is defence spending. Military applications are usually designed and manufactured to a higher specification than is required for the domestic market. A company culture devoted to defence does not therefore learn the lessons necessary to manufacture equipment at the price offered by companies exposed to the rigours of the commercial market. There are two effects to be noted. One is that the Defence Company is in a weak position to compete if the defence funding dries up. Secondly, from a national point of view, the defence companies can offer higher salaries to their employees and accordingly monopolise the best talent. Talent that would otherwise be available to compete with nations unhindered by the demands of the military.

Success factors.

The question arises as to why SE Asian industry has succeeded so well compared with many western industries. Cultural and financial investment attitudes are two factors and so is the JIT (Just in time) system [2], which was developed by Toyota in the 1950's, and adopted in many Japanese factories by the 1970's. Under this system components and resources are not supplied until they are needed. Consequently the cost of storage is minimised and errors in supply or specification can be corrected immediately they are discovered (a fast negative feedback loop). A production run of faulty components is halted and blame for failure more accurately identified. Another factor, however, is the engineering culture where a top down approach is replaced by a lateral organisation. It was reported that the job of management is to supply the services needed by the engineers. The company planning is the responsibility of the engineers since they are the people who are in touch with the technology and who are aware of its problems and potential. Management is there to provide the resources required.

Silicon Valley has illustrated the positive loop arising from the benefit of symbiosis. Expertise encourages the arrival of more expertise whether in the prime technology or in supporting skills. The pool of talent that is generated is available to the companies in the neighbourhood and movement between companies spreads the expertise upon which others can build.

A degree of negative feedback occurs as a nation becomes wealthier. The cost of labour rises and in turn increases the cost of goods to be exported. Countries with lower labour rates then become more able to compete. One response has been to licence the manufacture of goods in countries where the labour costs are lower. Japanese companies in particular licensed their previous out of date technology to surrounding Asian countries but maintained their technological lead by manufacturing the latest equipment at home. By this means the previous technology could still be marketed at a competitive price while the latest devices commanded a higher price due to their improved capability.

Counteracting effects.

Positive feedback loops, as the engines of industrial progress are of course not the only influence. Other effects are introduced which slow down the trend. One of the hindrances is the bureaucracy that develops, as the organisation is required to deal with ever more powerful technology. Contributions to the bureaucracy are received from legislation which introduce accountancy rules and other legal requirements aimed as safe guarding the user, the public and other businesses from unfair competition. Political intervention and political correctness are other factors.

At the time of writing, companies in continental Europe are burdened with extra costs in respect of social security. Their economic efficiency and rate of expansion has declined compared with former years. To this burden must be added the voluminous literature and patent applications for new ideas. The organisation of such literature required for a researcher to retrieve relevant material is such that it is often quicker to redesign a product and go it alone rather than spend time to check if it has been done before. The patent problems, which have been exacerbated by software patents, hold a threat over business since there is the potential to be sued and the cost of assessing prior art can be considerable, especially for a small company.

One of the problems of the legal process is that it can interfere with the natural market forces and is not subject to the correction of negative feedback loop on a continuing basis. Correction may be applied if a law is so bad that it falls into disrepute so that every one ignores it and it is ultimately repealed. Infringement of patents, for example, is considered by some companies to be a business risk that is worth taking. Factors in the infringers favour are the number of trivial patents that will not stand the test of inventiveness; the difficulty of identifying the infringing activity, and the cost of litigation, which may deter owners from prosecuting.

In other situations the law can become so draconian that it curtails legitimate business by stimulating litigation to the point where the cost of insurance is prohibitive. Medical litigation in the USA has shown this trend. The cost of legislation generated in Brussels may be so onerous that a business ceases to be viable and many may become bankrupt. If possible the market will seek an alternative way around the problem or find a way of minimising the sanctions. These alternatives may not be in the interests of anyone as again illustrated by the US health services where extra unnecessary treatment is given to make the doctors fire-proof in the event of litigation.

It would appear that a general principle is required in that the legislative body should suffer some of the consequences of its legislation. The principle is a manifestation of the negative loop, which applies a corrective influence to an undesirable trend. The problem is that the influence may be so delayed that it is too late to be effective in solving the issues.

Fashion.

The quote by Adam Smith that: any reasonable man will not buy a product more expensively when he can buy it more cheaply elsewhere; requires that product be carefully defined. Fashion has an unpredictable influence. A product must be considered not only as a physical item but also as an icon associated with some cultural interest. The most obvious case being the digital watch, which has achieved exceptional accuracy at a price that defeats alternative technology. It is evident that there are other considerations, such as style, that influence its value. The marketing department must necessarily take into account the influence of the customer's feelings of prestige not to mention the attitudes of a proportion of the population, who regard antique objects as a better investment than the latest offering.

Anticipating the whims of the market in clothing would seem especially difficult - unless the fashion industry dictates to the market the style of clothing it will wear. This appeared to happen for many years when people's feet were squashed into pointed shoes, when men's trousers got wet under a too short raincoat and women's dresses were discarded by the million because they were the wrong length.

The swing of the pendulum has an analogy to the way the width of lapels changed back and forth, or the length of skirts changed up and down; even though the swing was every few years rather than once a second.

There is an analogy here, in physical systems, to forced vibrations. Most systems have a natural frequency of vibration or oscillation. It may occur in our car at a certain road speed when a part of the car, or its contents, vibrate in sympathy with the drumming of the road wheels. The electric motor in our refrigerator may cause part of the casing to vibrate annoyingly. It is the same phenomenon that enables us to push a child's swing with the minimum of effort provided we do it in time with the natural period of the swing.

Vibration, oscillation or swings of the pendulum are different words for similar phenomena. If an object (or system) is energised at its natural frequency of oscillation then it will respond with maximum effect. It can be illustrated by violin string. If we were to play a musical instrument, such as a trombone (whose note could be changed continuously) then as the note approached the pitch of a string on a violin, the string would start to oscillate due to the pressure waves in the air emanating from the trombone. When the note is exactly in tune with the string then it will cause it to vibrate with maximum amplitude. If the note is further increased in frequency then the vibrations of the string will subside because the string is reluctant to vibrate at that higher frequency.

An example of this problem is observed in the time-honoured tradition of an army breaking step when crossing a bridge in case the rhythm of the marching coincides with the natural oscillation of the bridge.

In our analogy, the fashion industry is the army endeavouring to excite the consumer who is represented by the bridge. The industry would prefer the rate of change to be fast so that it sells more goods. The consumer is unwilling to change fashion at a rate that entails dumping good clothing before it has enjoyed adequate wear; this sets the fastest rate at which industry can introduce change. If industry were too slow, compared to the rate of consent, then, not only is it losing the opportunity to maximise sales, it also runs the risk of the customer becoming bored with the current fashion and experimenting of its own accord. The industry then loses its initiative in introducing fashion.

These comments have been, of course, painted with a broad brush and there is some evidence that views are changing. We are, in any case, considering the proportion of the population that conforms to the trends. On the fringes will be those for whom fashion is a way of life and who feel impelled to follow the nuances of their set. Accordingly there will be frequent minor, perhaps more subtle, changes in style which some of the wealthy can afford. In other sectors of the community, over-attention to fashion will be considered frivolous and a sign of immaturity.

Slavery to fashion appears to be changing. The younger generation has clear preferences such as trainers for footwear. The pin stripe suit of the city gave way to casual wear into which the vagaries of fashion will penetrated aided by the positive loop that is a feature of fashion.

At the other end of the scale will be people in straitened circumstances and some who buy their clothing second hand. If such clothing is discarded because it is going out of fashion then there will be a section of the community who will lag behind the current styles. This lag in fashion does not only apply to the poor or young families struggling to make ends meet, it can be seen in the varying styles of dress at an evening function. The infrequency, these days, with which many men don a dinner jacket limits the rate at which new styles are bought, not necessarily because they cannot afford a new one but because of the reluctance to throw away a perfectly good suit. This in spite of the efforts of the fashion industry to change the width and style of lapels every few years. Some of them will view a preoccupation with fashion with disdain and we may note the comment of one of the established rich that "if you buy good quality clothing it lasts and lasts". Most people in old age form another sector with little care for fashion as long as it is warm and comfortable. It ceases to be a factor that influences their lives.

A positive loop usually implies that there are winners and losers. It is clear that the fashion industry sets out to be the winner. If so why are the consumers the losers? Ill fitting shoes, unsuitable clothing and the pressure to discard perfectly adequate clothes are examples of loser situations. A fashion, which suits the young, may not suit the older person; a fashion for the slim will not suit others. Can the consumer break the loop and halt or reverse a fashion trend? By definition of fashion this will only be done if a significant number of people resist or demand a more suitable change.

It is an example of the crowd effect in which peer pressure accentuates the trend; the trend itself powered by the media and advertising. Conventional methods of limiting the loop gain imply limiting media exposure, compulsorily reducing advertising and restricting the influence that people have on each other. The introduction of a negative loop may be more feasible by calling attention to the disadvantages of a new fashion: for example medical conditions such as bunions from unsuitable footwear and the stupidity of a rain coat that gives you wet knees. In recent times the call for a sustainable planet should encourage people to keep clothing for longer.

Of course the consumer is not entirely powerless. If the fashion designers produce too extreme a change they will be shunned by the public and forced to modify their designs.

Fashion is also at work in the motor car industry except that there is a stronger influence from new technology. Whereas technology may, from time to time, offer new materials for the clothing industry which give some advantage, the motor industry thrives on it. New technology alone, however, is not enough since the fashion in styling can make or break the sales forecast.

When looking at overt features we see changes in style, which distinguish one year's model from another. The changes must not be too many, or too great, or else the public will lose track of the age of a style. In practice we see a basic design which classifies the model, and its era, and then there are small refinements added to differentiate subsequent years and provide an incentive for the fashion conscious owner to change before it is necessary. The change in basic design must not be too rapid, however, for like the fashion industry there will be customer resistance to change that cannot be afforded and it is necessary to tune into the frequency of change that customers will tolerate. These changes also provide a means of differentiating between a company's employees. Senior salesmen can see they are rewarded by a higher grade of car than their juniors. From the viewpoint of the employers of salesmen, the different added facilities must be sufficiently obvious for the desired effect but must not be so costly as to increase the company car budget over its limit. It is the job of the marketing staff of the motor manufacturers to optimise the differences in style and facilities so as to maximise their sales.

Like the clothing industry, the car industry is another example of forced change. For many years in the UK there has been the added thrust of government influence by the way of number plates that identify the year of registration. There must have been many industries that looked on with envy at this way of rigging the market to cause change at a greater rate than necessary. The sell by date used by the food industry is, we suppose, for more beneficial reasons than the change in the motor registration plate. One wonders how delighted the clothing industry would be if the government required that all raincoats be emblazoned with the year of manufacture. Would this encourage people to buy more raincoats, or might it create a cult, which glorifies the antique raincoat and shows disdain for the purchaser of an annual throwaway item?

Summary.

1. Initial conditions are vital for success
2. Market forecasts are subject to delayed feedback.
3. A nation's culture influences participation in industry.
4. Feedback to management changes as companies expand.
5. Symbiosis is an important ingredient for feedback loops.
6. Bureaucracy hinders the power of positive loops.
7. Fashion guides feedback.
8. Marketing often simulates forced vibrations.

References:

1. Hutton W, "The State We're In".
2. New Scientist circa. 1985.
3. http://www.ifm.eng.cam.ac.uk/dstools/process/jit.html

Chapter 16.   Finance.

"The world is a very complex system. It is easy to have too simple a view of it, and it is easy to do harm and to make things worse under the impulse to do good and make things better" KE Boulding

Vulnerability of financial institutions.

The liquidity of the money markets makes financial institutions vulnerable to feedback pressures. They trade largely on their reputation and it is important that it is not tarnished. A crisis in confidence is fertile ground for a positive loop as rumour influences confidence and a drop in confidence feeds more rumour, ultimately resulting in run on the banks. If the bank cannot realise its assets in the form of cash in time to meet demand then a crisis of confidence might occur. There is a history of bankruptcy following loss in confidence of an institution - whether or not the loss was founded on fact.

Insolvent Thrifts.

Another form of loop giving instability occurred with insolvent thrifts in the USA. The Thrifts, which included institutions such as savings and loans associations and mutual savings banks, were used to finance low cost mortgages for home ownership. The problem lay in providing low interest loans for the long-term house buyer to be financed by savings that were only available for the short term. When interest rates soared to over 10% in 1982 the cost of money to finance the long-term loans exceeded the returns obtainable on fixed rates of interest. Savings investors moved elsewhere to benefit from higher interest rates and the Thrifts had to engage in higher risk financing in order to recover a higher rate of interest. The rate of default was higher on these more risky loans and asset cover reduced to the point where the institutions were technically insolvent. A high interest rate regime meant also that assets were discounted by a higher percentage. Legislation was introduced permitting the asset cover to be reduced to 3% thereby letting a nonviable situation continue and compound the problem. Ultimately the taxpayer had to make up the difference.

The problem was analysed by Salam [1] who drew attention to the forbearance granted to thrifts by the regulating authorities. An outline of the issues is shown in figure 1. Prior to the 1970s the Thrifts were required to maintain a net worth (NW) of 5% of assets. This excess of assets over liabilities (some times referred to as capital or equity) was a prudent safety factor for the

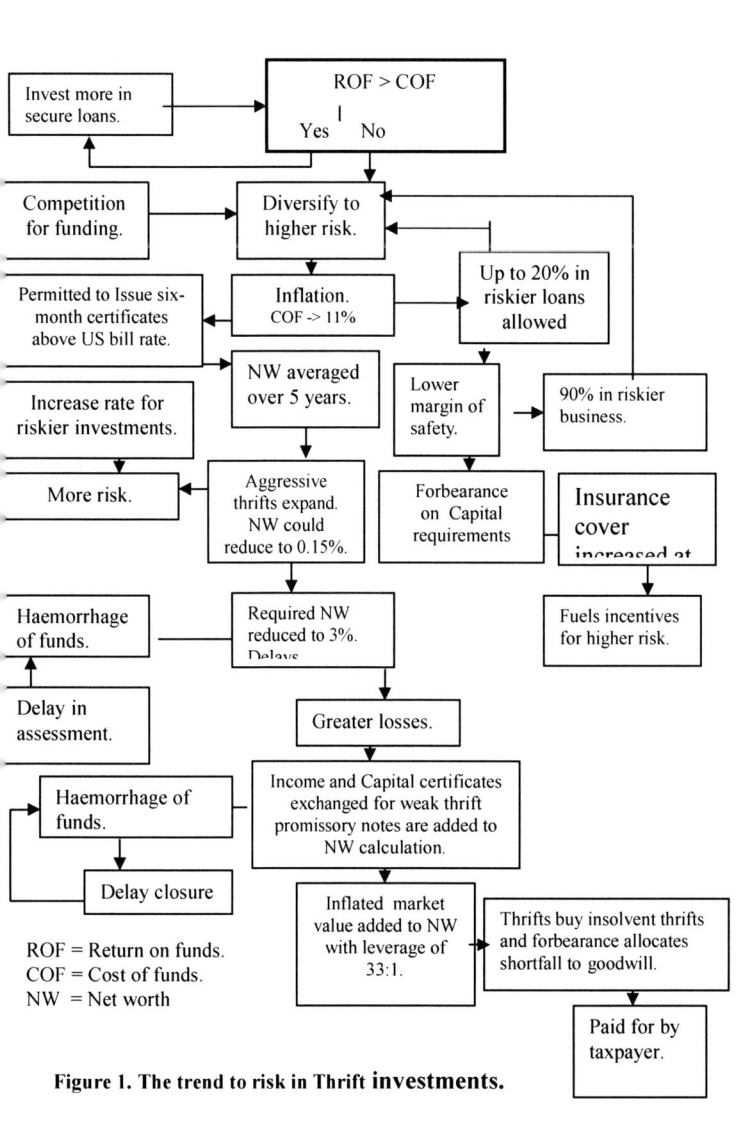

Figure 1. The trend to risk in Thrift investments.

ROF = Return on funds.
COF = Cost of funds.
NW = Net worth

security of depositors who kept their savings with the institution. Provided the return of funds (ROF) from long term loans for house mortgages was greater than the cost of funds (COF) for short term depositors the business was viable. When inflation increased the cost of funds to 11%, this could not be paid for by fixed long-term mortgages. The regulations were relaxed to allow Thrifts to invest 20% of assets in riskier loans that would return a higher rate of interest. By 1982 this was relaxed further to allow 90% to be spread over various commercial and financial investments.

Some help was given by allowing them to issue six month certificates above the US bill rate but the continued forbearance by the regulating authorities permitted the net worth to be reduced to 3% of assets which could be averaged over five years. This meant that if the Thrift was increasing business rapidly then the lower debts incurred in previous years would compensate for much higher debts in the current year. Accordingly NW for the current year could be considerably lower than 3%, implying that the debt to equity ratio could be greater than 33:1. This risk was further compounded for relatively new thrifts that had existed for less than 20 years. Under this provision the capital requirement could be reduced by the proportion of the 20 years that the Thrift had been covered by deposit insurance. Thrifts covered by only one year deposit insurance could reduce their NW to about 0.15%, implying a debt to capital ratio exceeding 600:1 The outcome of this forbearance by the regulating authorities encouraged the management of many Thrifts to take on riskier investments.

Supervision of the Thrifts was limited due to shortages of staff at the regulating authority. Consequently trends to insolvency were not discovered until much later when the losses became higher than would have been the case if action had been taken sooner. In order to prevent the insolvent Thrifts from going bankrupt, healthy thrifts were encouraged to take over the insolvent ones and allocate the difference, between open market value and book value, to goodwill. Management benefited from running larger assets and was encouraged by the assumption that the regulators who authorised this behaviour would not then close down a consequent ailing business. In effect the taxpayer paid for the goodwill in order to save the ailing thrifts from bankruptcy.

Whilst the basic problem lay in trying to pay for short term deposits with long term fixed loans the problem increased due to the delay in applying compensating feedback from the regulators. The simplest loop is one that compensates for the necessary rise in interest payable to depositors as shown in figure 2.

```
┌─────────────────────────┐
│ Difference between rates │◄─┐
│  for depositors and      │  │
│  mortgagees increases.   │  │
└────────────┬─────────────┘  │
             │                │
┌────────────▼─────────────┐  │
│  Adjust mortgage interest│──┘
│       to compensate.     │
└──────────────────────────┘
```

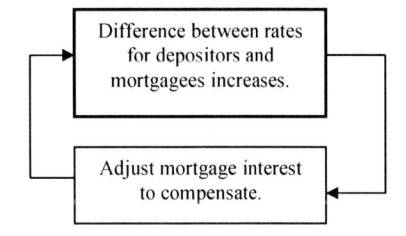

Figure 2. Maintaining financial viability.

The regulating authorities were intended to introduce compensating feedback by limiting the risk of a thrift to become insolvent. As with all negative loops it is necessary to apply the correction in time for it to be effective. The delays and forbearance in fact introduced a positive loop and encouraged Thrift management to take more risk, Figure 3.

```
                  ┌──────────────────────────┐
              ┌──►│ Thrift managers exceed the risk│
              │   │ that is prudent for the security of│
              │   │     their depositor's money.     │
              │   └──────────────┬───────────┘
              │                  │
┌─────────────┴────┐   ┌─────────▼─────────────┐
│ Shortage of regulating│   │ Regulator allows riskier │
│ staff causes further  │◄──│ behaviour to compensate for the│
│ delays and trend to   │   │ problem arising from fixed rate│
│ insolvency continues. │   │ mortgages. This delays │
└──────────────────┘   │ compensating action.  │
                       └───────────────────────┘
```

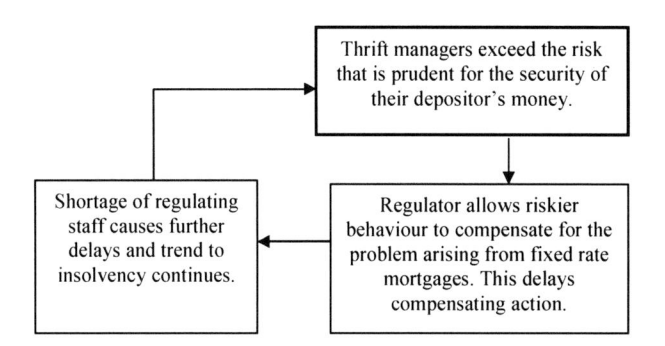

Figure 3. Delay in regulation of Thrifts.

It is difficult to see how modification to feedback loops can compensate for a flawed business model based upon fixed contracts that cannot be altered to reflect market conditions. With inflation, the value of money decreases so that the fixed rate mortgagee is, in effect, paying less as inflation progresses. The rate demanded by depositors reflects the influence of inflation in devaluing their deposits so that a greater rate of interest is required. On the other hand deflation would alternatively increase the value of the fixed rate payments and the depositors would expect less interest since the value of their deposit would rise. Given that deflation causes other problems it is appropriate to look at the basic issues that caused the problems in the first place.

The purpose of Thrifts was to promote home ownership by providing low cost mortgage financing. The encouragement of home-ownership is expected to provide the benefit of a more stable and responsible society. There will be a cost associated with this benefit. If the financing is at a lower cost than the market would provide then some benefactor must be financing the difference. The attempt in times of inflation to achieve greater profits in order to pay depositors a market rate must assume an inefficient market – or unusually astute managers who can beat the market. In an efficient market there will be a compensating feedback loop that determines the rate of return available for a particular degree of risk. The higher returns, expected from higher risk investments, must in the long term be countered by losses accompanying the risk; although there may be a premium to encourage the more risky behaviour.

Society at large is the beneficiary of stability of home ownership. It is also the one that pays for it whether by subsidising mortgage payments or meeting the bills when institutions become bankrupt. If the institution becomes bankrupt then the cost is likely to fall on relatively few; but if bailed out by the government then the cost is more widely distributed.

The problem with fixed rate long-term mortgages is that there is no compensating negative loop to ally the return on funds with the cost. Since fixed contracts have been signed (for the overall benefit of society) then society pays. One possibility would be to make the return on deposits tax free to encourage savers to invest at a rate of interest that is more compatible with the long term mortgages, alternatively the tax payer must subsidise the institution to make up the difference.

The crisis of 2008.

The financial turmoil of 2008 arising from the defaults on sub-prime loans introduced further issues into the realm of financial instability. The problem arose not from the altruism of providing home ownership for poorer families so much as the commission obtainable for the managers of the finance involved. More managers jumped on the bandwagon as the benefit to others became apparent. It provided motivation to fund construction companies to build houses in areas where they were not needed; especially during a downturn. The delay in the feedback, that would otherwise keep the situation under control, lay in the methods used to disguise the state of affairs.

Sub-prime liabilities were packaged as investments, which were sold onto other financial institutions. In accordance with many financial transactions these risky investments could be geared by borrowing money in order to help finance the purchase thus giving significant leverage to the gains to be made in a rising market, but also of course to the losses to be suffered in a falling market.

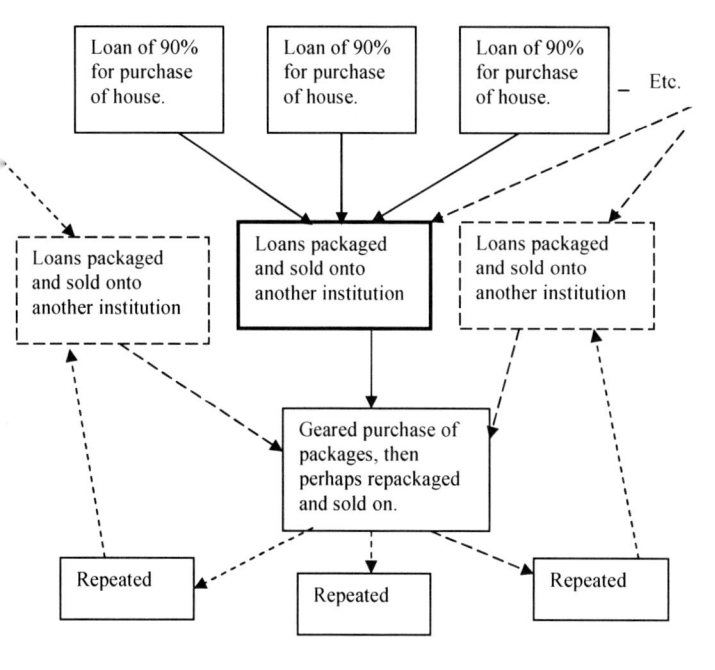

Figure 4. Recycling of geared investments.

The optimism prevailing in much of the financial world, after many years of a bull market, caused the risks to be ignored even though the people who had been sold mortgages would have difficulty in paying the interest - especially if the economy faltered and those people lost their jobs. When these risks were re-packaged as an investment in property and offered by a trusted institution the degree of risk was less apparent and an adequate degree of due diligence was not performed. The (risky) investment packages could be sold on to other financial institutions perhaps supported by loans from further institutions to give further gearing. It was possible that part of a package was recycled to one of the earlier institutions in the chain. The system lacked the transparency necessary for proper assessment and consequently it became difficult to unravel the risk that the banks had incurred – Figure 4.

Defaults on the sub-prime mortgages became losses for the institutions in a falling market. Their losses increased in accordance with the gearing and passed onto other institutions whose investment had also been geared. The development of complex derivatives ensured the losses incurred were such as to bankrupt many. A feedback loop of fear developed that prevented banks offering further loans to other banks and industry until their degree of solvency could be ascertained. The delay in assessing liabilities caused the circulation of money needed for liquidity to dry up until governments agreed to underwrite the banks' positions from tax payers' money. In the USA the House of Representatives agreed to enormous sums to bailout the banking system and governments in Europe similarly guaranteed the banks in order to restore confidence. It was necessary to break the positive loop of fear, Figure 5.

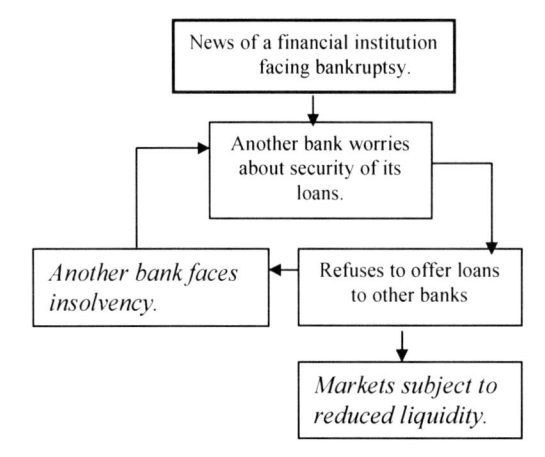

Figure 5. The positive loop of fear of default on loans.

Northern Rock and the run on the bank.

An early victim was Northern rock, which depended on wholesale finance to finance mortgages. The cause was not a flawed business model so much as being too dependent on wholesale short term loans when the sub-prime loans fiasco from the USA caused the liquidity provided by short term loans to dry up. The problem for the company lay in the panic depleting their liquid funds faster than they could replenish them from loans or by liquefying other assets. There was a run on the bank as queues of people assembled to withdraw their money. As the media drew attention to the length of the queues so people panicked and increased the length of the queues, Figure 6.

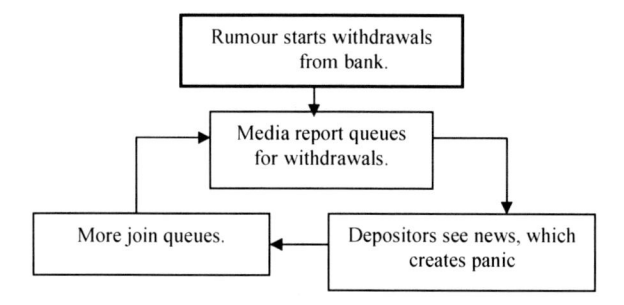

```
        ┌─────────────────────────┐
        │ Rumour starts withdrawals│
        │       from bank.         │
        └────────────┬─────────────┘
                     ▼
   ┌───► ┌─────────────────────────┐ ──┐
   │     │  Media report queues    │   │
   │     │    for withdrawals.     │   │
   │     └─────────────────────────┘   │
   │                                    ▼
┌──┴──────────────┐    ┌──────────────────────────┐
│ More join queues.│◄───│ Depositors see news, which│
│                 │    │      creates panic        │
└─────────────────┘    └──────────────────────────┘
```

Figure 6. The Panic Loop

The feedback loops of panic generating more panic are discussed elsewhere. The consequent loop for Northern Rock lay in the depletion of funds increasing the rate of depletion of funds. The task then for the bank is to limit the depletion of funds, Figure 7. The scoldent list might be:

Saturation: Put a limit on the rate of withdrawal of money.
Cut-off: by closing the bank's doors! More sensibly by removing investor's worries.
Open loop: loans from other banks to neutralise depletion of funds.
Low gain: by government guaranteeing deposits.
Delay: sufficient bureaucracy to delay payments until liquidity improves.
External force: take-over by another institution.
Negative feedback: regulation from authorities before the problem arises.
Theme change: Less risky style of management.

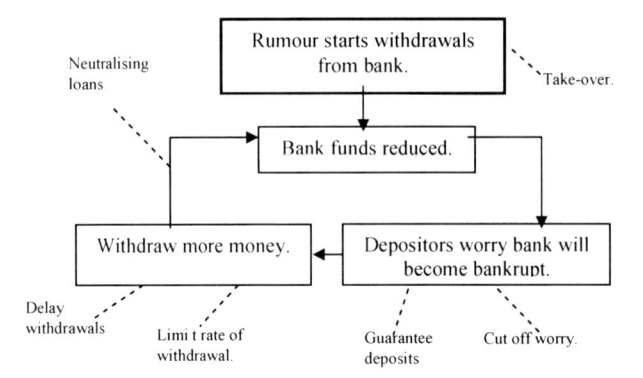

Figure 7. Loop for money withdrawal and counteractions.

Delay in response to credit.

Delay in the correcting mechanism of a system will cause oscillation in the response. The fluctuations in the economic cycle are an example as governments endeavour to maintain steady economic growth; a criterion by which they will be judged at election time. The financial controls available to the Chancellor, such as rate of interest or taxation, are instrumental in modifying future actions rather than modifying the past. In particular they are subject to error in estimating the state of the economy at the time.

The delay in collecting and correlating the data means that at any time the information is several months out of date and a recession may have changed to expansion in the meantime, so that an action based on the previous data may be the opposite of that required. Delay in correction means that the pendulum swings further than desired. It has been observed governments try to anticipate the problem and attempt to improve the method of control by small influences which have become known as "the notorious touch of the tiller".

A non-linear rise in income tax provides a degree of negative feedback, which helps to keep inflation more stable. If there is a rise in prices or wages and a corresponding rise in incomes then more people enter the upper tax bracket. If the tax system is progressive then a greater proportion of income goes in tax. Accordingly, inflation tends to raise government receipts more than its expenditures. The government absorbs cash so that less money is in the hands of public; which is deflationary.

The more serious trend is for a government to overspend on services during times of relative economic prosperity in the expectation that the prosperity will continue indefinitely. The effect of increasing taxation takes time to creep through the system. Increased taxation and regulation on industry leaves less investment available for increased output later as indicated in Figure 8. Johnson [2] has put it succinctly while commenting on the UK economy:

"in a time of prosperity we have taxed and regulated away the competitive strengths of our industries and squandered a comfortable future".

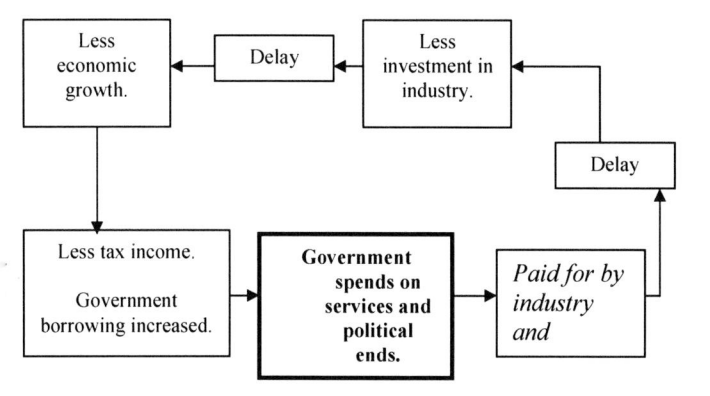

Figure 8. Excess delay in response to spending.

He further observes that deindustrialisation versus rising health costs and a bloated welfare state will be on a collision course. The loop gain necessary for industry to expand is reduced due to the resources leaking to taxation and bureaucracy as discussed in the industry chapter.

One of the potential time bombs lies in the pensions industry since not only have over-generous pensions been offered in the past but also the extended lifespan now enjoyed by many retired people is placing an unplanned burden on the pension providers. Some companies may become insolvent due to the shortfall in the pension fund. It is due to the successes of medical science and engineering that elongated lifespans have come about. This has not been without cost, which is likely to continue increasing as ever more expensive treatments are developed. Had such success been forecast then appropriate planning could have been put in place to fund the shortfall either by larger contributions or by raising the retirement age. The delay in feedback is primarily due to the lifetime of contracts offered early in a career, perhaps up to 40 years before retirement. The problem is further exacerbated by a falling birth rate if there are fewer people to fund the retirement of an increasing number of state pensioners. This problem should not be blamed on the pensioners since their contributions to their ultimate pension have probably been channelled away by successive governments into other more pressing projects, particularly ones that bring a short term benefit and consequent political gain to the ruling party.

Another cause for concern is the availability of credit. A credit card is a means of delaying accountability for debt. Whilst it is hoped the credit card companies only provide advances to people who can manage their finances adequately, there is evidence that the assessment is not always carried out with sufficient stringency. If the debts get out of hand then it is because the negative loop has been delayed. Zero delay implies no credit, the longer the delay the less influence the loop has on the debtor's behaviour.

Some positive loops.

The economics chapter has noted the tendency for financial matters to be stable in consequence of market forces. Such a desirable situation is likely - provided the partners in a financial agreement are sufficiently equal so as to be able to negotiate reasonable terms. This desirable situation evidently does not always occur. If one party is under duress due to shortage of funds then that party may be desperate to obtain funds whatever the terms. In consequence people with a bad credit record may be required to pay extortionate rates of interest on a loan. The nature of compound interest turns such a loan into a disaster if the loan cannot be repaid faster than the interest burden increases. Thus interest of 29% on a credit card will cause the loan to be doubled in about 4 years. A BBC panorama programme [3] quoted some mortgage lenders demanding an APR of 170%; a positive feedback loop of a truly vicious kind. Why anyone would be willing to enter into such an arrangement is hard to imagine unless the mortgagee believed house prices were set to double in less that 6 months.

Whereas the terms were not extortionate as above, a similar situation occurred in developing countries where loans, negotiated by banks, carried a rate of interest that increased the debt incurred with no prospect of retrieving the situation. Such situations are likely to occur where a country does not have the infrastructure to utilise the loan money efficiently. A more responsible assessment of a nation's potential is called for to determine the likely outcome of a loan. Such assessments are more likely when an investment is made in the expectation of a return dependent on performance.

The converse has been observed by Boulding [4] who noted that: "Wealth creates power and power destroys wealth". The cost of being a great power uses up wealth. It would seem to apply to nations who are burdened with the cost of administering a large empire. The cost of such activities is perhaps less likely to be monitored when other considerations are paramount, such as defence and standing in the world. A company subject to wealth draining activities is likely to act more quickly since it is usually accountable to shareholders sooner than a political party is accountable to its electorate.

Stability is also likely to be upset by monopoly. The factors in favour of a business may be small to begin with but with rising volume, and the benefit of mass purchase, a positive loop can arise against which smaller enterprises cannot compete. The imbalance does not get corrected by market forces and legislation has been needed to prevent undue exploitation of a near monopoly position.

McDonald [5] has noted the impact of genetics on insurance. If genetic analysis identifies the potential for illness then there will be a bias towards potentially ill people buying medical insurance. If the likelihood of illness is higher then the insurance company will raise the premiums. People whose genes are not conducive to illness will be less likely to insure so that the spread of risk is biased towards the potentially ill. A positive loop is thus created to make the premiums even higher - Figure 9.

This situation is perhaps another contender for the *scoldent* list.

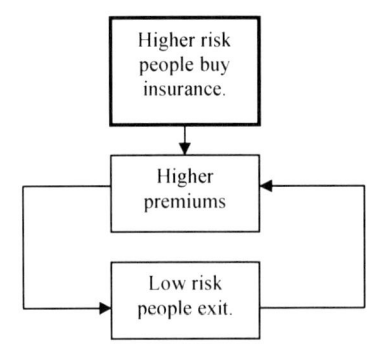

```
┌─────────────┐
│ Higher risk │
│ people buy  │
│ insurance.  │
└──────┬──────┘
       ▼
┌─────────────┐
│   Higher    │◄──┐
│  premiums   │   │
└──────┬──────┘   │
       │          │
       ▼          │
┌─────────────┐   │
│  Low risk   │───┘
│ people exit.│
└─────────────┘
```

Figure 9. Influence of genetic testing on health insurance.

1. *Saturation* will occur when the clients cannot afford to pay higher premiums and accordingly limit their cover, or pay, for example, the first £1000 of any treatment to keep the premiums manageable.

2. *Cut-off* will be a result of the insurer refusing cover or the client abandoning the scheme.

3. *Open loop* conditions apply if genetic testing is prohibited.

4. *Low loop gain* could result from government support for insurance, such as tax relief on contributions, or reallocation of a person's existing National Health Service entitlement to the private sector.

5. *Delay* in the loop would occur by placing an embargo on the publication of the test results for a period of time or by requiring insurance companies to agree no increase in premiums for a period of years.

6. *External influence* by government providing more funding or subsidising expensive treatments.

7. *Negative feedback* will occur if higher premiums encourage people to give up smoking to reduce cancer and overeating to reduce heart attacks and diabetes. Also in the long run by giving priority to research to improve the prevention and treatment of the more costly diseases.

8. *Theme change* by sufficient funds for a National Health Service that has the confidence of the people, who are motivated to minimise the costs.

Negative feedback.

One of the aspects of negative feedback loops is that they are usually set up to maintain a system at its optimum condition. This condition is achieved by measuring the error between the optimum and actual conditions and sending the error around the loop to correct the condition - Figure 10.

There may be several factors that influence changes; not least the delay that is incurred in assessing the costs involved and the costs of change. The error may not be quantified in precise terms, it may be simply the action of a free market that indicates when, for example, a price is too high so that people buy another brand. The optimum condition is then found by adjusting the price until sales versus costs reach a maximum - as discussed in the economics chapter.

Measurement of error arises in employment when the pay for a job has to be equated to the difficulty of the work and the expertise required. An employer needs to offer an attractive salary to a new employee, in part to overcome the

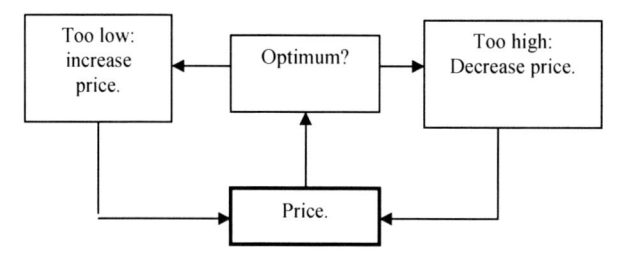

Figure 10. The negative feedback loops of market forces.

inertia of moving from an existing job and in part to overcome the cost of moving. Accordingly the initial salary will be higher than may be appropriate for the work to be performed, especially since there may be a learning period before the job is performed competently.

The poverty trap.

A worse situation in salary mismatching occurs with the poverty trap when financial subsidies are removed at a rate that gives no incentive to work harder to increase salary unless a significant jump in reward can be achieved. It is an example of legislation removing the feedback of market forces. A similar situation occurs with the change in stamp duty on house purchase in the UK when the price reaches a certain threshold, currently about £300,000. An anomaly occurs when the increase in stamp duty from 1% to 3% is charged on the whole amount rather than the increment over the threshold. The effect is to distort the housing market since anyone foolish enough to buy at, for example, £1000 over the threshold would be paying stamp duty at the rate of about 600% on the extra £1000. If it were only £100 over the threshold then the rate of duty would be about 6000%. Apart from distorting the market, the effect is to encourage people to disobey the law and allocate the increment to the purchase of notional contents to avoid the extortionate increase in stamp duty.

The rational approach to the increase in stamp duty is self-evident. The increased rate should be applied to the increment above the threshold. Such a system operates on salary when the rate of tax increases from about 20% to 40%. The increase is applied to the taxable income that (currently) exceeds about £30,000. If the same system were applied as for stamp duty then the 40% would be applied to the whole of the taxable income and create a poverty gap of unworkable proportions, not to mention a national outcry.

The poverty gap occurring due to the removal of benefits with rising income is more difficult to correct. One solution [6] is to give everyone the benefit as a form of national wage (to which a lower earned income would be added) and then raise extra tax to pay for it. The effect is to remove the distortion that the poverty gap creates. Provided the tax burden is not loaded onto industry, it improves the economics for the employment of low skilled workers since the financial burden to industry can be commensurate with the workers' skills; as discussed in the appendix to chapter 13 on employment.

Summary.

1. Feedback in the financial world is rapid.
2. A stabilising loop is necessary to balance assets and liabilities.
3. A financial contract must anticipate future trends.
4. The feedback loop of rumour can be disastrous for an institution.
5. Delay in correcting mechanisms will cause oscillation of the system.
6. Credit delays compensating feedback.
7. Compound interest can lead to extortionate demands.
8. Insurance dedicated to the genetically risky may not be sustainable.
9. The discontinuity in subsidised employment contributes to the poverty trap.

References.

[1] Salam AW, "Congress, regulators, RAP, and savings and loan debacle". The CPA Journal, January 1994.
[2] Johnson L. "Crash of 87, how to profit from it", 1988.

[3] BBC1 Panorama "The Borrowers - Britain deep in debt." 28-1-01
[4] Boulding K E. "Business and economic systems", p109.

[5] Macdonald, A.S. (1999) "Modelling the impact of genetics on insurance." North American Actuarial Journal, 3:1, 83-101.

[6] Grover D., " Optimising Employment in the Microelectronics Age. ".
....Computer Weekly 1979, and revised in Computer Age 1980.

Chapter 17.   Financial systems.

Bonds.

Financial systems are perhaps the most responsive to feedback. With the advent of computers the response can be essentially instantaneous and feedback loops can be both positive and negative.

An example of negative feedback maintaining stability is the issue of bonds by governments. A loan to the government is considered the safest investment and accordingly the rate of interest offered is expected to be less than for more risky ones. The bond prices are nevertheless subject to market fluctuations in interest.

A government wishing to raise money might issue a bond for £100 subject to paying a fixed rate of interest for the life of the bond. By way of example the interest rate on the £100 might be 5% for a bond with a life of 10 years (the rate of 5% is known as the coupon). After the 10 years the government repays the £100 to the owner of the bond. In the meantime the bond can be sold on to another at a price that reflects its value in terms of the income yielded as interest. If the bank rate were raised so that the return on a low risk loan becomes 6% then a bond offering only 5% would be unattractive and would not sell. Accordingly the price of the bond would reduce to about £83 so that the annual £5, payable on the bond, would represent 6% of the price of £83.

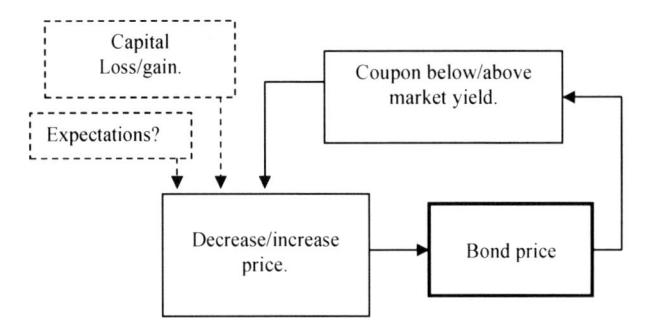

Figure 1. Adjustment to bond price.

Alternatively if the no risk interest rate reduces to 4% then a bond becomes more attractive and would be expected to sell for about £125 because the annual payment of £5 (the coupon) represents a yield of 4%, namely 4% of the £125 invested. This simple feedback loop is shown in figure 1.

The above scenario is not quite so simple since the bond has to be redeemed on maturity. Accordingly someone who buys a bond near the end of its 10-year term will get the agreed value of £100. A price of £83 during a period of a 6% market rate is then even more attractive to the buyer who would gain another £17 on maturity. Accordingly the price would rise above £83 to reflect this benefit. The situation is further complicated by taxation. Whereas the interest payment would be taxable, the £17 benefit would be a capital gain and only be subject to tax when the capital gains allowance is exceeded. A higher rate taxpayer would therefore be willing to pay more for a short dated bond than a price that simply reflects the yield otherwise expected.

This example of a feedback loop is unusual since (whilst most loops incur a delay in response) investors may anticipate changes in interest rate that will affect the price of bonds and accordingly act early. If interest rates are expected to fall then the buyer who acts early will enjoy the benefit of a rising bond price, these acts themselves tend to increase the price of bonds before the interest rate is decreased. Alternatively if interest rates are expected to rise then it is beneficial to sell early before the bond price falls.

The Stock market.

It is perhaps tempting to regard the rise and fall of the stock market as an example of the pendulum. It is of course a very complex system that responds to multiple influences that confuse the observer, especially in the short term. Nevertheless there are times when an overall picture seems predictable, at least on a statistical basis. Many people profit by speculating on the market (and accordingly some people must lose).

Efforts to anticipate market trends have caused the publication of many books and occupied the minds of countless investors. It is apparent that certain trends can be forecast with reasonable certainty, and equally certain that those who study the behaviour of the market will profit more (or lose less) than those who blindly take the advice of others.

Financial systems tend to respond quickly to changes in influence. The comparative ease with which money can be transferred allows a financial system to compensate for changes in circumstances very quickly. Indeed financial systems not only respond quickly; they may anticipate changes before they happen (sometimes wrongly). Systems that require the manufacture and movement of hardware are, by comparison, slow to respond.

The money market is the most responsive of all because there is no delay in the production of a commodity. The response has been increased further with the advent of computers that process numerous transactions per second and accordingly market prices respond equally quickly. It is fertile ground for a positive loop if news and rumour cause a run on the market.

The expert trader is more alive to the trends in the market. Typically the expert will judge the beginning of a bull market before the novice and accordingly buy when prices are more favourable. The influence of numerous investors feeds back into the system and causes prices to rise further. More investors notice the trend and make their contribution and add their influence to the positive loop. Eventually cautious investors notice the movement in the market and decide they are missing out. They start investing towards the top of the bull trend.

In the meantime the expert is watching for signs that the bull market is ending and the procedure is reversed as they start selling. The descent is usually steeper than the rise since there may be a measure of panic (implying greater gain in the positive feedback loop) as investors see their capital being eroded. The picture, of course, is not as simple as this since there may be many false starts and many surprises that influence prices before the majority react.

The positive feedback influence spoils, to some extent, the careful and responsible efforts made to evaluate stock. Insofar as the price of a share is equated to the no risk rate of interest obtainable in the market there is a form of benchmark available. The elements of reward and risk are nevertheless so variable that the relationship may be obscure. Factors that feed back into the share price such as: the rate of dividend; the expected future rate; expected earnings; risk in the market and the overall economic outlook should, when taken together, yield a profit that bears some relation to the interest the equivalent capital would receive in a safe investment such as a government bond. The expectation is doubtless higher than for a risk-free investment if only to compensate for the time and work required to monitor the market and pay commissions. The simple diagram in fig. 2 illustrates the loop.

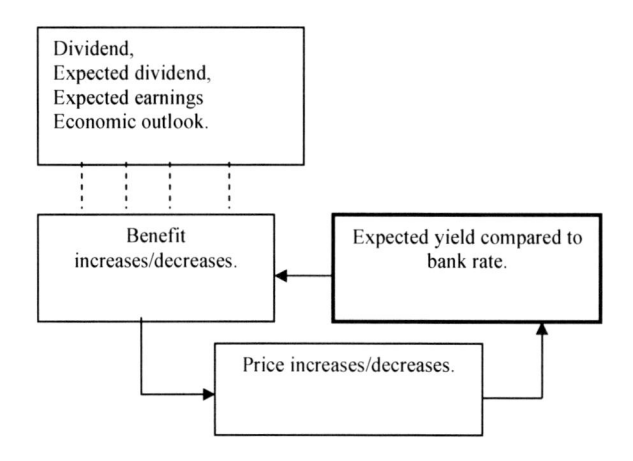

```
┌─────────────────────────┐
│ Dividend,               │
│ Expected dividend,      │
│ Expected earnings       │
│ Economic outlook.       │
└─────────────────────────┘
    ┆  ┆  ┆  ┆
┌─────────────────┐      ┌───────────────────────────┐
│    Benefit      │◄─────│ Expected yield compared to│
│increases/decreases.│    │       bank rate.          │
└─────────────────┘      └───────────────────────────┘
         │                           ▲
         │        ┌──────────────────────────┐
         └───────►│ Price increases/decreases.│──┘
                  └──────────────────────────┘
```

Figure 2. Some factors affecting share price.

Added to the complexity of the market are the activities of the speculators who bet on the likely movement in the market. It is possible that the speculator helps to make the market more stable than it would otherwise be. Whilst going short on a stock may push the price down, the downward influence is counteracted when it is necessary to buy the stock back.

The Crash of '87.

Unstable conditions can develop if corrective influences do not keep a bull market in a viable state. A notable example was the crash of 1987 [1] which was intensified by the use of computer sell orders that respond when prices reduce to a predetermined level. The sales reduced the prices further and triggered further sell orders. Whilst the crash happened quickly once started there had been signs that the market was overvalued to a dangerous degree so that a correction was overdue. As discussed above a bond price maintains a fair market value in the light of interest rates. The yield on stocks and shares is expected to be higher to compensate for the extra risk. Accordingly when the price of stocks rose to a level where the average yield was comparable to the return on bonds then it was an indication that prices were too high. A further indicator was the high average price to earnings ratio (P/E), which on American stocks rose to 23, which was considered high at the time.

On October 19th 1987, known as Black Monday, the Dow Jones industrial average dropped 508 points - a 22.6% loss. It was much larger than the losses in 1929 that sent the world into a depression. Such a loss is expected to stimulate a pendulum response to initiate a partial recovery but by the end of the week the average was still down by nearly 300 points.

As Johnson [1] noted: computers played a crucial role in the severity of the crash. By 1987 the NYSE was completely computerised, as were most other markets. That meant trades could be executed at a volume unheard of in the previous decade. A sell-off that would have taken days only a few years earlier could now occur in a matter of hours. As stock prices plummeted on October 19, mutual fund managers had to dump stocks for cash to pay off investors redeeming fund shares, while margin calls forced investors who had bought stock on credit to sell out.

The positive loop that is apparent in this case was not so severe on the Tokyo stock exchange. It was considered more resilient because many shares are held in cross shareholdings. These are bought by businesses with mutual interests so as to form co-operative relationships and guard against predators. They are tokens of good faith and long term support. 10% were held by 73 insurance companies, which the government could manipulate in a crisis. It was a patriotic duty not to sell. This is equivalent to low gain in the positive feedback loop.

Arbitrage.

The arbitrageur profits by buying and selling stocks when their price is different on two or more markets. Provided the selling price on one exchange is higher than the buying price on another then a profit can be made (from which trading charges have to be subtracted). Computer programs have been developed that monitor the markets to identify opportunities when prices differ.

An example of arbitrage [2] occurs with the New York stock market and the futures market in Chicago. When the price of a stock in New York and its corresponding future in Chicago are not synchronised then it is possible to buy one at a lower price and sell an equivalent one at a higher price. The effect of this is to bring free market discipline (a negative loop) into the pricing so that the prices converge.

A Futures contract is an agreement to buy or sell a commodity or share at an agreed price on a defined date in the future. Futures are used by speculators or by people wishing to hedge their position in case the price of a commodity goes against their interests. They provide a form of insurance so that a business can plan ahead in the knowledge that commodities will not change significantly in price. In a falling market the price of futures may be less than the present day commodity price. Accordingly a form of arbitrage is possible by buying the low cost futures and selling the higher priced current stock. Such actions will tend to increase the cost of the futures and lower the selling price of current stock until it no longer becomes profitable to speculate. This applies so long as the market is stable. In the event of a crash when confidence is lost then the price of futures may reflect the lowering price of current stock. If a panic sets in then the futures may trade lower and lower as short sellers take advantage of the lowering price. In 1987, with the aid of computers programs, traders exacerbated the situation. The software writers had not anticipated conditions fed by panic during a crash and failed to counteract the feedback loop.

Derivatives.

Market forces are ubiquitous forms of negative feedback loop since if the price of a product increases above a fair value then it will be ignored in favour of a more favourable product. The market force tends to act so as to maintain prices at a fair value. The financial markets are systems in which the feedback occurs very quickly and the prices are fine-tuned to take account not only of present value but also risk and future prospects. Insurance is also a factor in the calculations. The premium is the price of nullifying risk and will be represented as a loss to be offset against profits. Although not specified as such the premium, for options and warrants, is a form of insurance for the buyer to prevent unacceptable losses if a trade should be a disaster.

Derivatives are contracts to purchase or sell shares subject to certain conditions. The prices of the contracts are based on the underlying share price and the future expectations. It may not be necessary to actually buy or sell shares since, subject to a premium, the contractor can buy an option to do so if he/she chooses. The contract can be sold onto another party at a later date when its price has reflected the change in the underlying share price.

Options.

An option is a contract giving the buyer the right, but not the obligation, to buy or sell a share (or other asset) at an agreed price on or before a particular date. They have similarities to shares insofar as they can be traded in a similar manner. Apart from loss of voting rights the main difference is that the option expires at a certain date defined in the contract. The option has added value over a share since the buyer of the option can delay making a decision until it is apparent where the share price is going. The premium reflects the added value, which is a benefit for which a price has to be paid

The two main options are a *Call* and a *Put*. A Call Option permits the owner (of the option) to buy a share at a specific price (known as the strike price) on or before a certain date. The owner can *call* on another person to give him the share for the price specified in the options contract. The call will only be made if the share price has risen above the strike price in the meantime. It gives the owner the retrospective right to buy.

Figure 3 illustrates an example where a *call option* cost 10p per share for a strike price of 100p. The investment makes a loss until the share price reaches 110p. Thereafter the option holder can make a profit by buying the shares at 100p and selling them on the market.

Conversely a Put Option permits the owner (of the option) to sell a share at a specific price on or before a certain date. The owner can *put* the share in the hands of another person in consideration of receiving payment at the price specified in the contract. The put will only be made if the share price has fallen below the strike price. It gives the option holder the retrospective right to sell.

These rights, that options contracts convey, may be viewed as an insurance policy against making the wrong decision (to buy or sell shares) at an earlier stage and accordingly a premium is payable for the benefit of the insurance.

The person or institution with which the option owner has the contract is known as the writer of the contract. The writer receives the premium in consideration of taking the risk that a share price moves to or beyond the strike price. If an option holder chooses to exercise an option, then the writer must sell or buy the shares at the price previously agreed. Alternatively the option holder can sell the contract in the market at a price that reflects the benefit of the contract in respect of the new underlying share price.

Covered warrants.

The covered warrant is a further example of an options contract that also incorporates gearing. The price reflects several factors such as the underlying share price; the volatility of the share price; the time available for the warrant to run; dividends and interest rates. A warrant (as for options contracts) can be a *Call* or a *Put*.

Gearing.

A geared investment is one in which the value of the investment changes at a greater rate than the share price. A familiar form of geared investment occurs when a house buyer purchases a mortgage. If the deposit is 10% then a 2% increase in house prices will give a 20% increase in the value of the investment. The gearing in this case is 10 (less payments of interest in the intervening period). Whereas the gearing is very much to the buyer's benefit when house prices are rising, the percentage losses, during a housing slump, are also magnified by 10.

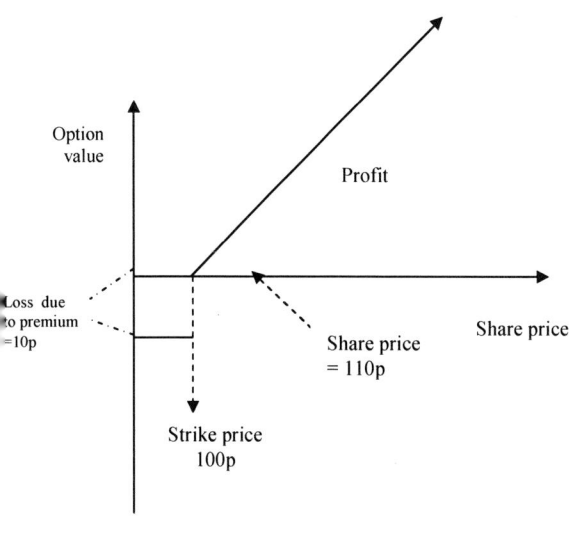

Figure 3. Value of option as function of underlying share price.

There is an analogy to mechanical gear wheels. If a gear wheel with 100 teeth is meshed with a wheel of ten teeth then for every revolution of the larger wheel the smaller wheel must revolve ten times. The same principle applies to the lever shown in figure 4. If the lever is pivoted at O and points A & B are 10 and 100 cms from O, then raising A by 1 cm will raise B by 10 cms. This magnifying effect makes the warrant a more lively investment than a share since not only do profits change more quickly, losses do as well. Gearing of a warrant reflects the ratio of the share price to the warrant price. If the price of the underlying share changes by 1p and the warrant price also changes by 1p then the warrant changes by a much greater percentage than does the underlying share. The ratio of the prices is the gearing.

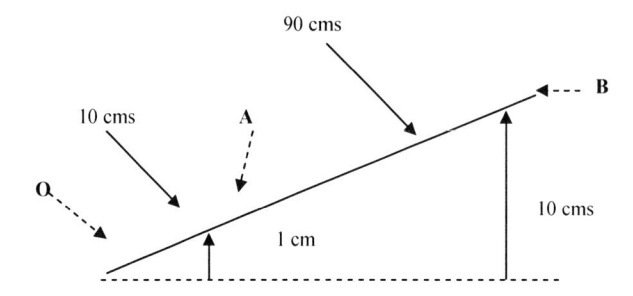

Figure 4. Gearing.

A gearing of 10 implies 10 times increase in the gain in the feedback loop. For a relatively small deposit the profits or losses (as a percentage of the deposit) will be much greater than the change in the underlying share price. The premium paid depends on the strike price chosen. The profit from a Call transaction does not increase linearly with share price (as shown in figure 5). The further away the strike price is from the current share price the smaller the premium since it is less likely that the share will appreciate to the point of profit. As the share price increases, the rate of warrant increase accelerates and changes rapidly in the region of the strike price (shown as 100p). Volatility in the share price also adds value to the warrant since it becomes more likely that (at least momentarily) the share price will reach a profitable level. The time left for the warrant to run is also reflected in the price. The longer the time to expiry, of the warrant, the more chance there is of the share price increasing. The amount the time factor adds to the price is known as the time value. It is greatest at the beginning of the warrant period and reduces to zero at the end of the period.

Figure 5 is a simplified chart. The warrant's value will additionally reduce in value due to reduction in time to expiry and increase in value if the share price increases in volatility.

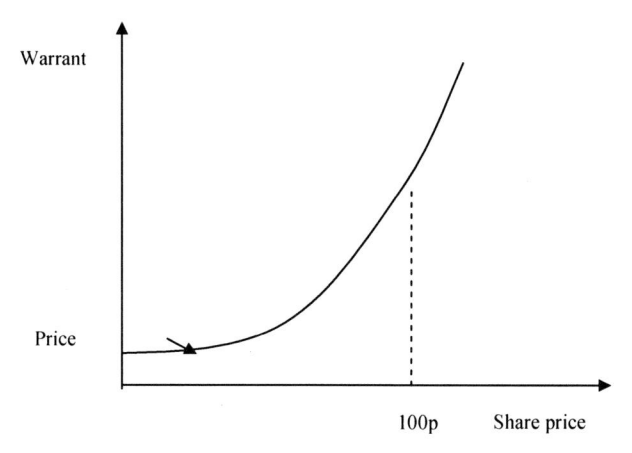

Figure 5. Change in warrant price

When the strike price of a warrant is more than the share price then the warrant is known as being out-of-the-money. If the share price is much lower than the strike price then the warrant may be worth very little. In these circumstances it would be an anomaly for an out-of-the-money warrant to increase by 1p when the share increases by 1p. It would otherwise be more beneficial to buy the most out-of-the-money warrant since the cheapest price gives the highest gearing. This issue is counteracted by the notion of effective gearing, sometimes called leverage.

There are two factors affecting performance: firstly the spread (the difference between the price offered for buying in or selling) does not diminish in proportion to the drop in price of the warrant. Accordingly the spread becomes a greater percentage of the price offered and it will be longer before a transaction moves into profit. In cases where the share has dropped considerably the ratio can be infinite – this occurs when the bid price has fallen to zero.

Returning to leverage, figure 6 is figure 3 with the lever replaced by a flexible fishing rod. If the rod has a fish on the line then the end will bend under the weight of the fish. For low effective gearing (reflected in out-of-the-money warrants) the fishing rod is weak. It bends so that point B does not rise ten times as quickly as point A. If point B is only raised by 2 cms then whilst the "gearing" of the rod is 10 the effective gearing is only 2 (only 20% of the gearing). To take the analogy further the fisherman seeking a large fish of more value would choose a much stiffer rod. It would bend only slightly under the weight of the fish so that if point A is raised by 9 cms: the effective gearing is increased to 9 (it is increased to 90% of the gearing).

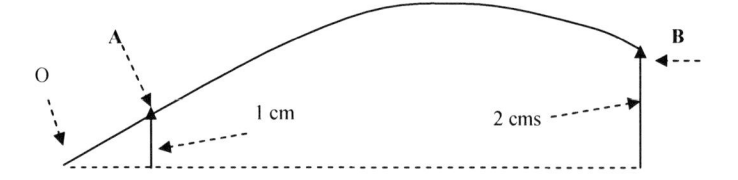

Figure 6. Effective gearing.

The stiffness is a measure of how much the level of the fishing line changes in response to a movement in the fishing rod. If a rod with 100% stiffness is one that does not bend then the line will move the full amount expected. If the stiffness is only 1% then the line will only move 1% of the amount. The analogy of stiffness in covered warrants is known as the delta. Delta, which is quoted by institutions selling warrants, can vary between 0 and 100%, and when multiplied by the gearing gives the effective gearing or leverage. Delta is low for warrants that are out of the money and approaches 100% for warrants that are well in the money (well above the strike price). The effect is to make the risk/benefit ratio more proportionate.

Summary.

1. Bond prices are subject to a negative feedback loop, which reflects value.
2. The stock market is subject to numerous loops and particularly to crowd psychology at extremes of the cycle.
3. Automated control of financial transactions must anticipate all likely scenarios.
4. Derivatives offer gearing that magnifies the effect of positive loops.
5. Options offer a means of compensating for changes in the stock market.
6. Warrants reflect the totality of effects on a share price.

References.

[1] Johnson, Luke. "The Crash of 87"
[2] Wikipedia - Arbitrage.
[3] Société Générale "S G Warrants".

Chapter 18.   Legislative issues.

Legislative problems.

Legislation is likely to interfere in a feedback loop insofar as it is intended to restrict the natural behaviour of people, or markets, which are normally candidates for loop control. Legislation is necessary when social or economic pressure is insufficient to control anti-social behaviour, or for cases where a positive loop may run out of control: such as a business monopoly. The difficulty is to introduce legislation that deals with the problem without hindering legitimate activity. As discussed in the chapter on companies, any form of bureaucracy whether in the form of employment law, taxation or human rights will reduce the gain of the loop, which determines the rate of growth of a business.

Whether other loops are desirable is often a matter of political opinion. There are, however, clear cases of clumsy legislation, which introduce effects that are detrimental to the community. Some examples of undesirable effects were cardboard housing, the poverty trap, and trade union excesses.

There are numerous examples of legislation restricting free trade and social movement. Whether it is a tariff on selected goods, specific taxes or, for example, legislation on minimum wages. The difficulty of optimising legislation for the social good is evident from the problems of the past and the differing views of political parties. The reasons for the different approaches may be in order to right perceived social wrongs, or to maximise the wealth of a nation rather than redistribute it (justified in the belief that some of the increased wealth will filter down to the lower paid).

The relatively high cost of living in an advanced society is in part due to the competition for scarce resources such as land and accommodation and in part due to the minimum standards that are ordained by certain authorities. If those standards are set too high then a proportion of the population will not be able to afford them. The situation is aggravated by, for example, the powers of local authorities to condemn housing considered (by the authority) unfit for habitation.

For many years some homeless people were living in cardboard boxes on wasteland due to the shortage of housing. This together with the number of homeless people sleeping in shop doorways pointed to an absence of awareness of the nation's true requirements in regard to housing. A factor was the legislation that defined minimum facilities for buildings. Stories were circulating about inspectors condemning houses, which were then demolished, on the pretext of inadequate lighting in corridors and similar factors. It is apparent that a badly lit house is preferable to a cardboard box or shop doorway. In a free market the substandard housing would have found its own occupants grateful for a roof over their heads. The legislation on housing took little account of their needs. The setting of minimum standards, before the people and the economy can adequately support them, is an example of remoteness between legislators and the people affected.

Is this an example of delayed feedback where a faster corrective response would have changed the policy in time? At a time of economic recovery the authority might feel justified in introducing draconian measures to improve the housing lot. If, however, they were run as a business, with the need to survive, then the potential impact of recession would be taken into account and appropriate allowances made.

The distribution of wealth from taxation and social security contributions has been the subject of criticism. People who contributed to the health service over their working life expected to be looked after when they became ill and were admitted to a nursing home. People who were responsible and saved for their old age have been penalised by being required to spend their savings until their capital has been reduced to a sufficiently low level

The poverty gap caused by the withdrawal of benefits, at a greater rate than recipients can increase their salary, has been a well-known disincentive to work harder. The more lenient withdrawal at the same rate as salary increases is not the kind of incentive that most people expect. It is a difficult problem to overcome, given the size of the benefit on offer and the need not to burden the taxpayer unduly. It is nevertheless one that needs to be addressed in order to motivate people to move out of the benefit culture.

The legislation, which led to the UK Trade Union excesses of the 1970's was no doubt the result of the pendulum swinging too far from problems in former times when employees were unduly exploited. An excessive movement of the pendulum is, as previously noted, the result of delay in

corrective influences. Such delays allow resentment, and resolve, to multiply to the point where excessive compensation is enacted as shown in figure 1.

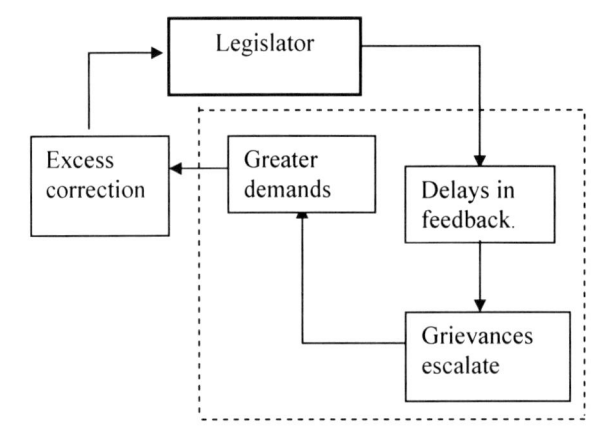

Figure 1. Excessive correction due to delay in feedback.

Data delay and future perception.

Social legislation, often based on perceived inequity in the past, introduces much uncharted territory in which it is difficult to foresee the consequences. Inevitably this is an area in which circumstances are so variable that it is not feasible to define a best procedure for every situation. An authoritarian attitude often prevails in which the people who dictate the procedures are unaffected by the circumstances, and therefore are unlikely to suffer the consequences when things go wrong.

Difficulties also arise due to the problem of acquiring accurate data. The channels for this data might be biased by political opinions; by the media exaggerating circumstances; by a situation that is too complex to be comprehended adequately or by data that is out-of-date by the time it is collected. Such a situation may be worse than having no data at all. Legislation based on the feedback of false data might be erroneously trusted whereas a system with no feedback will be seen to be what it is and assessed accordingly.

Data may not be merely out of date it may be up-to-date history. Such situations occur when people are trusted to act responsibly subject to being accountable for their actions. Accountability is necessarily a response to the past. It is a substitute for direct control by employing someone to do their best under the threat of sanctions if they fail or do not perform well enough. The retrospective sanctions thus imply delay in the feedback loop. The preferred route must be to employ someone who benefits directly by the actions taken and in accordance with the goals that are set. One way is to employ someone who not only has the expertise but also a share in the profits enjoyed by following the correct path (and consequently suffers if the outcome is wrong).

A democratic government is necessarily based upon a negative feedback loop in which the opinions of the majority of the population are fed back to government by the members of parliament who are representing the electorate; or by the power of the media which perhaps commands more attention. By this means left and right leaning parties do not depart too far from a central policy so as not to alienate a majority of the population. Circumstances may cause the policy to swing to the left or right depending on recent history but a large swing would imply a greater correction than is desirable under vigilant government. Loop theory would lay the blame on delayed feedback, either because the data needed was difficult to obtain or because the government was not vigilant to the prevailing circumstances.

UK residents have been fortunate to have a relatively stable system of government. The two main political parties maintain a sufficient presence to be influential and their policies are tending to a similar base. An important influence here must be the comparatively short time of four years between elections. The delay in feedback is (hopefully) not long enough for extremes to develop before being accountable to the electorate. The swings of the pendulum could be made even shorter if elections were more frequent say every two years. Not in order to elect a new government, which would cause excessive disruption too frequently, but on a rolling basis whereby 50% were elected every two years (or 25% per annum). More frequent election would enable the electorate to effectively participate in a referendum of the legislation to be enacted. There is of course an argument that it is necessary for a government to have sufficient time to legislate for necessary but unpopular measures that would not be supported by those parts of the electorate that did not understand the needs and objectives.

Local councils, which are familiar with the needs of their locality, are expected to be better at dealing with local problems than a national government. In part this is due to the immediacy of the feedback and in part due to their familiarity with the culture of the local community; so that action appropriate to that culture can be enacted. In contrast the remoteness of Brussels, from many parts of Europe, will lead to greater delays in dealing with the special needs of sections of the European community. The likelihood that people of different cultures will be happy with a broad-brush legislation is optimistic and a degree of social unrest is surely to be expected. Accountability to the electorate is an important mechanism, which, in Europe, needs strengthening.

Control of the economy would ideally be based on perfect data regarding the prosperity of industry and commerce, the level of imports and exports, and the psychology of the people; to name but a few factors. In practice the difficulty of capturing the data, and particularly of capturing it in time, poses significant problems for implementing a stable strategy. A delay in financial data may lead to the impression that measures need to be taken against recession when the country is, in reality, enjoying an upturn in the economic cycle, and vice versa. Known as the notorious touch of the tiller, past attempts to correct an economic trend sometimes made the trend worse. It is not possible to know where the economy is at the moment. The measures were often too much and too late. Consequently swings in the economic cycle were inevitable - a symptom of delay in the negative loop.

Complexity and diminishing returns.

Even if data is accurate legislation suffers from the problem of predictability. A new situation presents new possibilities, not all of which can be foreseen when the legislation is enacted. Not only is the future unsure, some in the legal profession counteract the good intentions of the legislators by seeking loopholes in the law for the benefit of their clients. The legislators learn from the experience and counteract the problem as the legislation is tightened up the next time round. The law becomes more complex and more lawyers are required - an example of a loop that is of doubtful benefit to the community. Eventually a positive loop must be curtailed. There will always be an end to such a loop. Possible outcomes are:

1. It becomes so cumbersome that it is unworkable;
2. too much effort is applied to taking avoiding action to the detriment of the nation;
3. the realisation of diminishing returns as the law becomes evermore complex so that the legislation is simplified to be more consistent with natural forces;
4. the law is seen to be harmful and the legislation is scrapped.

Some problems were illustrated in an article [1] reviewing the outcome of the Criminal Justice and Public Order Act designed to crack down on crime and prevent public disorder. The legislation was declared to have suffered major defeats in the courts and key issues are to be challenged in the European Court of Human Rights. Police in some areas preferred to utilise the many bylaws and common law that they had always used. Other forces, aware of the controversy surrounding the new legislation did not want to be seen to be using the new powers. The main reasons appear to be that some provisions were impractical to implement; there was ambiguity in the drafting and confusion amongst the police about implementation.

For example the Act on trespass that criminalises groups of more than 20 could be bypassed if the groups broke up into groups of less than 20. The power of eviction of travellers was reduced by a High Court ruling declaring that the basic human needs and welfare of travellers had to be taken into account before evicting them.

Where legislation is effective it may nevertheless create problems. As discussed previously with respect to the power of the trade unions in the UK during the 1970's, the tendency of legislation to override the normal corrective action of the negative loop can have serious consequences. These consequences arose because of the unions' immunity in law to the economic damage inflicted on industry due to strike action. Whereas the trade unions were founded on the need to contain the excesses of industrial exploitation the pendulum had swung too far in favour of the unions to the point where it was damaging to the economy. A factor in such a swing must be the grudge born by people, or relatives of people, who suffered previously. Another factor is the absence of a compensating loop in a party that is funded by the people most likely to benefit from legislation that gave unions immunity. As ever, the greater the swing of the pendulum one way the greater the swing in the other direction and the Thatcher government had a mandate to curtail the power of the unions to the point where they could not inflict so much damage to the electorate.

The Rent (Control of Increases) Act 1969 is an example of the swing of the pendulum destroying market forces to the detriment of the people it was intended to benefit. Rachmanism, as it came to be known, arose from the activities of gangs who ejected people from rented accommodation in order to let it out at a significantly higher rent. In consequence legislation was introduced to limit these activities. A landlord became unable to eject problematic tenants. Other landlords who observed the problems were withdrawing their property from the market rather than becoming committed to tenants who could not be moved. A positive loop was in operation where the fear of acquiring tenants, who could not be ejected, increased as the availability of alternative accommodation dried up as illustrated in figure 2.

```
┌─────────────────┐     ┌─────────────────┐
│ More property   │◄────│ Other landlords │◄──┐
│ withdrawn from  │     │ observe problem.│   │
│ market.         │     └─────────────────┘   │
└─────────────────┘                           │
        │         ┌──────────────────────────────┐
        └────────►│ Increased inability to move  │
                  │ tenants to alternative       │
                  │ accommodation.               │
                  └──────────────────────────────┘
```

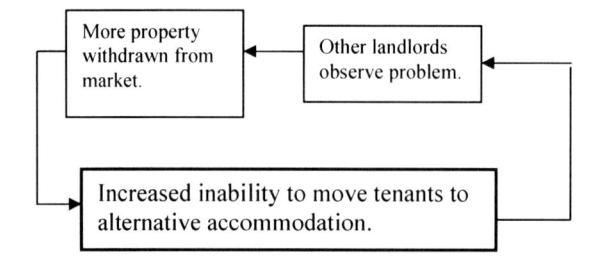

Figure 2. Legislation increasing the accommodation problem.

A further factor was the embargo on rent increases. As inflation increased the rent became increasingly uneconomic. It did not cover the cost of maintaining the property, which fell into disrepair, or was withdrawn from the market if possible. The protection for the tenant became self-defeating insofar as tenants could not move even if they wanted to. The Act had become detrimental to the people it was meant to help. A positive loop was in being. The recovery of the situation awaited the compensating loop whereby the shortage encouraged the provision of more property. This awaited the freer market legislation many years later.

Social legislation, often intended to improve the living conditions of people in need, has had its share of unintended consequences. The poverty trap is a major example and arises when taxation on incremental income rises to more than 100%. The situation arose because of the level of benefits, deemed necessary for low income families, was such that it had to be reduced quickly when their income reached a specified level.

This perverse situation can be simulated in electronics. It is the engineering equivalent to a no man's land in which a system can never dwell. The effect is equivalent to a brick wall, which opposes any incentive to earn more income until a sufficient jump has been made to "get over the wall" and reduce the incremental tax to a less debilitating level.

The provision of a 100% subsidy to people who are out of work has the potential to create more problems. Whilst many people will endeavour to obtain work to take them out of the subsidy position there is the danger of creating an underclass who are satisfied to live permanently on a subsidy. Such a subsidy is equivalent to saturating the system as discussed elsewhere in this book. The effect of saturation is to cut off feedback and consequently remove sanctions for bad behaviour. It is important to avoid putting a person in a position where they have nothing to lose.

There has been a tendency for social services to provide greater benefits to unemployed people than are enjoyed by those who pay their own way. Maintenance of property and equipment is often better than the employed can afford but who may anyway perform the work themselves. There is an anomaly that it is people living on social benefit who have the work done for them, when they are the people who have more time on their hands and who might benefit from a sense of doing useful work. Such a level of support, however, offers a way of introducing sanctions for bad behaviour by the threat of moving a family to less opulent surroundings. There is a clear need to provide incentives to be self-reliant. The option to jump a housing queue by virtue of being a one-parent family might also be seen as a disincentive to self-reliance.

Litigation.

The theme of success breeding success will be seen in the US where litigation is more rife. Not only is the potential litigator informed by the media of the awards obtained by suing for damages, there are also lawyers eager to earn a fee by representing them. The damages secured encourage more litigation and people in various occupations have to pay higher insurance premiums to protect themselves. Numerous examples have been noted in the press.

In 2003 it was reported [4] that American doctors in West Virginia hit by often-frivolous malpractice lawsuits went on strike over crippling insurance premiums. The state was quoted as a hotbed of ambulance chasing lawyers, and several hospitals were forced to transfer patients to neighbouring jurisdictions because of the shortage of medical staff. The American College of Obstetricians and Gynaecologists noted that in year 2000 the average medical liability award had risen to over £600,000. Similar sums were awarded for "neurologically impaired" children who were alleged to have suffered trauma during childbirth. In one case the jury awarded a child £64.5 million. It is considered that many juries were unable to comprehend concepts such as genetic birth defects. A consequence of the litigation was that many obstetricians resigned, causing a serious shortage. Similar cases occurred with radiologists who were sued for failing to spot early signs of breast cancer.

A consequence of these awards is that it becomes necessary for medical staff, who continue in practice, to insure against litigation and thereby increase the cost of medical treatment. A further factor is that surgeons feel obliged to make unnecessary precautions in order to be fireproof and exempt from prosecution. The escalation in damages necessitating higher insurance premiums and therefore higher medical bills is, of course, paid for by the general public. Nor are the average damage receipts representative of the higher costs since there is a form of gearing - necessary to pay for the legal fees and the unnecessary precautionary medical treatment. One outcome in the USA has been for some states to cap damages for "non-economic" losses at about £300,000.

The trend to defensive medicine to protect doctors from being sued is not in the best interests of the patients or a National Health Service. Unnecessary tests are made and unnecessary drugs are prescribed. In some cases surgery is recommended in case the patient does not make a full recovery, since the doctor will look better in court if the extra actions are taken. These extra treatments are not without risk to the patients. Too many x-rays can be harmful, antibiotics can cause stomach upsets and Caesareans can cause complications. It is noted that in a health system with limited budgets, such as a National Health Service, one unnecessary procedure performed is one less necessary one that cannot be.

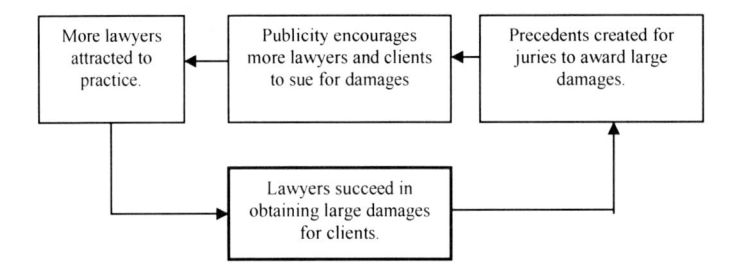

Figure 3. The compensation loop.

The feedback loop causing the problem is evidently the encouragement given to lawyers and their clients based upon the success of previous litigation coupled with the large number of lawyers attracted to the practice who need to generate business to pay their salaries - figure 3.

Evidently the loop cannot keep on increasing. Otherwise a point must come when all existing practitioners resign and no one will enter the medical profession.

Can the Scoldent list generate any ideas to combat the problem? Some possibilities are:

Saturation	Limit medic's ability to pay damages.
Cut-off	Legislate maximum compensation.
Open loop	No advertising of successful awards.
Low gain	Limit size of award.
Delay	Priority to most deserving cases.
External force	Tribunal to determine compensation.
Negative feedback	Educate juries on medical problems. Refuse treatment for lawyers.
Theme change	National compensation scheme.

Saturation is by limiting the money available. Legislation to limit the size of awards to reasonable levels is perhaps the most practical methods of keeping the practice within acceptable bounds.

The loop phenomenon is fed by advertising or by word of mouth of the financial benefits that accrue from litigation, which also set precedents for juries making future awards. Low gain of the loop would occur if the size of award were limited possibly by removing juries from the assessment process. There have been moves to abolish juries on the grounds that they do not have the experience to assess damages. Delay in the loop is probably already significant, but the trivial cases could be given low priority, and perhaps delayed indefinitely.

Negative feedback means encouraging the parties involved to behave reasonably. This may mean educating juries on the medical problems and the realisation that insurance companies are not a bottomless pit of money - unless they charge the public higher premiums for insurance. A proposal has been made in the USA for medics to refuse to treat lawyers - presumably until they mend their ways. If a black list of lawyers is drawn up, this could also apply to patients who seek compensation for trivial problems.

Theme change is already practised in Scandinavia where a no fault compensation scheme pays modest sums for injuries. The UK Criminal injuries Compensation board is an example where people who suffer harm are given a cash award automatically.

Other suggestions that have been made are:

- A full and open investigation into what went wrong; free remedial treatment by a National Health Service and payments to compensate for pain and suffering.

- Subsidised insurance premiums for doctors in order to stem the haemorrhage of staff. This would be the opposite of saturation and, whilst keeping necessary medical staff, would appear to aggravate the excessive awards problem.

The further compensation culture.

Watts [2] has estimated that, over four years, premiums for employer's liability insurance has risen between 50% and 500%. About 40% of the claims on policies are to pay legal fees. Whether it is a consequence of fashion, the me-too mentality feedback loop or the influence of no-win no-fee lawyers, the effect on firms can be disastrous. So high are some of the premiums that it is not viable for a business to pay them. The consequence of no insurance may be bankruptcy not to mention the sanctions for disobeying the law that requires insurance for paying out for accidents or injuries in the work place, as well as industrial diseases.

It is suggested that the rises are the result of government policies since they make it easier to claim for the most trivial of injuries or inconveniences. By raising the level of awards the government has encouraged litigation. Many of the claims are for injuries that at one time would have been considered a natural hazard that was unfortunate.

The potential for the compensation culture was given a boost when 200 people were given legal aid to sue a tobacco company [5]. It appeared to confirm that we are not responsible for our voluntary actions. It was, Hardman declared: *"an example of culpaphilia - the obsession to place responsibility on anyone but ourselves. The implication that self-abuse could be someone else's fault is a dangerous precedent that could escalate into the costliest legal action in history."* It could emulate the American experience where incredible sums are paid out in damages for self-inflicted problems: be it the spilling of hot coffee, selling equipment, which was subsequently misused, or criminals incurring injury while trying to escape from the law.

Johnson [3] quotes employers biggest headache as: *"vexatious litigant employees jumping on the payout bandwagon, egged on by grasping lawyers and a flawed system"*. In the USA it was mooted that in two years there would be one million lawyers and since *"these 'professionals' need to make a living they manufacture legal actions and lobby politicians to pass new laws. Since many politicians are lawyers - members of the same club- they are happy to oblige"*. The worry is that UK residents *"read about the huge compensation payments against the medical profession in the USA and fancy their chances here"*. The outcome is likely to be more expensive medical treatment and a less caring attitude by the profession.

The bandwagon effect was illustrated in the asbestos litigation in the USA [11]. The uncontrolled escalation of claims resulted in the bankruptcy of numerous companies. After the main asbestos manufacturers had been made bankrupt the trial lawyers were reported to have targeted hundreds of American companies with little if any connection with the problem. The cost of the litigation and consequent bankruptcies has been the loss of over 50,000 jobs and loss of earnings to many more. Much of the money has been paid to people who showed no signs of illness but who could claim some exposure to asbestos. These excess payments and the attorney's fees reduced payment to genuine sufferers from asbestos related illness. By 2004 legislation was being considered to control the situation and ensure a fairer distribution funds.

A difficult situation arises when the "injury" cannot be fully assessed. The normal compensatory action, that informed opinion provides, breaks down when the injury cannot be measured. For example when the litigant suffers backache, stress or discrimination. Examples are the trauma alleged to have been suffered by a father who witnessed his daughters' drowning and was awarded over £1 million in compensation. A woman army officer was awarded £300,000 for being forced out due to pregnancy. An award it was noted that far exceeded the likely compensation of £20,000 for the loss of an eye. A European court ruling that compensation, in discrimination cases, could be limitless only raises the potential for me-too cases that want to get on the bandwagon of generous payouts.

The difference in attitude to business and government is illustrated by a judgement for the social services. The decision was made to restrict the capacity of children and their parents to sue for negligence or breach of statutory duty in respect of mistakes made in exercising social services functions [7]. The judge
was concerned that allowing such claims to be made would prejudice the resources available for authorities to carry out their function imposed on them by parliament... ... the court would not impose a private law duty of care on local authorities performing their public law function of caring for children in need. The fear was that it would generate a detrimentally defensive frame of mind among those responsible for carrying out those functions.

When families have been destroyed by some social services the need for a feedback loop to prevent abuse is obvious.

Excess legislation.

Excess legislation interferes with free market forces and consequently in the operation of compensating feedback loops to maintain stability. Johnston [6] is scathing in his criticism: The trend for government to tell people how to live has been taking precedence over its primary role to run the country competently, ensuring that the nation is secure and that its people are safe to walk the streets and live in their homes unmolested. He notes:
.. the streets are less safe, more motorists are jailed than burglars, we have no clear idea whether we are allowed to defend our homes against intruders, public services remain in decline despite the vast sums spent on them and anyone wanting to start a business, a charity or a nursery school is confronted with too many rules and regulations as to make the effort hardly worth the candle.

The excessive law making has introduced so much bureaucracy that it is self-defeating to the point where different laws are sometimes in contention. He quotes the historian Gibbon:
A Locracian who proposed any new law stood forth in the assembly of the people with a cord around his neck and if the law was rejected the innovator was instantly strangled.
It was considered this helped guarantee the citizen freedom from petty interference with their affairs.

An editorial [10] drew attention to the problem of laws on access. HSBC had been providing a mobile bank for outlying villages in Cornwall. The Disability Discrimination Act required the bank to provide a new vehicle and back-up facilities to allow wheelchair access. This would have cost £500,000, which was non-economic and the bank withdrew the service. Accordingly the older villagers had the hardship of travelling longer distances to a bank. It is another example of lack of feedback to the legislating authority.

Human rights.

The escalation of violence and immunity of troublemakers was well underway in 1994 [8] when a policeman was fined for cuffing a young troublemaker who was harassing a woman in her seventies. The magistrate and colleagues on the bench were not the ones who experienced the hooliganism - they were not the ones to suffer from the consequences of their decisions. A telephone poll revealed 97% supported the policeman's action and only 3% against.

Burrows [9] reported that there are whole neighbourhoods that are subject to vandalism and hooliganism without redress. Violence is available to the illegitimate operator
...while law-abiding adults are unable by law to lift a hand to show that violence can also be used towards a moral end..... It is supremely important that the ability to use physical force is not confined to bad eggs while those on the side of decency and civic order are restricted to weak and demonstrably ineffective punishments. The boneless response to youthful male aggression, the nagging, wheedling and bribing of young males to make them behave only produces contempt .... Very few people think that pacifism in the face of an aggressor is effective.

An American psychologist, Irving Janis [12], has described the establishment's view as the result of groupthink, whereby a small group of like-minded individuals are recruited around an idea (this is discussed more fully in the chapter on psychology). They share feelings of moral superiority and a sense of mission. It is said that such a group masterminded the anti-corporal punishment legislation in the teeth of opposition from teachers and parents. Subsequently aiming to prevent parents having the right to smack their children. A small group working with glossy brochures, selective quotes and media personalities created the impression of a considerable force to convince professionals in the fields of child care, social work, fostering and child-minding. In contrast bouncers in pubs and night-clubs have the power to molest people and this has earned them the respect of the hooligan mob.

Summary.

1. Legislation interferes with natural compensating systems.
2. Legislation is subject to the difficulty of forecasting future situations.
3. There is a danger that legislators are separated from the consequences of their work.
4. Delayed feedback can distort the response.
5. Immediacy of feedback in a local jurisdiction is preferable to a national one.

6. Increasing complexity gives diminishing returns in efficacy.
7. The increasing feedback loop of litigation is a potential disaster for society.
8. The compensation culture has damaging sociological consequences.
9. Human rights legislation has produced controversial results.

References.

[1] Mills H., "It takes a bad act to make the law a farce". Independent, 26/9/95
[2] Watts R., "Soaring premiums are making employer's cover a liability".
[3] Johnson L., "The Lawyers will kill us" May 1998.
[4] "US doctors strike over lawsuits", World News, Daily Telegraph, 3/1/2003.
[5] Hardman R., "Warning: this could damage our health". DT 1/2/95.
[6] Johnston P., "The Prescott fiefdom no one wants". DT 26/1/2004.
[7] Baker and Henderson, "No Claims", Community Care 7/4/1994.
[8] Muir H., "Old fashioned bobby wins Britain's backing". DT 15/6/1994.
[9] Burrows L., "Yes, we can bring back smacking". DT.
[10] "Access law disables last mobile bank". DT 6/2/2005.
[11] "The Public Policy Solution to Runaway Asbestos Litigation", Issue Backgrounder, The Independence Institute, Vol. 12,1 January 2004.
[12] Irving Janis, "Victims of Groupthink, A psychological study of Foreign Policy Decisions." Houghton Mifflin, 1972.

Chapter 19. Feedback mechanisms in physiology.

The prime objective of the negative feedback loop is to provide stability by correcting deviations from a desired state. There are many such loops operating in the human body, and in the animal kingdom, in order to maintain temperature and other conditions within a narrow band at which physiological systems operate efficiently. The name given to this system in medical circles is homeostasis from the Greek "self-governing".

Muscle control.

Muscle activity is perhaps the most obvious application of feedback in the body. Many actions require feedback from vision or touch to monitor and correct for movement of hands or limbs. For this to operate it is necessary for at least two muscles to be antagonistic. As a flexor muscle contracts when lifting a load an extensor muscle must become active and pull in the opposite direction to prevent the movement exceeding the required function. In some cases where the movement has been practised many times it is possible that the action is remembered sufficiently for visual feedback to be unnecessary, although the strength of grip is likely to be monitored. This simple action has, however, been refined to give a faster response than can be achieved by feeding information through the brain.

Muscle spindles are specialised fibres that run the length of the muscle. They generate an electrical signal in response to changes in length of a muscle. They are important for monitoring the change in stress experienced when the load is suddenly changed. A person carrying a tray, for example, needs to react quickly if a heavy object such as a coffee pot is placed on it. In a case like this the muscles for holding the tray are just sufficiently tensed to combat the weight of the tray. The extra weight of the coffee pot will momentarily lengthen the muscles, which in turn lengthen the muscle spindles. This lengthening causes spindles to generate a signal that increases muscle tension to maintain the tray in position. It has been found, Hammond [1], that the response is much faster than can be achieved by conscious monitoring of the action via the brain. It is believed that a spinal reflex to give the necessary speed achieves the response.

Homeostasis

The prime control is from the hypothalamus, situated in the brain. Its function is to process information obtained from sensors such as nerves to determine the operations to be performed by the autonomic nervous system. This system regulates, in addition to temperature, various physiological functions such as heart rate, blood pressure, and concentration of salts in the blood. These are all functions of which we are normally unaware, except perhaps heartbeat in response to fear, or perspiration on a hot day.

Temperature control.

The control of temperature is achieved in several ways, and animals, depending on their make up and whether they are warm or cold-blooded, use different methods. In humans the main heat loss is through the skin and this can be controlled by evaporation of perspiration and by dilation of the blood vessels under the skin to distribute, more efficiently, the heat generated by the body. Losses through the skin are estimated to be about 77% of the total for humans, [2]. In addition respiration accounts for about 20%, and 3% is by other means such as the passage of urine. Animals because of their fur, and birds because of their feathers, necessarily lose most heat by panting.

The maintenance of an optimum temperature is important for the efficient operation of various physiological processes. Heat is generated by the action of muscles including the heart, which since it never rests contributes a significant amount of heat. The brain, various organs and the digestion of food also contribute. The heat is conducted around the body by the flow of blood and the rate of distribution of heat is determined by the degree to which the blood vessels are dilated. When more dilated the cutaneous vessels distribute more heat to the surface of the skin where it will be lost to the environment. The role of the thalamus is to determine whether the body should to be cooled by inducing perspiration and dilation. Alternatively whether it should to be warmed by shivering, contraction of the vessels and generation of "goose pimples" to cause erection of hair so that more air is trapped to insulate the surface of the skin as shown in Figure 1.

For cold-blooded animals this criterion is less important. They nevertheless need to be warm for their muscles to operate efficiently. Hence lizards and snakes amongst others bask in the sun before they are ready for hunting. Alternatively if too hot then they seek shelter in order to maintain a suitable temperature. Whether these animals are consciously in the feedback loop, or perform their actions subconsciously, is another question. They are nevertheless performing the actions necessary for a compensating loop.

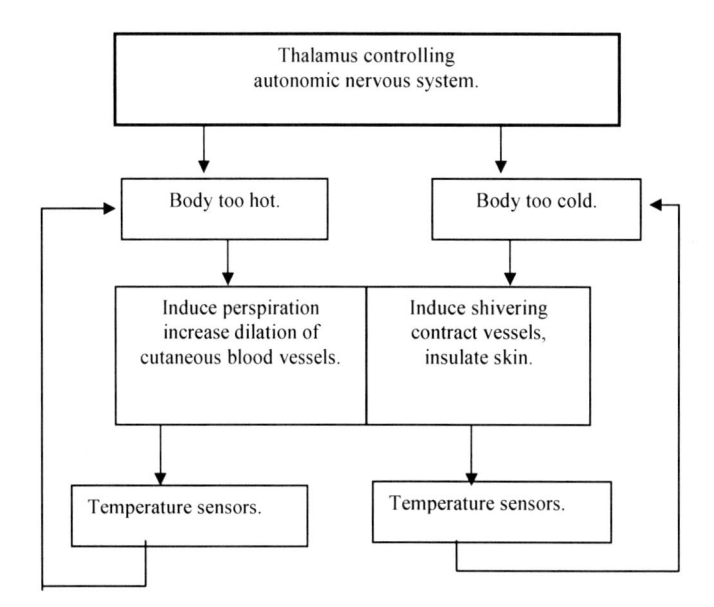

```
          ┌─────────────────────────────┐
          │    Thalamus controlling     │
          │  autonomic nervous system.  │
          └─────────────────────────────┘
              │                │
              ▼                ▼
     ┌──────────────┐   ┌──────────────┐
     │ Body too hot.│   │Body too cold.│
     └──────────────┘   └──────────────┘
```

Figure 1. Temperature control of the body.

For warm-blooded animals this loop only operates over a limited temperature range. Once outside this range the organs cease to operate and the heat producing mechanisms fail thus allowing the body to cool further to take on the characteristics of an unstable positive feedback loop. Similarly if too hot then rigidity sets in, the cooling mechanisms cease and the body fails to apply corrective action.

There is a danger of the feedback loop being cut off if the body temperature varies by 12 degrees below or above the normal temperature of 37 degrees C due to hyperthermia or heat exhaustion. If due to hypothermia the temperature of the body falls to about 25 degrees C the nervous system of heat generation becomes paralysed. At high temperatures metabolism increases to a rate where exhaustion ensues. At about 50 degrees C the muscles become rigid, the organs cannot operate and death follows.

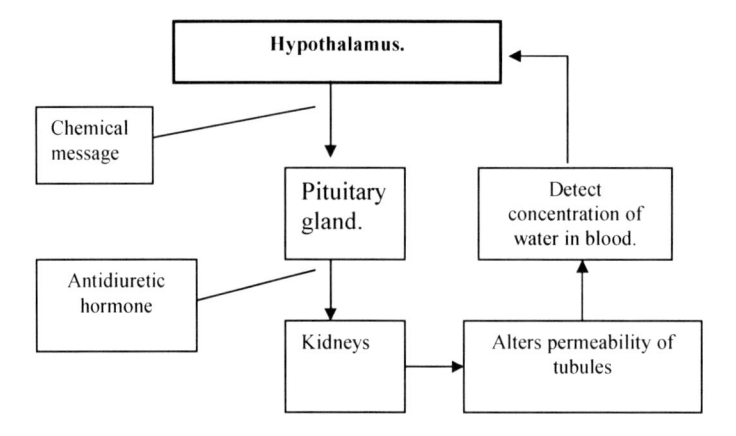

Figure 2. Homeostatic control of water concentration in blood.

Water concentration.

The concentration of water in the blood is detected as it passes through the brain by osmoreceptors, which lie in the hypothalamus region. The hypothalamus sends chemical messages to the pituitary gland, which in turn secretes Antidiuretic hormone (ADH) to control tubules within the kidney. If more water is required in the blood stream then high concentrations of ADH are used to make the tubules more permeable. If less water is required then the concentration of ADH is reduced to make them less permeable. The action is illustrated in Figure 2.

The kidneys are also controlled to maintain a stable balance of sodium and water in the body. If the concentration of sodium is too high then the excess is excreted in the urine.

Equivalent actions are performed to maintain the balance between acidity and alkalinity. If the blood is too acid then the tubular cells add bicarbonate, if too alkaline then the bicarbonate is excreted.

An important feedback mechanism for healthy people is the monitoring of blood glucose concentration. Alpha and beta cells in the pancreas normally control this. Most carbohydrates in food are rapidly digested to glucose, the principal sugar in blood. Insulin is produced by beta cells in the pancreas in response to rising levels of glucose. Insulin is the hormone that regulates the uptake of glucose - primarily into muscle and fat cells. It makes it possible for most body tissues to remove glucose from the blood for use as fuel, for conversion to other molecules and for storage against future requirements. It initiates the conversion of glucose to glycogen for storage in the liver and muscle cells. When glucose levels are low, alpha cells cause the liver to start the reverse process of converting glycogen to glucose. The feedback loop is shown in figure 3.

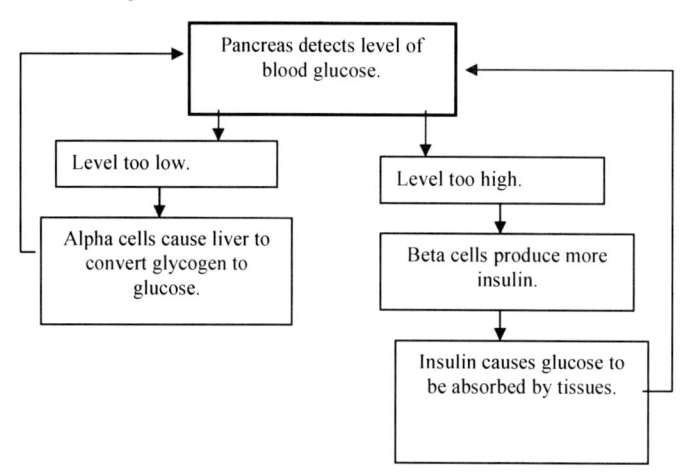

Figure 3. Regulation of blood glucose.

Unstable conditions.

Diabetes is a serious condition where the homeostatic feedback loop has failed. The generation of insulin is insufficient to cope with the glucose level in the blood. Diabetes type 1, an inherited autoimmune disorder, is usually diagnosed in childhood and young adolescence. The body's immune system attacks the beta cells in the Islets of Langerhans of the pancreas, damaging them sufficiently to reduce insulin production. Type 1 is treated with insulin injections, adjustment of life style and careful monitoring of blood glucose levels.

In type 2 diabetes the body cells are resistant to insulin and do not respond appropriately. The symptoms are less noticeable since they develop gradually so that there is a danger of severe complications such as renal failure and coronary artery disease.

The negative feedback loop for controlling glucose level in the blood at that stage is no longer automatic (the feedback loop is broken at "A" in figure 4).. Human intervention is required, either by the patient or a supervisor. It is necessary to be aware of the signs such as frequent urination and increased thirst. This results from the high glucose content which is excreted by the kidneys and requires water to carry it causing increased fluid loss. The loss in blood volume will be replaced by water held in the body cells causing dehydration. Insulin deficiency leading to hyperglycemia is a dangerous complication that if not treated can lead to death

A difficulty in treating diabetes is in estimating the quantity of insulin required since this will vary depending on the food eaten, the amount of exercise taken and the timing of the injections. Hypoglycaemia in a diabetic patient arises from poor management of the disease - too much or poorly timed insulin, too much exercise, not enough food or poor timing of either. If glucose levels are low the patient may experience agitation, sweating and a feeling of dread and panic. Consciousness may be altered or even lost, leading to seizure, coma and even death. A lump of sugar or sweet drink will rapidly reduce the symptoms provided they are taken in time. Alternatively an injection of glucagon causes the liver to convert its glycogen to glucose in the blood.

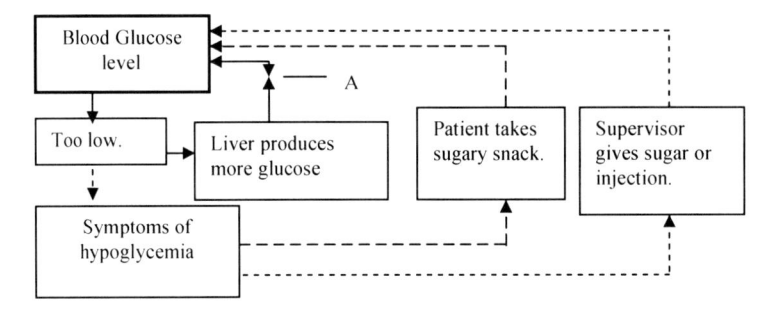

Figure 4. Treatment for hypoglycemia.

Other life threatening illnesses occur when bacteria or cancer cells start to exceed the threshold above which the immune system cannot cope. Since such cells double their number each time they divide, this gives a positive loop where the rate of increase is exponential once the threshold of the immune system is passed.

The action of homeostasis to maintain the body in optimum condition can be destroyed by external influences that cause the system to run out of control. Two of these were mentioned under the biofeedback section where hypothermia and hyperthermia overcome the compensating mechanisms that increase or decrease temperature towards the normal of 37 degrees C.

Biofeedback.

Biofeedback was investigated extensively in the 1960s [4]. It is a technique for applying sensors to detect conditions in the body and using the signals obtained to give feedback to the person. With training this feedback can be used to control unconscious actions and cure adverse conditions. The patient can control the nervous system in a shorter period of time than would be possible without it. The average person achieves control in a matter of hours whilst the Yogi may take years of contemplation to achieve control of his brainwaves. Miller [5] showed that the involuntary autonomic nervous system could be controlled to influence eye pupils, heart rate, blood vessels, stomach and endocrine glands amongst others.

In general if a problem is related to some particular activity of the body then with instrumentation the patient can monitor that activity. The instrumentation can be used to control sound, light or a meter so that the patient becomes aware of what in other circumstances may be a sub-conscious activity such as heart rate and blood pressure.

For many years it has been suspected that humans have more control over their nervous system than previously expected. The placebo problem whereby a patient recovers by swallowing bogus tablets just as well as a patient receiving genuine medicine may be evidence of this.

Phillips [6] found that people could even control, to some extent, when they died; especially when there was an event that they wished to live for. He found a significant dip in deaths before birthdays and a significant peak afterwards. It was concluded that humans can exercise a certain amount of voluntary control over their health.

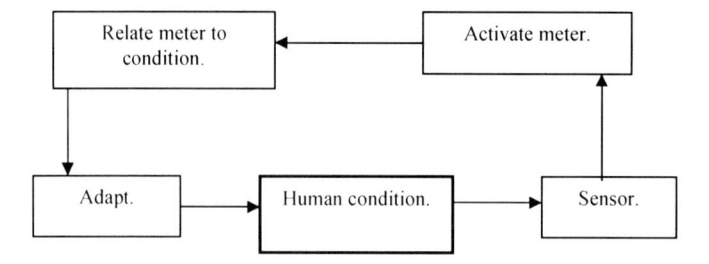

Figure 5. Biofeedback loop.

The simplest method for biofeedback uses a device that measures the galvanic skin response across a person's fingertips. The response is a function of minute amounts of perspiration on the skin. The tenser the person is, the more perspiration there is to conduct electricity. This reduces as the person becomes calmer. The signal from the electrodes is used to control a light or a buzzer. The system can be adjusted to give a sound that is moderately audible at the beginning of the session. If the person becomes tenser, more perspiration is produced and the signal becomes stronger. If the person becomes calmer and there is less perspiration, the sound becomes quieter until it eventually disappears.

In practice patients are told to stop the sound. By experimentation they find that the sound gets louder if they become tense and softer if they relax. In the course of time they realise that the sound is associated with certain mental states and if they think appropriately then the sound can die away. Once the method has been learnt then the system is made more sensitive so that the patient has to apply their learnt method to relax even more to make the sound disappear. Eventually they are able to achieve relaxation without the relying on the system.

Achieving relaxation was often found to be difficult since instructing a patient to relax often caused them to become tense in case they did not perform the instruction. In another experiment students were given feedback by playing back the amplified sound of their breathing. They were able to reduce the tension in their muscles better with the feedback and achieved a more relaxed state as a result. An alternative to this form of feedback used an electromyogram (EMG) [8] with which two electrodes were placed on the forehead to detect any movement of the frontalis muscle. The voltage detected by the electrodes was used to control the pitch of a tone that rose when the muscle contracted and fell when it relaxed. The frontalis muscle was chosen because it was "a crucial barometer of the patients relaxation level". If the frontalis is relaxed so also will be the scalp, neck and upper body. The relaxation criterion was also used to help people who had extreme anxiety over public speaking and at social gatherings.

More recently [11] the EMG has been utilized to rehabilitate patients paralysed by stroke. Even when a person has no sensation in a paralysed limb and cannot move it voluntarily, an EMG can often detect some electrical activity in the muscles. The EMG machine amplifies the electrical sound emitting from the paralysed limb, and as the patients become aware of the activity, their nervous systems may be able to stimulate more muscle activity. Eventually, new nerve endings may grow in the affected muscles and the patient regains some mobility.

For migraine and tension headaches temperature sensors were placed on the forehead and index finger [9]. A meter indicated the difference in temperature. The patient learned to make the forehead cooler than the hand (by in fact trying to make the hand warmer than the forehead) by watching the needle of the meter. 80% of migraine sufferers were reported to have improved.

It was shown that a person could be trained in a matter of days to cause the temperature of one hand to rise five to ten degrees higher than that of the other hand, while not contracting the hand muscles. When people, trained in biofeedback, cause their hands to quickly become warmer than normal, they can reduce the intensity of a migraine attack. The blood in a migraine attack is diverted from the blood vessels in the head to the hands and arms. People can be taught to use this method to prevent headaches within a week provided there is not chronic tension that also needs treatment by relaxation.

Blood pressure control was achieved by using the conventional cuff on the patient's arm and then feeding the result to coloured lights [10]. If the red light flashed then the patient was lowering blood pressure, the aim was to keep the red light flashing as long as possible.

The techniques have also been applied to insomnia, muscular tics and heart disease. The insomniacs were connected to an electroencephalograph so that the waves generated by the brain could be monitored. The patient would observe the wave patterns and by this means learn to achieve the wave patterns associated with sleep. With this training patients could fall asleep in less than 10% of the time previously taken.

The patients with tics were given a pair of earphones so that they could hear their muscles contracting. The feedback was used to reduce the rate of tics until complete control was achieved.

Patients with irregular heart rates learned to control the rate by coloured lights. The heartbeat was converted into electrical signals, which were used to illuminate red, yellow and green lights. The patient was taught to slow the rate when the red light was on, and increase it when the green was lit. The goal was to maintain the rate in the middle of the range; indicated by a constant yellow light.

Another experiment was conducted to control sub-vocalisation - the tendency to mouth words silently while reading, which limits reading speed to about 150 words/minute. Electrodes are placed on the neck either side of the vocal chords to records minute electrical signals that indicate mouthing. By using these signals to control a sound the patient was made aware of the problem. Whispering would cause the sound, but relaxing would cause the sound to stop. The patient learnt how to inhibit the sound that warned of sub-vocalising and consequently the method of preventing it.

Neurofeedback.

Neurofeedback [11] is a variation on the conventional biofeedback. It has been tested less and is more controversial. Also known as brain-wave training or Electroencephlagraphic (EEG) biofeedback, it is considered that it may be useful as a safe, drug-free alternative for the treatment of migraines.

In practice the user is rewarded for producing desirable brain-wave patterns. Electronic sensors are placed on the head. A form of computer game is controlled by the patterns produced by the EEG machine. If the mind is relaxed and focused, the computer responds by sending Pac-Manlike characters across the screen but if the mind drifts, then nothing happens. Neurofeedback is thought to reset brain-wave patterns that are associated with certain illnesses. 20 to 40 hour-long sessions may be required to succeed but once achieved then it is claimed the benefit is permanent.

Summary.
1. Homeostasis is a negative feedback loop for maintaining body functions.
2. Homeostasis maintains temperature, concentration of water and salts etc. to be within acceptable bounds for the body to function normally.
3. When a function falls outside the acceptable limits, such as in hypothermia, then a positive loop takes over and control is lost.

4. Diabetes is caused by the loss of automatic control of concentrations of sugar or insulin.
5. Biofeedback is a negative feedback loop that helps the patient to control many body functions such as heart rate.

References.
1. Hammond P H et al, "Nervous Gradation of Muscular Contraction", British Medical Bulletin, 1956, 12,3.
2. www.Wikipedia.org
3. Cannon W B, "The Wisdom of the Body". 1932
4. Karlins M. & Andrews M., "Biofeedback", Abacus books 1975.
5. Miller N., "Learning of visceral and glandular responses" Science 1969, 163, p434
6. Phillips D., "Dying as a form of social behaviour, Princeton University, 1969.
7. Wright P. "Neal Miller", The Guardian 4, 4, 2002.
8. Budzynski T, et al. "Feedback induced muscles relaxation". J. Behaviour therapy & experimental psychiatry, 1970,1,205-11.
9. Green E. et al, "Feedback technique for deep muscle relaxation". Psychophysiology, 1969, 371-7.
10. Shapiro D. et al, "Effects of feedback and reinforcement on the control of human systolic blood pressure". Science, 1969, 163, 588-90.
11. http://www.holistic-online.com/Biofeedback.htm

Chapter 20.   Environment.

Natural hazards.

Many years ago I was driving on a dirt track through the Rocky Mountains in the USA. My sedan had the soft suspension that was usual in American cars. At a bend in the road I hit a long set of corrugations. All the wheels bounced and I started sliding towards the outside of the bend where there was a 15 foot drop. It was as though I was on a skidpan and the rear of the car was heading towards the edge. Powering the wheels in these circumstances is not recommended since they are likely to lose any chance of a grip on the road but that chance was unlikely anyway. In situations like this, time seems to pass slowly probably because one concentrates the mind exclusively on the problem. I reasoned that anything that would reduce my motion towards the edge would help. I raced the back wheels to eject up as much dirt and stones behind me as possible so as to act like a jet and give a reactive force to make the car go forwards. It worked and I lived to tell the tale. I drove more carefully for the rest of the journey.

My problem was due to a positive loop. Corrugations on a road surface are formed when the wheels of vehicles hit a bump and leave the road to land again further along. If the road surface is soft the pressure on the road, where the wheels land, can cause a slight depression. Subsequently further vehicles pass along and their wheels hit the depressions to repeat the process causing a deeper rut. As the rut deepens the reaction of the wheels is greater. Eventually a set of corrugations is made that continues until they reach a surface that is hard enough to resist the pressure. Such corrugations can be dangerous since, with the wheels bouncing, traction and braking are lost and the vehicle can behave as though it is on a slippery surface.

Naturally occurring loops are apparent in other spheres. The generation of waves on the sea is enhanced by the effect of the wind as the waves increase in size and provide greater resistance to the air movement. As the wave steepens so the effect of the air on the water increases. The same phenomena can be seen in sand drifts. The wind makes the sand pile up. The higher the dune the greater the resistance to the air and accordingly the greater the force of the air on the sand to cause it to rise higher. The increase in height in both cases lasts until the effect of gravity equals the effect of the wind on the water or sand.

Other effects are less dramatic than the air movements. Ox-bow lakes on the Mississippi and in other countries are an example. As the curve in the river is formed the water on the outside of the curve eats away at the ground and extends the curve further. This creates a sharper bend and the bank is further eroded. In a suitable terrain a loop is formed which gets bypassed as the beginning and end of the loop are eroded towards each other.

Interference with established ecology can disturb the stability of the environment. Excessive farming using fertilisers compromised the quality and cohesion of the soil in the American mid-West. It was blamed for the subsequent dust bowls. In other areas, the encroachment of the desert advances when trees are cut down and changes in vegetation fail to protect the ground from erosion.

The disappearance of rain forests is also expected to generate a feedback loop. In a lecture, by Meade [1] on the effect of logging on the ecology of the Amazon rain forest, he suggested that reduction of the forest would have a cumulative effect. The climate is determined by the easterly winds that bring rain from the Atlantic. The subsequent evaporation from the leaves of the rain forest is greater than from a similar expanse of water. In consequence there is significant rainfall onto the rest of the land. Without the rain forest, the recycling would not occur and the region would become arid.

Global warming.

Positive loops are to be found throughout the environment [2] [3]. One of the more obvious is the melting of snow. Clean snow, being white, absorbs little heat from the sun and accordingly remains as snow. When darkened by dirt, grass or earth showing through, it absorbs more heat from the sun and accordingly melts faster to reveal more dark material, which further hastens the melting. The effect is important in relation to the ice caps at the poles. As more ice melts so water from the ocean takes its place and this absorbs more heat. It contributes to the increase in global warming, which over a period of time changes the earth's climate and raises the sea level to the point where low lying countries are threatened with flooding.

The greenhouse gas that has been demonised in causing global warming is carbon dioxide. Methane and water vapour, however, are more potent candidates and are a major cause of a feedback loop. Carbon dioxide may be credited with starting the warming but the other gases amplify the effect (and there are other factors at work). [Ref. 1]

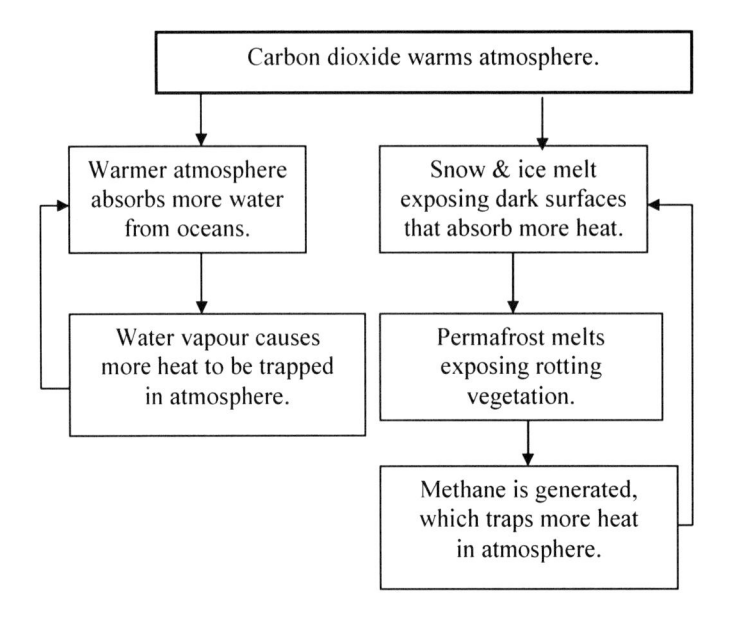

```
                  ┌─────────────────────────────────────┐
                  │  Carbon dioxide warms atmosphere.   │
                  └─────────────────────────────────────┘
                       │                    │
                       ▼                    ▼
         ┌──────────────────────┐  ┌──────────────────────┐
         │  Warmer atmosphere   │  │   Snow & ice melt    │
    ───▶ │  absorbs more water  │  │ exposing dark surfaces│ ◀───
         │    from oceans.      │  │  that absorb more heat│
         └──────────────────────┘  └──────────────────────┘
                       │                    │
                       ▼                    ▼
         ┌──────────────────────┐  ┌──────────────────────┐
         │  Water vapour causes │  │   Permafrost melts   │
    ──── │ more heat to be trapped│ │  exposing rotting    │
         │   in atmosphere.     │  │    vegetation.       │
         └──────────────────────┘  └──────────────────────┘
                                            │
                                            ▼
                                  ┌──────────────────────┐
                                  │  Methane is generated,│
                                  │ which traps more heat │──
                                  │    in atmosphere.    │
                                  └──────────────────────┘
```

Figure 1. A simplified view of Global warming.

It had been expected that trees would grow more quickly in an atmosphere richer in carbon dioxide. A negative compensating loop would then arise as the trees sequestered more carbon in wood. There is however evidence that trees will not thrive above a certain temperature. Above this temperature a counteracting positive loop will arise.

The water vapour in the atmosphere increases as the sea water surface warms up. This water vapour is a potent greenhouse gas that causes further heating as shown in figure 1. Further damage is caused when the permafrost thaws exposing vegetation in the arctic regions which then rots forming methane to give another positive loop.

Hurricanes, typhoons, cyclones and tornadoes.

Hurricanes, known as typhoons in the Pacific and cyclones in the Indian Ocean, are defined as tropical storms in which the wind speeds exceed 118 Kms per hour [Ref.2].
They are typically 200 - 2000 Kms wide with a calm centre known as the eye, which is 20 - 100 Kms in diameter. They originate about 6 degrees from the equator where the Coriolis force from the earth's rotation causes the vortex to spin.

The hurricane and its aliases are examples of small disturbances that increase in power as long as their feedback loop operates. They are dependent on a warm sea surface and become more prevalent as the temperature increases. Initially latent heat is released from rainfall in a warm climate. This heat causes an updraft in air that draws moisture from the sea surface. Latent heat from this moist air is released causing the air to rise further in temperature and increase the intensity of the updraft as shown in figure 2.

```
┌─────────────────────────┐
│ Latent heat released from│
│ rainfall in warm climate.│
└──────────┬──────────────┘
           │
           ▼
┌─────────────────────────┐
│ Heated air rises drawing │
│ moist air from warm sea  │
│        surface.          │
└──────────┬──────────────┘
           │
           ▼
┌─────────────────────────┐
│ Latent heat from moist air│
│    increases updraft.    │
└─────────────────────────┘
```

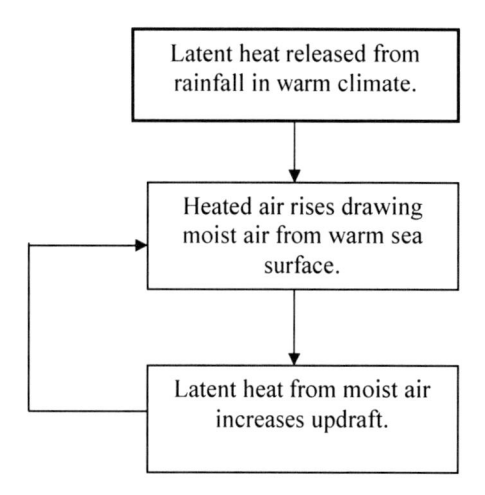

Figure 2. Formation of hurricanes.

A hurricane is reliant on the raised temperature of the atmosphere and sea in the tropics to provide the moisture that maintains its power. As it moves away from the equator its power diminishes; either because the sea becomes too cold for the water to vaporise in sufficient quantity or the hurricane moves over dry land where there is no water to form the vapour.

The formation of tornadoes is less clear since they are formed over dry land and are more vicious than hurricanes. They are typically 200 - 300 metres wide with winds in the vortex of several hundred Kms per hour, although the vortex itself moves at only about 50 Kms per hour. They are considered to be caused by the cool dry air from mountains meeting moist air from warmer latitudes

Road congestion or public transport.

The debate on congested roads presents a dilemma. Overcrowding should be a disincentive to use the car but it doesn't seem to work; or rather, it doesn't work well enough for comfort. Is there a positive loop effect in the transport problem?

The approach to the problem may be better illustrated by considering the disincentives that act against either the car or public transport - as shown in table 1:

Disincentive to use public transport.	Disincentive to owning and using a car.
Wait for local transport (if available). Distance to station/ bus stop. Wet weather. Need to carry shopping/luggage. Security especially at night. Cost of several passengers. Cost of parking at station	Road congestion. Cost of car and fuel. Cost of parking. Non-availability of parking. Accident rate & insurance costs. Time wasted behind wheel. Vandalism of vehicle. Availability of taxis & public transport.

Table 1. Disincentives.

Perhaps the greatest disadvantage of public transport is its non-availability when needed. When this means waiting in the rain for a bus, or walking (in the rain) a significant distance to a bus stop, public transport is not much of a competitor. Added to this is the inconvenience of carrying luggage or shopping. Security, especially at night if walking home in the dark, is a worry in areas where crime is prevalent.

Bus delays are perhaps one of the more frustrating issues since the comfort of bus stops is not an incentive to use them. It is not usually the fault of the bus company if there are delays, but of the congested road conditions - Figure 3.

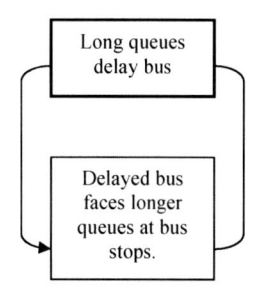

There is often a positive loop operating when the roads are busy. If a bus is delayed, more passengers are waiting at a bus stop and they take longer to board the bus. The bus is therefore delayed further, and this increases the number of passengers at the next stop. The following buses are not delayed by this problem and accordingly catch up on the first one. The long-suffering passengers see the familiar procession of several buses arriving at the same time.

Figure 3. Bus Delays.

The rise in car congestion over the years suggests there is a positive loop in operation, although *congestion* is not the influence going round the loop. The influence has to be the feature that causes congestion namely the desire to own and use a car -Figure 4.

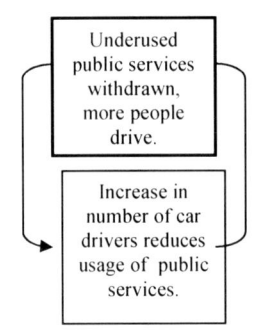

[Diagram: A feedback loop showing two boxes — "Underused public services withdrawn, more people drive." connected to "Increase in number of car drivers reduces usage of public services."]

A positive loop operating on car ownership is shown in figure 4. The withdrawal of public services, as car ownership rises, is the culprit. The loop gain is then increased further as non-drivers perceive the advantages enjoyed by an increasing number of car owners - the fashion for ownership might also be a factor.

Figure 4. Motivation for car use.

Town planners have of course made many efforts to counter the traffic problem. Motorways and dual carriageways increase throughput and towns are bypassed so they will suffer less traffic. The contention at crossroads is reduced by flyovers and under-passes and to some extent by roundabouts and traffic lights. On the other hand government has some influence by taxing petrol, licensing car use and charging for parking. Should more be done to reduce traffic or will this damage the economy?

Evidently the incentives to cease using a car are frustrated by the lack of alternatives to meet the user's needs. If public transport is inadequate then there may be no alternative to a car. Why is public transport inadequate since there was a time when people were dependent on it? The obvious answer is convenience; being able to choose the time and destination for a journey. This convenience, however, is being eroded by the time wasted due to congestion and the difficulty and cost in parking near the desired destination. A part of the problem may be fashion. School children are taken to school by car. This is a trend that has been reinforced by the media as discussed in chapter 15. It is a factor that increases the crowding of the roadway at those times of the day. The siting of places of work away from public transport is another.

The frustration of car use may increase incentive to use public transport but this has to await the building of the infrastructure. Punitive taxes have been suggested as a way to increase the incentive to take the train or bus. In London, at the beginning of the 21st century, congestion charges were introduced. This had the effect of reducing the traffic and enabling buses to travel more freely.

It was, however, in an area already supplied with substantial public transport. In other areas there is a mismatch between the provision of public transport and the needs of a population that has spread geographically beyond the bounds that were formerly served. It is evidently necessary to provide more flexibility that emulates the benefit of car ownership.

Disincentives for the car.

Although much has been done to make travel by road more efficient, the disadvantages of using a car in towns are numerous. Road congestion, as has been mentioned, should be a big disincentive. Also the problem of parking once in the vicinity of the destination is not only frustrating it also adds to the congestion if it is necessary to search for a parking place. The cost of parking is often high in the cities which, when added to the cost of car ownership and fuel, should make public transport more appealing. The insurance cost is significant especially since road accidents are more frequent than for air or rail transport; in some areas vandalism is a further cost. A salutary lesson is to calculate the time wasted behind the wheel of a car. A person driving to work for an hour each day spends nearly 500 hours behind the wheel each year; equivalent to fourteen 35-hour weeks. In spite of these disadvantages the car is still often more popular than public transport where it is possible to do something useful, such as reading a book. One interpretation of this is that there is insufficient gain in the negative loop; the other is that there must be something seriously wrong with transport planning.

Counter measures.

The positive loop causing congestion was identified in figure 4. Can any of the methods of the scoldent set counteract the trend?

Saturation	Congestion.
Cut-off	Prohibition?
Open-loop	Rail stations or bus stops near to destination.
Low Gain	Reduce incentive to use a car by better alternatives
Delay in feedback	?
External force or influence	Compulsory sharing of transport.
Negative feedback loop	Increase public transport.
Theme change.	Use of communal minibuses, luggage delivery.

Table 2. Counter measures.

Saturation occurs when there are congested routes that cannot cope with the volume of traffic.

Cut-off implies prohibition It may be unpopular but it is a practice in some cities where only emergency services are allowed to operate when, for example, the level of atmospheric pollution reaches dangerous levels.

An open loop would occur if the incentive to drive could be removed altogether, for example if a journey's start and destination were next to a station or bus stop. Whilst this is unlikely, since the wait for a bus might be inevitable, the most that would be achieved would be a reduction in *loop gain* by the alternative of providing a better public service. Evidently a frequent minibus service is better than an infrequent conventional one.

External influence encouraged the sharing of transport during crises of petrol supply and may be considered to be justified when pollution levels are threatening the health of the population.

A negative feedback loop would most satisfactorily be achieved by motivating motorists to use public transport by upgrading it to a level where it is the preferred method of travel.

A theme change arises from a change in attitudes and planning. Travelators at airports are such an example although not economic in other situations. There are some services that share minibuses between several paying passengers. The problem of finding sufficient compatible journeys could be eased when all the population is on the Internet and computers could devise optimum combinations of passengers and destinations. A major issue is the movement of luggage and shopping and there is already a move to provide delivery services reminiscent of times when fewer people owned a car. Shopping on the Internet (combined with a delivery service) is a clear example of theme change.

A true analysis of the situation would consider the total picture in terms of the cost of time wasted and the benefit that a subsidised transport system would provide. Thus increases in taxation on car use might be put to subsidising taxis or minibuses until the transfer of custom was considered sufficient. On this basis a balance would be achieved between environmental benefit and benefit to the economy.

The Total Picture.

Some of the themes mentioned above are not likely to obtain acceptance unless there are substantial benefits to be derived from them. It is necessary to look at the total picture and assess the overall cost/benefit to both people and the economy. If alternative schemes are to penalise the car driver further then money derived from the penalty must feed back to fund an alternative scheme of transport.

We are close to the position where technology can make it efficient to share transport with the minimum inconvenience. There are already travel sharing schemes in operation that are more convenient than the public transport system. Parents share the school run; coach parties are arranged for holidays and theatre outings; and the package holiday business thrives on them. In some towns, buses are provided to transport motorists to the town centre from an out-of-town parking area. Most of these schemes are prearranged and lack the flexibility to compete with the car in other situations.

The boating community use GPS (Global Positioning System) to identify where they are on the chart or map within a few metres. The technology can advise on speed and the expected time of arrival at a destination. The mobile phone can perform some of these functions and could be designed to incorporate the facilities offered by GPS and also be linked to the Internet. Route finding systems are presently available for the car driver.

In a future scenario the public could access a central computer system, which could optimise the route for a taxi or minibus to follow when picking up several passengers. Such a system could be funded by penalising car usage in proportion to the congestion problem and by billing users of a taxi or minibus a realistic charge to prevent the system being abused, as shown in figure 5

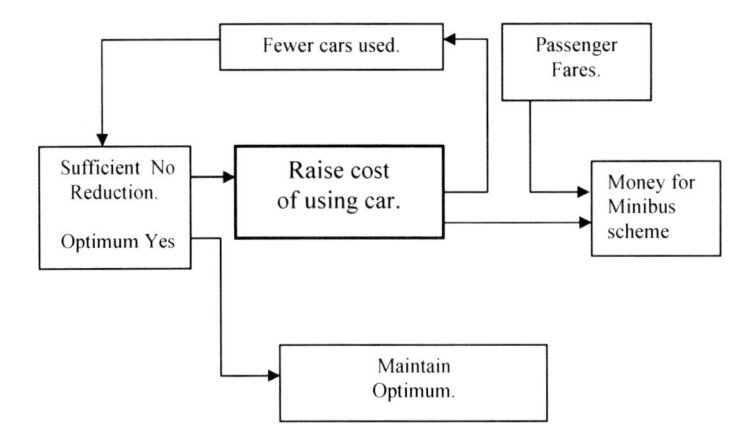

Figure 5. Control of congestion.

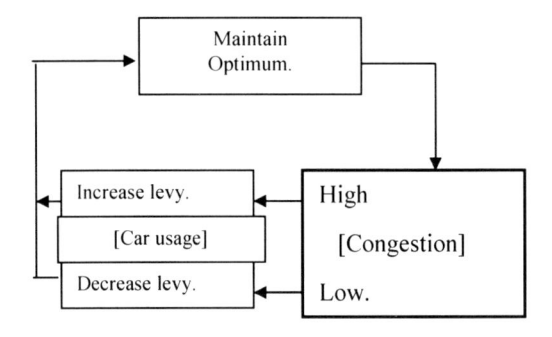

(a)
Figure 6. Maintaining optimum.

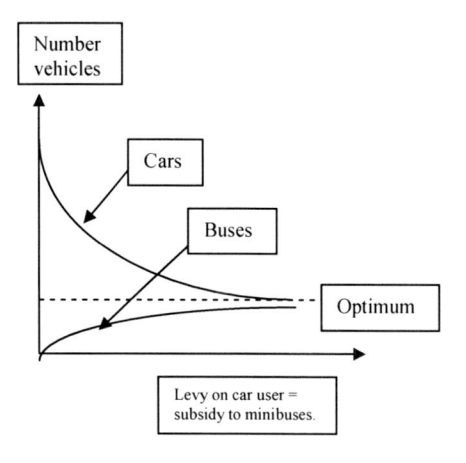

(b)
Figure 6. Maintaining optimum.

As the cost of using a car is raised, fewer cars are used until there is a sufficient reduction to reduce congestion to an acceptable level. The money raised together with passenger fares is used to supply a minibus alternative transport scheme. Once the optimum is reached the levy for car usage can be raised or lowered to maintain it, as shown in figure 7a. A minibus could perhaps, on average, carry four times the number of people carried in a car. The graph in figure 7b. supposes the number of cars reduces four times faster than the number of minibuses increases.

It may appear, at first sight that this is yet another burden on the motorist. It need not be a burden provided the money, from penalties for using the car, is channelled into the alternative forms of transport from which the motorist can benefit. Provided the money received from motorists and passengers is not siphoned off to pay for other amenities the system should settle at an optimum position. Assessing the optimum fee or levy for car use may be difficult since different towns with different environments and populations may require different levies. It is evident that a scheme must be subsidised at the beginning and the levies increased gradually to assess their effect. If the levy for car usage it too high then too few motorists will be available to fund the scheme.

The reducing car population and increasing minibus usage should provide the information needed to assess the appropriate levy. As mentioned before the optima will differ for different towns. Those with extensive car parking facilities would be optimised with fewer minibuses and the converse applies. Since the minibuses would be in service continually, no parking facilities would be needed for them other than the points for setting down and picking up passengers.

Table 3 looks at the overall cost of using a car. As more money is channelled from car usage to alternative transport so it becomes more advantageous for the motorist to use that transport. Continued use of the car would imply that it is for a purpose that justifies the increased cost.

Overall costs of car.	Benefits of minibus.
Time wasted due to congestion. Time spent looking for parking place. Time spent walking from parking place. Cost of car and tax. Cost of fuel. Insurance. Frustration, tension and road rage. Pollution.	Fewer cars, less congestion. Delivery to and from destination. Better service for non-drivers. Efficient organisation with mobile phones and GPS positioning. Flexibility compared to bus/train. Efficient employment of drivers. Luggage delivery.

Table 3. Costs versus benefits derived from change of system.

On the assumption that sharing minibuses is a lower cost to the economy, an optimum can be achieved when sufficient drivers find it economic to change to flexible public transport. Taxing the car driver to fund the alternative transport should reduce congestion. The service should cause less hassle than envisaged in the costs side of table 3. It is likely that the time taken for a journey would be less than the total time incurred by using the car (in a congested environment) and parking and walking from it.

The Motorway.

One of the situations that should be self-limiting is the overcrowded motorway. A problem, however, for any road with restricted access, is the lack of feedback of current conditions. The slip road feeding a motorway usually gives no indication of the density of traffic beyond. Once in the queue to enter the motorway it is too late. This can be countered to some extent by traffic information from the local radio station provided by motorists already in the predicament (if they can use their mobile phones when stationery) or alternatively from a helicopter pilot at greater cost. The same situation occurs when road works block traffic, although sometimes advance warnings and alternative routes are suggested.

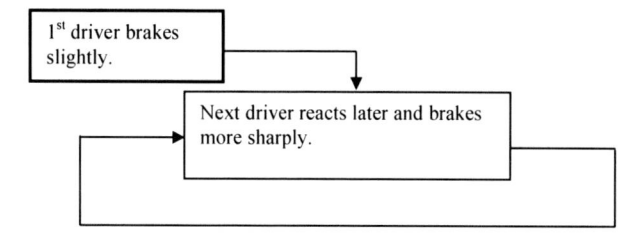

```
┌─────────────────┐
│ 1st driver brakes│
│ slightly.       │──────────┐
└─────────────────┘          │
                             ▼
         ┌──────────────────────────────────┐
     ┌──►│ Next driver reacts later and brakes│
     │   │ more sharply.                    │
     │   └──────────────────────────────────┘
     │                                      │
     └──────────────────────────────────────┘
```

Figure 7. Cumulative effect of braking.

Positive loops are to be found in the start/stop mode of a crowded motorway. It is often found that traffic comes to a standstill for no apparent reason. The problem lies in the tendency for some drivers to follow too closely behind the car in front. Thus if a first car slows down slightly then the delay before the driver of a second car (following too closely behind) reacts means the second driver has to brake more heavily as shown in figure 7. The effect happens again with a third car until eventually a driver further down the line must stop completely. This effect is cumulative until there is a driver with sufficient space to maintain a relatively constant speed so that the loop action is reduced.

Population issues.

In 1980 Isaac Asimov [5] made estimates of the rise in the rate that the population would increase: he noted that before agriculture was organised the rate of population increase was 0.02% per year and would have taken 35,000 years to double in size. By 1900 with the industrial revolution: the rate of increase was 1% per year, a doubling in 70 years. He extrapolated the figures to estimate a world population of 50 billion in 2050 and 1.2 trillion by 2280. The trend implied that the weight of the population in 1,800 years would equal the weight of the earth. This may be an unusually graphic way of saying that something has to be done and clearly something will occur to limit the population increase long before then.

His other statistics drew attention to the consequences of increase in life expectancy in the USA. Based on the statistics for that country he estimated that over a period of 100 years the population would triple while the people over 65 would increase tenfold. It should be noted that whilst the population increase is a consequence of a positive loop (when people on average have more than two children), the increase in the ratio of people over 65 is not the result of a loop so much as the improvements in medicine and living standards.

As long ago as 1838 P F Verhulot devised the following population equation to assess the stress suffered by over-population: $DP/dt = a.P - b.P^2$

Where $a.P$ represents population growth proportional to P and $b.P^2$ represents conflict and stress that show sigmoid growth. It implies that beyond a certain level, war is inevitable. It is interesting to note that zero population growth occurs when the population $= a/b$. This implies that the population is sufficiently dispersed that the opportunity for mating is curtailed. It is relevant to the dispersal of fish in the ocean due to overfishing.

It is, of course, right to draw attention to the problems to be expected if the rate of population increase continues at the same rate. It is a classic positive loop in which the rate of population increase is proportional to the population; the condition for an exponential increase which is certain to cause disaster unless countered by some limiting factors such as a negative loop in some form or other. In fact the population explosion that has been threatened for many years has slowed down and food production has increased to the level where the expected shortage has not materialised in most of the developed countries. Global warming is expected to reverse this trend.

Some aspects of population control are shown in the scoldent list, table 4, for countering the effect of the positive loop. The factors in the table (influential in keeping the population more constant) are likely to be interlinked.

Saturation	Of food, water and housing.
Cut-off	Deaths due to war and famine.
Open-loop	Infertility or premature death.
Low Gain	Birth control.
Delay in feedback	Late marriage.
External force or influence	Compulsory sterilisation or infanticide.
Negative feedback loop	Disease and war due to overcrowding.
Theme change.	State control of childbirth or women choosing a career instead of family.

Table 4. Population control.

The influence around the loop is the desire or willingness to have more children.

Saturation of the supply of food and, water and housing demotivates for children and will occur as resources are fully taken up.
Cut off of food and water is more drastic and occurs as a result of drought or war.
Open loop will occur if the population is infertile or dies before child-bearing age.
Low gain implies some measure of birth control, preferably by cultural influence.
Delay will result from later marriages, often due to economic circumstances such as difficulty in housing.
External force: compulsory sterilisation and infanticide have been practised in some countries.
Negative feedback: An ever increasing population and the resultant over crowding is a factor in disease and also in conflict leading to war.

Saturation of the food and water supply can to lead to war if the population increases. Famine leads to conflict resulting from the competition for scarce resources and is likely to be the cause of premature deaths. The wars resulting from politics, and religious or cultural differences, also play their part.

Overcrowding is often associated with lack of hygiene if the public services are over-stretched. It is a potent way of increasing disease and the chance of an epidemic that will reduce the population

An innocuous method of controlling population by birth control might be achieved if people limited their families in accordance with reductions in space available for housing and food production. It has been noted that 25% of the population did not marry in bad times and this had a stabilising effect on the burden placed on the economy. Also late marriage due to difficulties in affording housing gives a delay in the loop that reduces the rate of increase.

Additional factors may counteract an expected change in population. Thus attempts to limit population, by encouraging smaller families, has been thwarted in some countries by people who see many children as an insurance policy for their old age. In some cases compulsory sterilisation and infanticide have been practised in order to cope with the problem.

Social policies have an effect on the population of sections of society. A trend has been noted towards single motherhood. A factor to be considered is how cultural attitudes encourage young women to become mothers at too early an age and without the means to support a child. The example set by them may be followed by others and set a trend that it is difficult to stop. Social policies may also perpetuate an underclass by removing the incentive to become self-reliant and limit offspring to those the parents can afford. Figure 8 illustrates the influences on population in one diagram. The factors on the left increase population and those on the right of the diagram tend to reduce it.

Methods of containing population levels may not always give the desired result due to the delay in responding to the incentives. An interesting study was the simulation of the rabbit/fox population. In this example it is supposed that there is an excess number of rabbits which a population of foxes will reduce. Since there is an ample food supply for the foxes, they multiply to create large numbers of offspring, which can initially be sustained by the rabbit population. After a time the fox population increases to a level that causes the rabbits to decline in numbers. Eventually there are so few rabbits that many foxes starve to death. The fox population declines and the rabbits breed again to produce large numbers. As a result the populations of each animal appear in cycles, resembling the oscillations caused by the pendulum.

This drastic behaviour is hopefully not to be expected of humans although there may some resemblance in the rise and decline of nations where resources are analogous to the rabbits. The delay in the negative feedback in population control will be realised by the period between successive generations of families.

The problems have been delayed in part by the increased efficiency of food production and in part by increasingly effective methods of contraception. Economic factors are also important. Whereas it seems a contradiction that economically successful societies should limit their population more than those who are more deprived; there are reasons for this. The economically successful societies place a burden on their members insofar as a certain standard of living is expected before raising a family. There is therefore a tendency for people to stay in education longer and delay marriage until they are financially able to meet the demands expected by society. The greater opportunities for women also appear to be a factor in reducing the number who bear children.

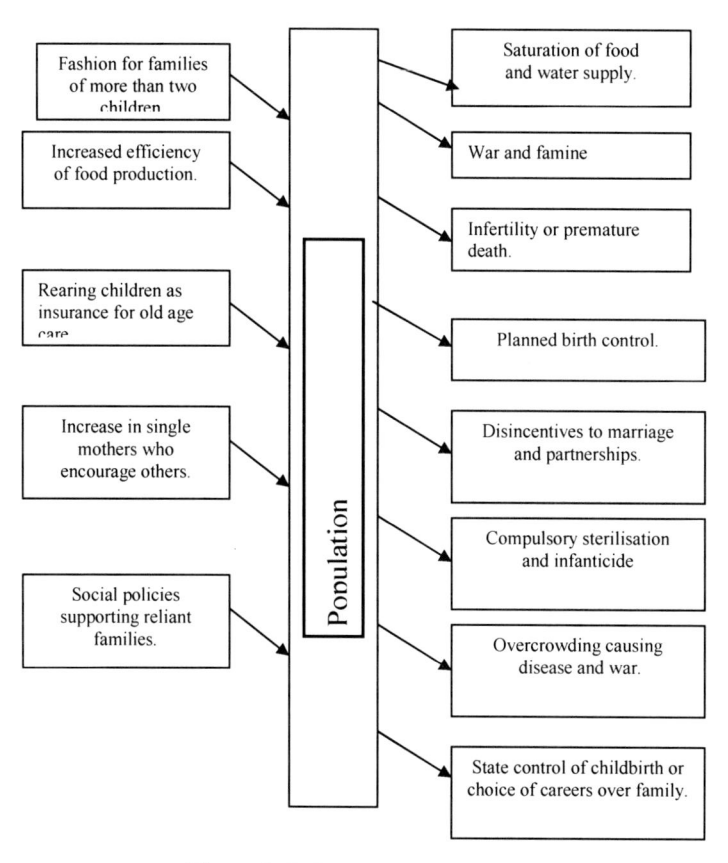

Figure 8. Influences on population.

Survival issues.

As has been observed previously a successful venture requires a positive loop in order to survive. This equally well applies to species as well as inanimate systems. The numbers of animals in a species is a balance between population explosion due to breeding of multiple offspring and the loss of numbers due to predators and disease. The balance, between the inbuilt positive loop consequent upon breeding in humans, and the losses due disease has been upset by the advances in science, medical services and improvements in hygiene. Population control now must be achieved by a more conscious effort.

A particular issue regarding population lies in the quantity of harmful bacteria, which multiply in true exponential style when given the opportunity. Much of this is kept at bay by the body's immune system. If, however, the population of bacteria exceeds the threshold beyond which the immune system can cope, then a dangerous problem arises. It is well known that drugs such as penicillin that have been effective in countering the invasion of bacteria have been subject to problems due to mutants of bacteria, some of which are resistant to known drugs.

There are of course diseases such as AIDS. These have decimated the population in some African states. A contagious disease, such as this, is a candidate for a positive loop since the spread is proportional to human contact and the more people with the disease the more it will spread. The problem is exacerbated by the frequency of air travel that conducts disease from one region to other parts of the world. The potential for an influenza pandemic is discussed in chapter 23.

Summary.

1. Positive loops create many natural hazards.
2. Positive feedback is likely to accelerate global warming.
3. Global warming increases the energy available to generate hurricanes.
4. More positive incentives are needed to popularise public transport.
5. Driver discipline can help flow of traffic and reduce hazards.
6. Modern technology should offer more efficient methods to improve people movement.
7. Population subject to a continuing positive loop will end in a disaster.
8. Epidemics are powered by positive loops.

References.

[1] R Meade "The effect of logging on the ecology of the Amazon rain forest."
[2] Gibbon, J & M "Inside Science, number 120", New Scientist 22/5/99.
[3] New Scientist Global Supplement, 28/4/01
[4] Fox D., "Saved by the trees", New Scientist, 27/10/2007, pp 42-6.
[5] Asimov, Isaac "A Choice of Catastrophes." Hutchinson 1980.

Chapter 21. Information Technology.

Information loops.

In your everyday life you are giving opinions to colleagues.
Your opinion may be passed on to others without reference to yourself. There may be an occasion when the opinion travels full circle and is offered back to you as a piece of new found wisdom. It, of course, supports your original hypothesis. If you have a high opinion of your influence you may recognise that it is a repetition of your views which have come back to you. On the other hand if you are of a modest disposition you might regard the comment as an independent one which supports your original hypothesis. Your belief in the hypothesis is thereby strengthened and you are in a positive feedback information loop [1].

A manifestation of this loop in public life is the rumour. As the rumour spreads so its alleged validity is increased and significant damage can be caused before the rumour is scotched. The importance of this kind of event is perhaps greatest in the financial world where the information network is world-wide and public confidence in a financial institution is vital to its well being. The rumour in this case may not be by word of mouth but by the movement in share prices, or change in the exchange rate, which is notified instantaneously over computer networks. Runs on banks have traditionally started on the basis of rumour which can be self fulfilling if the bank does not have sufficient liquid funds to meet the demand.

Positive loops in computer systems are important enough to require further examination. A programmed computer system has features in common with government legislation. In both cases the designers, or legislators, are endeavouring to forecast the future by anticipating all the events to which their system will be subjected. A further feature is that their systems also constrain freedom of action. It becomes possible, in a badly designed system, for these constraints to inhibit the correcting influences that may otherwise occur. An example of such a correcting influence is the negative feedback that occurs in a free market.

Stock market.

The stock market crash of 1987 was aggravated due to the US Futures Market being subject to pre-programmed computer control. Computer sell orders were triggered by the rate of decrease of prices. As prices lowered so more sell orders were triggered thereby exacerbating the fall in prices. The problem arose because the systems analysts/designers did not take into account the effect of the data that could be input to the system in those circumstances. The computer controlled actions happened faster than a human could comprehend - by the time comprehension had been achieved significant orders had been executed. This is a very simple feedback loop as shown in figure 1.

```
    ┌──────────────────┐
──▶ │  Drop in price.  │ ──┐
│   └──────────────────┘   │
│   ┌──────────────────┐   │
└── │  Trigger sell    │ ◀─┘
    │  order.          │
    └──────────────────┘
```

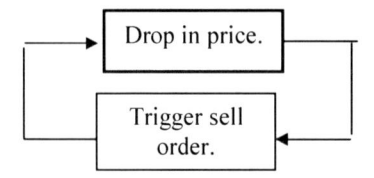

Figure 1. Stock market Crash.

Systems overload (or chaos breeding chaos).

Perhaps the most problematic loop is one where chaos increases chaos. Not only does the problem expand dramatically but also computer systems are often designed to update records after each operation. In this scenario a false record can generate others. Eventually all records may be false so that it is impossible to recover (other than by back-ups that can be referred to in an emergency).

One of the examples of this occurred with the London Ambulance callout and computer scheduling system. In part this was due to staff entering incomplete information from which the computer would calculate the most appropriate ambulance to send to an emergency. This was assessed in terms of distance from the scene, equipment required and experience of the crew. Errors accumulated until responses were so delayed that repeat requests were being made from one accident scene. If these repeats were treated as a new accident a further ambulance would be dispatched to the same accident. As this scenario continued fewer and fewer ambulances were available for other accidents and the number of duplicated calls multiplied which compounded the problem as shown in figure 2.

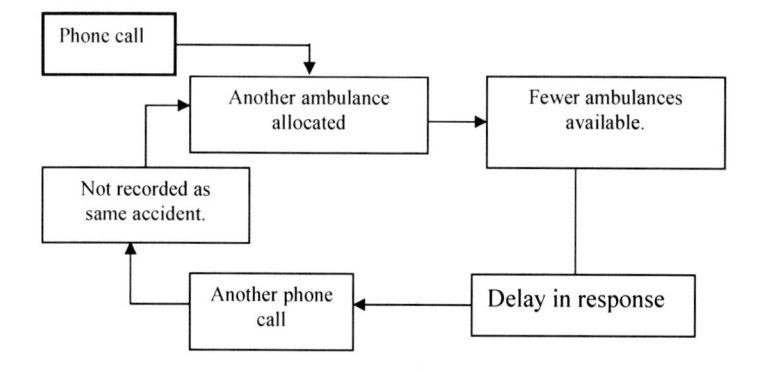

Figure 2. London Ambulance problem.

A similar example of chaos spreading chaos occurred with a wholesale book distributor. The distributor received books from publishers and distributed them to booksellers as required. When a computer system was installed the staff were not adequately prepared to operate in accordance with the computer system which was designed to record the number of books taken from a particular location and update the stock record. When staff took short cuts the records were wrongly updated. The computer might declare a full pallet when it was out of stock and vice versa. Some books would not be ordered when required and others were ordered unnecessarily. Customers did not receive the books they ordered and the locations of hundreds of books were lost. The scene was set for increased chaos, the extent of which can be envisaged since the warehouse contained 25 million books.

In the 1960s one of the earliest examples of an unintended positive loop in a computer system occurred with project MAC at Massachusetts Institute of Technology. In this early project for a "Multi-Access Computer", an operating system was developed to allocate computing power to different programs in turn so that the computer would appear to be servicing several users at the same time. A system of priorities was incorporated according to the urgency of the program. It was found, however, that the computer operated at a fraction of its expected power. Eventually the operating system was diagnosed to be the problem. It was spending so much computing power to decide on the allocation of resource to each program that there was little left for the programs themselves. The problem was compounded by the increasing demand as the queue of unserviced programs increased.

These problems arise because the programs are designed to be open ended. The programmer has to anticipate, without the benefit of hindsight, the situations that might arise. It is of course routine development procedure to test out programs under the expected operating conditions and perhaps a test may be regarded as a form of feedback loop insofar as it provides corrective action that leads to further correction.

It is possible, to some extent, to design programs that incorporate feedback loops in order to adapt to circumstances, but still it is necessary to anticipate the circumstances that the program has to adapt to. An interactive program goes one step further. The user is now able to steer the program in accordance with circumstances at the time. A diversion from the expected course can be seen and corrective action taken. The comparative slowness of the human being slows the system down but this may be the price for correct procedure.

An interesting example occurs in fighter aircraft. It is found that the response time of the plane can be made faster if it is inherently unstable. Such planes are so unstable that a pilot cannot respond quickly enough to counteract the instability. A computer system can be designed to operate the plane and convert the pilot's instructions into a form that achieves the objective while at the same time compensating for any adverse action from the instability of the aircraft.

At the other end of the speed scale is the sea going freighter. The steering characteristics of these enormous ships change with the loading. These are ships that take several miles to stop, and respond to the rudder very slowly. An empty ship will be higher in the water and respond to the rudder differently. A human cannot assess the response sufficiently quickly, in a crowded seaway, to control the steering accurately. Computer control systems have been developed that can adapt to the changed characteristics by the feedback that they receive. The response to the steering commands alters and these changes can be measured from the ship's initial responses, and responses subsequently refined as the ship gets underway.

Beneficial loops.

A beneficial aspect of positive loops in information arises with the design of computers. Laying out the computer circuitry is a complex process. The fabrication of the components requires precise calculation and positioning of the different layers of the semiconductor. The optimum wiring to connect the components must be calculated so that there are no short circuits or lengthy connections that would degrade the performance of the circuit. Replication of this process a million times without a mistake is a job for the computer. In consequence the computer can be used to replicate faster and more powerful computers; resulting in the exponential increase in computing power which has been doubling every 3 -4 years.

The computer literate are able to take advantage of this power to generate their own feedback loop. As Milsum [3] has noted the privileged few use wealth and power to accumulate more wealth and power in contrast to the poor who, on low incomes with greater susceptibility to disease, lack of education and poor working efficiency are unlikely to enjoy relative improvement. As so often happens with a positive loop there can be a downside and it is possible sociological problems will arise if computer illiterate people are disadvantaged to an excessive extent.

In a lecture to the British Association, Cochrane [4], has drawn attention to the mushrooming of business for users of the Internet. Here the interaction of users, and ease of contact with others, is likely to cause the activity to rise in proportion to the number of people engaged in the activity - a classical criterion for exponential increase. Unfortunately such a situation also favours the spread of the computer virus and spam in similar quantities.

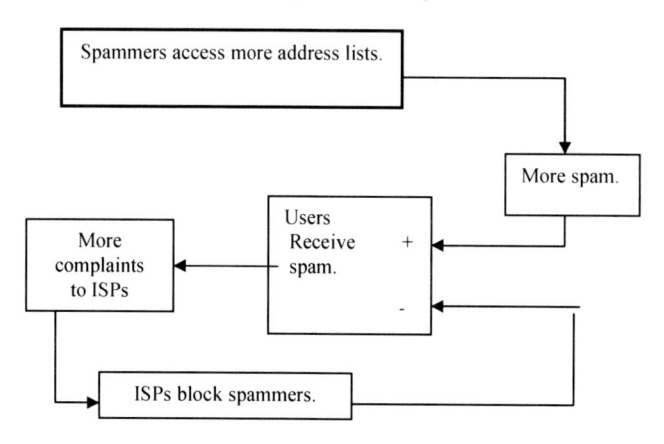

Figure 3. Addressing the spam problem.

The problem is aggravated if the virus writer gains access to the address list of the infected user in order to spread the virus further [5]. There is nevertheless some counteraction consequent on the rise in number of users since there are then more people to report on the prevalence of a virus. The cost of the problem has also motivated the Internet Service Providers (ISPs) to scan email for virus content. On a similar vein is the rise in Spam. Defining the threshold in nuisance value that an email causes is easier when numerous users report unwanted messages from the same originator Figure 3. The ISP then knows which messages to block.

Malicious users pasting erroneous information, perhaps, to downgrade the reputation of a competitor might also degrade the system. The effect of erroneous views is to dilute the valid information and reduce the gain of the loop. The validity of information on the online encyclopaedia Wikipedia sometimes suffered the problem of erroneous information put on by, or edited by malicious users. Steps have been taken to avoid this problem by using only trusted editors.

Feedback loops arise when search engines such as Google cite more popular sites at the beginning of the pages of hits [6]. Since searchers are unlikely to explore numerous pages the first few achieve priority and become more cited and more popular Figure 4. This feedback loop can give a disproportionate popularity to a few sites at the expense of the less visited ones. One solution proposed is to introduce some randomness into the search so those sites lower down the list can get a posting near the top occasionally.

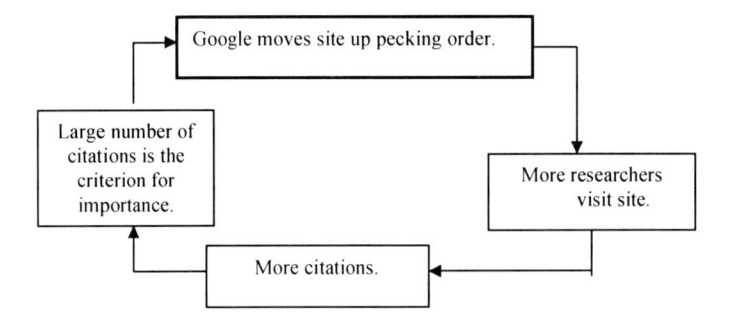

Figure 4. Preferential citation loop.

The scoldent list to limit the bias towards a few sites might follow the following theme:

Saturation: Limit rate of citation.
Cut off: Limit number of citations.
Open loop Remove criteria of importance.
Low gain Introduce randomness.
Delay: Slow update.
External force: Legislation, rulings, trade body.
Negative feedback: Action by disadvantaged sites.
Theme change: Panel decision.

Saturation here implies limiting the rate that further citations are quoted, whilst cut-off would place a limit on the number of citations shown for a site. It would become an open loop if the criterion of importance were removed. Randomness in the selection of sites that are given priority would dilute the effect of the number of citations. Slow update would seem to have a similar effect to saturation in delaying the appearance of recent citations.

A trade body or other authority would be the external force to administrate a system that gave more prominence to lower cited sites. Compensating feedback in this scenario will arise when managers of low cited sites take action to raise their profile. Such actions might be by enhancing keyword data to increase their hit rate or by collaborating with like-minded individuals to cite each other.

Data overload.

The sheer quantity of data available is itself an impediment to achievement. One of the problems in industry and government establishments is the difficulty of cataloguing and searching data to find what is relevant. The issue was noted by Toffler [6] who advised that as long ago as the 1970s, 100,000 US government reports were filed per annum together with 450,000 articles, books, and papers. He estimated this was added to at the rate of about 60 million pages per annum worldwide. There is evidently too much information for easy access. No doubt there are many more today. If it is too difficult to retrieve the information that is wanted then there will be more duplication of effort and, no doubt, more reports. On top of this is the vast number of emails. These are easy to produce and send to multiple users who may not welcome the information. This escalation opposes the efficiency of the information system. It contributes to the operational overheads in a business and reduces the profits and efficiency. It is as though a beneficial process has the seeds of destruction that will limit its efficiency. In loop terms, the gain of the engine of the business loop is reduced - Figure 5. The next step was to introduce systems to evaluate the relevant data and compensate for the problem.

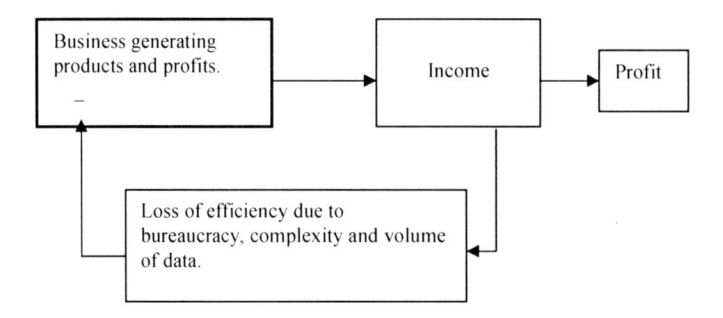

Figure 5. Profitable business loop.

Attempts have been made to compensate for this volume of data by software systems that automatically assess the importance of the data received in an attempt to prioritise and channel the information appropriately.

Information processing systems have many uses. For example market forecasting can benefit from feedback by monitoring the browsing of users. If the features that people are seeking can be identified then manufacturers can prepare for the future demand: for example people browsing for a car of a certain colour such as blue with various other features [8]. Manufacturers can then prepare for extra sales of blue cars with those features, which will probably sell in 1 to 6 months time.

Counteracting influences.

The difficulty of comprehending computing systems is shared by many. Reasonably educated people have difficulty in understanding some of the computing facilities on offer. Accordingly, analogously to a business, the effectiveness of the systems is less than it could be.

The greater danger is presented by a system that is so complex that the users do not fully understand the outcome of a computer response. The complexity of some systems is such that a human cannot adequately assess the validity of the results. The solution sometimes adopted is to independently program an alternative system using different procedures, when possible, and then check each system against the other in order to give confidence in the outcome.

It must be noted that a compensating negative feedback loop in a digital system may not remove all errors. In conventional analogue systems, reduction of errors to a small amount may be acceptable. In a digital information system, one small error maybe a vital piece on information. It is necessary to have a system that is error proof.

The problem was noted in computer aided design systems, circa 1970; especially in finite element analysis. Here a medium is divided into numerous small elements and the distribution of stress (or other quantity) analysed. Different programs were found to give different results. The validity of computer output in this example was of such importance that the system was checked against one that has been developed by an independent design team. This was to guard against errors in the design philosophy as much as programming errors. Faults due to hardware failure are more easily corrected by having 3 systems and taking the majority verdict when one differs from the others.
Auto-control of aircraft and space flight are examples of the need for certainty.

The speed of computing today is so great that the time required for comprehension and correction may be an unacceptable overhead that unduly slows the system down. In this situation users are more likely to ignore a trend that is self-replicating. Evidently the ambulance problem would not have arisen if staff had taken the time to check whether a vehicle had already been allocated to a particular accident, and the book distribution staff had understood the importance of complying with computer system.

The Internet and the hype surrounding it are dominating our experience of information technology. On the one hand are the Public Relations that encourage us to go online and on the other is the enormous quantity of information available - much of it orientated to advertising and some aimed to make the user spend more than necessary on telephone bills. The advertising and hype form part of a positive loop either because the user wants to be part of the crowd or is afraid of missing out on the services that might be available. Mixed in with this soup of opportunity are those who see the Internet as a way of making a quick buck and who disguise the cost of making the connection to their site. Others have posted misleading company information on the Internet and benefited from the temporary change in share price. These situations arise because the expansion of the system has been too fast for everyone to appreciate the dangers and for the necessary regulations to be enacted.

The greater the power the greater the potential damage and so the immense power of some computer systems should cause us to question whether there is the possibility of a positive loop which could run out of control. There are remarkably few cases reported with such a problem. This is not to be interpreted as the absence of problems since the normal commercial companies (and many institutions) will not publicise their mistakes in case they damage their image.

Summary.

1. A rumour is an information loop.
2. Pre-programmed computer control can cause havoc if not adequately assessed.
3. Chaos breeds further chaos.
4. Computers breed faster computers.
5. Electronic communication leads to information overload.
6. Complexity reduces human comprehension.
7. The potential for cyber crime increases with complexity.
8. Human computer interaction maintains a degree of negative feedback.

References.

1. Grover D., "Information systems and stability", Computer Bulletin, Dec 1993,   pp24-25
2. Collins T. & Bicknell D., "Crash", Tiptree books.
3. Milsum JM., "A General systems approach to feedback and mutual causality" p.93
4. Cochrane P., British Association for Advancement of Science. 200
5. Bradbury D., "Strength in numbers", IT Now (formerly The Computer Bulletin) Sept. 2004, pp18-19.
6. Krieger K., "The net reloaded", New Scientist 1st July 2006, pp 40-43.
7. Toffler A., "Future shock", The Bodley Head,1977.
8. Fayyad, Usama, "Searching for the next big hit." New Scientist, 2/9/2006.

Chapter 22.   MATCHING.

Efficiency issues

The concept of matching is an important one for increasing the efficiency of an enterprise, improving communications or maximising the effect of a commodity. It is used in the coupling of the aerial cable to a television, and an audio amplifier to a loudspeaker, where it is desired to transfer as much of the signal power as possible. It has analogies in many other walks of life.

The gearbox in a car is necessary to match the speed of the engine to the speed of the road wheels. Most of the time it will not be a precise match since the gear box can only be changed in steps. It would be preferable for the engine to run constantly at its most efficient speed and then alter the gearbox continuously as the speed of the car alters. This is the aim of the Torotrak transmission [1], which is claimed to introduce a fuel saving of up to 28% and less pollution.

The advantage of gears is evident when riding a bicycle up hill. Changing gear not only makes it easier to cycle but if the hill is very steep it can make the difference between cycling and walking. The aim is to match a person's ability to power the cycle to the extent required to move it. If the gear is too high then they may not have enough strength to turn the pedals on a hill - so the transfer of power is zero; alternatively if the gear ratio is too low then they would be unable to turn the pedals fast enough. It may be that the gear ratio is not optimum (since it moves up and down in steps) and it would be preferred to have a gear marginally higher or lower but the best choice would have to be made from what is available.

An analogy to this is the relative merit of steps versus a sloping path. A set of steps dictates the length and height of climb we have to attempt. For young children and older people the steps may be too steep for comfort. Alternatively an athlete may find them too shallow and climb the steps two at a time. A slope on the other hand lets everyone choose the length of stride that is most comfortable. People can "match" the energy to be expended in climbing compared to the energy they have available.

A yacht is designed to move through the water most efficiently at a certain angle of heel. If the heel is greater then the resistance of the hull in the water is increased and if less then it implies that more sail area could be used to extract energy from the wind. Accordingly the yachtsman endeavours to match the sail area to the wind strength so as to achieve the optimum performance that is possible for a particular wind speed.

The theme of matching can be extended to the interaction between people so as to optimise the benefits. On occasions matches have been arranged between a chess master and about ten comparative novices. This provides a degree of matching since it exercises the chess master's ability to decide a move in perhaps a tenth of the time required by the novice. Otherwise (compassion aside) the master is likely to win so quickly that the match is of no benefit to anyone. Similarly it is better if two tennis players are matched since otherwise the weaker player ends up retrieving the ball from the back of the court most of the time and the strong player gets little practice at returning a shot. Some improvement in matching might be achieved by setting the strong player against a doubles team.

Optimisation

Since matching is closely related to optimising a system it is to be expected that a negative feedback loop, which is designed to correct departures from optimum conditions, will also achieve a degree of matching. Thus an atomic power plant has to be matched to the power required by the electricity grid and a negative feedback loop will be used to control the fuel rods so as to generate the amount of power required.

A manufacturer must match the quantity of product produced to the requirements of the market. If too little is produced then there is lost opportunity, if too much (especially if they are perishable goods) then product is wasted. In either case the manufacturer's business is not optimum - it is not matched to the market. The sales and marketing departments will form part of a negative feedback loop for controlling the amount manufactured but this will have a delay since the information on the market has to be collected and communicated to the manufacturing management. This delay will cause the rate of production to oscillate about a mean. This will not matter if the goods can be stored in a warehouse, or deep freeze, provided that average production is equivalent to market take-up. The warehouse, in effect, acts as a buffer before the goods enter the market.

Different forms of matching occur in many aspects of everyday life. The employer employee relationship is such an example. It is expected that the salary paid will match the value of the employee to the company. It will not be a precise match, however, since at different stages of the employment the value of the employee will change (and the salary may be slow to follow suit). In typical circumstances there are impediments to changing jobs such as the need to find something more suitable, the cost and inconvenience of moving house and the problem of learning to cope in a new environment. Such impediments introduce a delay based upon the reluctance of an employee to move and, as noted previously, delay in a negative feedback loop causes oscillation. The oscillation swings about the mean where the mean in this example is the salary that matches the value of the employee.

To give incentive (in a typical situation) for a person to change jobs the new employer must offer a higher salary than is immediately justified in order to compensate for the burden of moving. A new employee will take time to learn the ropes of a new environment and will not contribute much of value for maybe six months. In fact the need, for existing employees to teach the newcomer the company's procedures, will introduce a cost associated with the reduced productivity of existing staff.

The pendulum of value has moved to one extreme. As the newcomer learns the ropes and contributes value to the company the pendulum swings to the mid point where salary and contribution are matched. In the course of time the salary may not keep up with the rise in expertise and the pendulum swings to the other side where the salary is less than the employees contribution. In some companies this disparity is based upon the assessment of the employees reluctance to move. The time period over which these events occur varies widely with different types of jobs and may range from a few hours for basic functions to as much as two years for some management posts.

Various other situations are candidates for matching. It is required between the fuel fed to a fire and the temperature required; the speed of vehicles on a motorway can be controlled to match to the density of traffic so as to optimise the throughput; the clarinet player must match the flow of air past the reed so as to deflect the reed to its optimum deflection for quality of tone. Too little and the reed does not vibrate; too much and harmonics are generated which gives a harsh tone. These are situations in which the behaviour may be already have been learned so that direct control can be used rather than feedback.

A degree of matching is important in human relations. People will be more comfortable if the behaviour patterns of acquaintances conform to their own. This does not mean that they have to have the same attributes, a better match is made of people who are opposites but have similar interests. If one person is talkative then the other must be a good listener.
The optimum transfer of information will only occur if they have similar intellectual ability. A highly qualified academic might not deliver a lecture that can be readily understood by pupils. A newly qualified teacher on the other hand may be more matched to their ability and understand the student's problems.

The art of negotiation is concerned with matching the burdens and benefits between two (or more) parties. The needs of one party must be satisfied by the capabilities or assets of the other. How well this is achieved depends on the skills of the negotiators. A good negotiation is of benefit to both parties. If matching is not achieved then, in a free market, the losing party will be able to seek better terms elsewhere.

Connectivity.

Matching has been discussed for its ability to transfer power or information from one entity to another. There is another factor that affects transfer and that is slop that often makes the transfer less effective.

An illustration is shown in figure 1 where a connecting rod is being used to move a piston back and forth. Ideally the pin on the end of the piston will fit into the hole exactly without any gap. In practice there will always be some gap even if it is only a fraction of a millimetre. The hole is shown exaggerated as an oval in the figure with a gap "d"; i.e. the rod has to move a distance "d" before the piston is moved. On the return journey it again has to move by d before the piston takes up the movement. If the total movement possible for the rod is, for example, 10 times the value d then there is a loss of 10% in the effect of the rod on the piston. If this connection is but one in a series of connections and each contributes some slop then all the slops adds up and can become a serious defect.

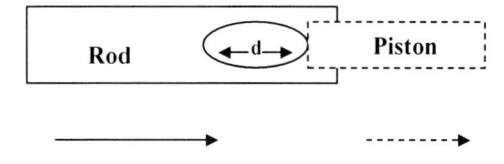

Figure 1

The effect is particularly noticeable when the movement is magnified either by levers or gears that multiply rotation of, for example, the hands of a clock. It will be found that the minute hand can be moved backwards and forwards by a fraction of a minute and this will introduce an error depending on whether gravity is acting so as to hold back the minute hand or is advancing it.

An analogy to slop is to be found in a railway timetable for a service that operates a "flexible time" policy. Figure 2 illustrates a journey on trains A, B and C. The shortest journey time would occur if the train times were connected so that a train left as soon as passengers had transferred from the previous train, i.e. the connectivity is maximum. The expected journey times as shown by the solid lines, however, are predetermined by the timetable and show a delay between trains which adds to the total journey time. These delays reduce the connectivity of the system. The dotted lines show the amount by which a train may be late. If for this example it is supposed that the timetable is organised so that train "B" only starts when it is certain train "A" has arrived, so that connections can be made, then this represents slop in the system analogous to the gap in the slot driving the piston above.

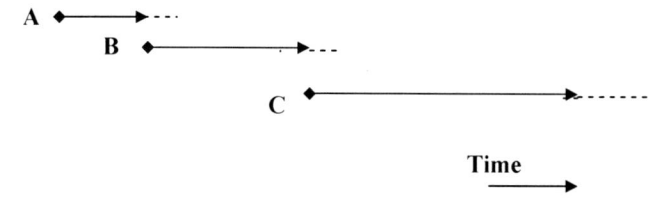

Figure 2.

The effect of slop will depend on the situation. The slop in the minute hand of an old grandfather clock may be about 30 seconds. The slop (or play) in the steering wheel of a car may be sufficient for it to fail its MOT. In a car engine slop between the piston rod and the crankshaft will lead to failure of the bush connecting them. The delay caused by a late train may be sufficient to lose the next connection.

Whilst the error in a grandfather clock may be acceptable, the connecting rod in a car engine has to be manufactured to a fine tolerance although there has to be a minute gap in order for the crankshaft to move and not seize up. It is the oil between the surfaces that solves the problem.

Slop in a system also applies to the transfer of information between people. The slop in this case is the variation in the meaning of words. If the listener is unsure of the exact meaning of a word used by the speaker then slight variations may be put on the meaning of the information. For people who are matched by having a similar upbringing and experience, the precise meaning of a word is likely to be shared. It will not require further explanation and the information will have been transmitted as efficiently as possible. The ultimate is likely to be seen in people who work closely together and develop a form of shorthand (or short sentence) to convey information.

The Price of Perfection.

Matching is relevant to the degree of perfection it is sensible to aim for. A higher specification for a product increases the cost of the product. Efficient engineering matches the specification to the need in order to keep the cost to a minimum.

In chapter 3 the cost of fish as the oceans stocks were depleted was shown to

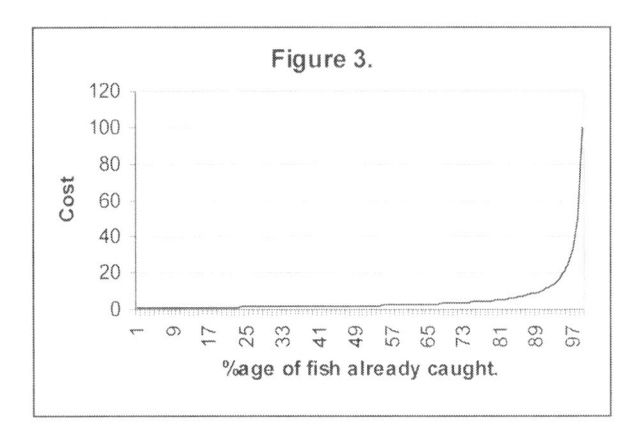

Figure 3.

[Graph: Cost vs %age of fish already caught, showing an exponential rise near 100%]

reach an excessive price due to the difficulty of catching scarce fish in the vastness of the ocean as illustrated in figure 3. This is a graph that is applicable to all situations in which the difficulty of achievement is proportional to the scarcity of a resource. Whether this is the cost of depleted fish; the cost of land in a free market or the price of coffee after frosts have killed the plants.

There is also a price to be paid for improving the accuracy and reliability of a system's components; the price of perfection is usually unacceptable. This can be a problem when a customer expects a product to be perfect every the time. Food should not have foreign bodies in it; computer software should not have bugs. An absolute guarantee is not possible.

The point is made more graphically by Turney [2]. He notes that grain certified by the US Department of Agriculture may contain small quantities of stones, pieces of glass, unknown foreign substances and *"10 or more rodent pellets, bird droppings or an equivalent quantity of other animal filth per 1000 grams"*

Attempts to write computer software that is bug free are particularly over ambitious. Not only is it extremely difficult to write thousands of lines of code that are perfect in every way but changes in the operating environment and the need to operate in conjunction with other software make it impossible to predict every requirement.

The problem for a manufacturer was illustrated at a meeting concerning the testing of transistors. These were electronic components that had three wires for making connections. The inspector at the factory would miss perhaps 2% of the errors. Accordingly another inspector could retest them so that 2% of the 2% would be missed (giving 0.04% with errors). This process could not go on indefinitely because a stage would be reached where the further act of testing introduced more errors - usually because some wires would fracture when twisted yet again.

The lesson to be learned from this example is that it is impossible to achieve absolute reliability in anything; and as the reliability is improved, to perhaps 99% or 99.9%, so the cost goes up at an increasing rate. In fact when the reliability approaches 100% the cost increases even faster than an exponential rate as shown in figure 4.

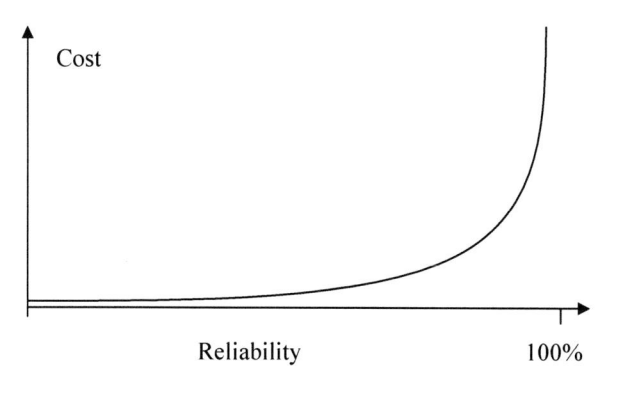

Figure 4.

A point will be reached where other aspects of the situation suffer because money or time is not available to address other problems. An exception would seem to be the aircraft industry that has achieved a remarkable degree of safety exceeding 99.9% - It is however an industry in which the high costs of maintenance and organisation are justified to the extent of triplicating critical controls. Even here there is an adverse reaction since an aircraft's components are so costly that an unscrupulous black market industry has emerged that channels inferior components into the maintenance service.

Excessive zeal for perfection often causes more problems than it solves. Legislation to control the behaviour of people may reach the point where no one can remember all the rules. If it becomes too cumbersome it is ineffective. The influence from Brussels falls into this category. Attempts at covering every situation make legislation cumbersome and costly. In figure 5, instead of reliability the horizontal axis is the percentage of activities legislated for; the vertical axis is a measure of ineffectiveness. This also implies increased cost and reduces the funds available for other perhaps more important activities. In this diagram, 100% implies that a citizen would have to follow rules for every action taken.

Ineffectiveness
(and cost)

%age of activities legislated for.   100%

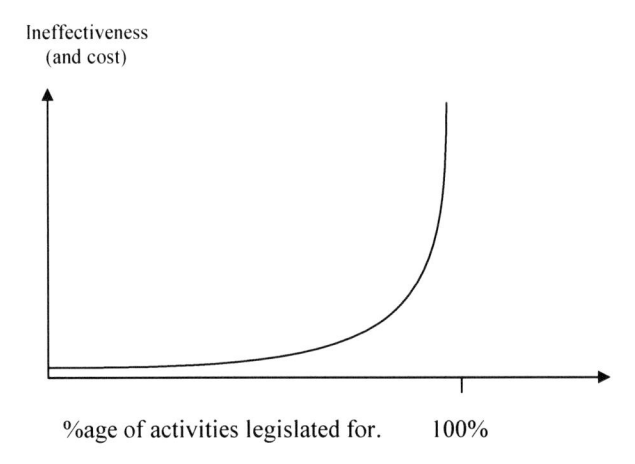

Figure 5. Legislation versus cost.

Too many rules may cause a business, such as farming, to go bankrupt; alternatively people spend too much time finding a way to avoid the rules so that the economy suffers. An example of this problem occurred when punitive taxation was in vogue; it became more profitable to spend time avoiding tax than working at a productive task. Attempts to reduce the speed limit of motor vehicles would be expected to reduce the damage caused by accidents - but not if the limit is reduced to the level where people fall asleep at the wheel, or become so irritated that they take extra risks.

These attempts to achieve perfection, detailed ruling or 100% reliability are usually examples where the excessive efforts are not matched to the needs of the community. The burden of this zeal is realised as bureaucracy that hinders the growth of a positive loop in industry or alternatively delays the feedback from a negative loop - making the correcting influence less effective.

Summary.

1. Matching enables a person or system to operate at their most efficient.
2. Matching optimises the transmission of power or information.
3. An aim of business is to match supply and demand.
4. Slop in a system reduces its efficiency.
5. The goal of perfection is unobtainable and will introduce excessive costs.
6. The compensation culture is based on the expectation of perfection in others.

References:

[1] http://www.torotrak.com/IVT/works/
[2] Turney, Jon "Pandora's lunchbox", - a review of "A consumer's guide to GM food" by Alan McHughen.

Chapter 23. The Future.

"There are known knowns.
These are things we know that we know.
There are known unknowns.
That is to say, there are things that we know we don't know.
But there are also unknown unknowns.
There are things we don't know we don't know. "
Donald Rumsfeld

Legislation and planning.

Many people already deal in the future. Legislators and planners fall into this category. The problem for the planners is not only in anticipating the influence of foreseeable situations but also in unexpected events. In addition are problems caused by various sectors of the criminal classes who seek to destroy or damage.

The legislators evidently have a different problem in that other members of their profession will try to undermine the intent of the legislation in the interests of their clients. The problem is greater in new fields of legislation where the scope extends over uncharted territory and the outcome is dependent on the interpretation by the courts. Although well-established territory has been sufficiently explored for the interpretation to be well known, particular circumstances may modify the outcome.

Trend in litigation.

The most worrying trend that has developed at the time of writing is the degree of litigation and the influence of the ambulance chasing lawyers. Even then the influence would not be so problematic were it not for the considerable sums of money often awarded in damages. The feedback to generate more sensible settlements, when it came, was from the insurance companies who were increasing premiums at a substantial rate to the point where some companies could not afford the cover and had to cease trading. The problem lay in the absence of feedback to the assessors of damages or juries who quoted unrealistic sums. Whether the excessive sums were influenced by past awards it is difficult to tell but if a feedback loop was in operation then it played a part in a situation that was spiralling out of control. The UK National Health Service management is known to be concerned that the damages awarded in cases of medical malpractice could push the NHS further into bankruptcy. The smaller funds left for the service would imply a poorer service and presumably a greater likelihood of inadequate treatment. The other positive loop lies with the people who were successful in seeking damages and the outcome influencing other people to pursue litigation, particularly when the awards were reported by the media.

Consumption.

The use of energy is a continuing concern. A loop is in operation in respect of every consumer item. Whether people consume more to keep up with a fashion or are simply envious of the life style that the consumption of more energy permits - the result is the same. Examples of the extra comforts enjoyed from the use of energy are noticed by others who seek to enjoy the same benefits. The developed countries have set an example of excessive consumption that is likely to be emulated by the developing nations. Petrol consumption for cars and oil consumption for electricity heating and plastics are examples of a trend that will reach its limit in a few decades when the supply runs out. There are attempts by engineers to design more efficient systems. Modern design methods produce better cars with more efficient engines that use less fuel. Whether larger aircraft that spread the energy used amongst more people will give an energy saving depends on other factors. It is likely that the saving will be nullified by more people being able to afford flights.

Resources.

Many of the predictions for the future consider the consequences of limitations in the world's resources to provide energy, food and water for a growing population. Alternatively if not a growth in population then a growth in the expectations of the existing population. The extent of the world's oil resources is well researched and the consequences sufficiently well understood to generate a plan of action to find alternative sources of energy. At the time of writing the alternative sources proposed are generally more expensive than oil but as oil becomes scarcer the costs of extraction will rise until the alternatives become financially viable. This may be seen as a compensating loop in which the demand for oil decreases as the cost rises. It is one in which the delay in feedback is small in comparison with the time scale of the developments. Consequently it is likely to be manageable albeit not without some adaptation to absorb the increase in prices.

There will be other influences that will offset the increase such as more efficient engineering design that use less material resources. Other factors in this equation are the distribution costs of energy; thus although solar panels, wave machines and wind generators are more expensive methods of electricity production, there are compensating factors such as the local availability of electricity without the need for power lines for its distribution. In addition a local source of power can be fed back into the electricity grid and help compensate for the cost of the installation.

Estimates of world population increase are not as dire as formerly predicted. There is evidence that the rate of increase is stabilising and is declining in the more developed countries. The bigger problem lies in the expectations of the population in the less developed countries as they become wealthier and seek to emulate the behaviour of some Western nations. A further problem may lie in the declining birth rate in countries where life expectancy is increasing. The burden of maintaining pensions will rest on fewer workers. Here the feedback loop is needed to adjust pension contracts and retirement age to be compatible with the funds available. There has been a mismatch between the relatively quick advance in medical sciences that has raised life expectancy in a short time compared with the life time of the subjects and the lead time before a baby matures and is ready to be a net contributor to the economy. Unfortunately the increase in life expectancy has not been matched by a decrease in dependency in old age. The spiralling cost of nursing home care is a problem for the future. It is also a situation where patients do not have a strong negotiating position and are often at the mercy of a management trying to cut costs.

Food and water are likely to be subject to advances in technology that produce greater yields; whether by genetically modified crops or better methods of desalination of seawater. In respect of water it is estimated that more water is wasted than is required for the world population. A sensationalist media has castigated genetically modified foods but if starvation were to appear on the horizon then opinions are likely to change. The sensationalist reports should be compared with a meeting of the British Association where a meeting of over 100 scientists voted in favour, of eating genetically modified foods, unanimously bar one abstention (by a publisher).

Human rights.

Some trends in the future are to be expected in retaliation to current events. Analogous to the swing of the pendulum: the greater the deviation from the norm the greater is the correction likely to be. It is perhaps inherent in these situations that feedback is delayed and consequently the departure from the norm is greater than will be tolerated. It seems likely that political correctness and human rights stemmed from injustices seen in the past. The pendulum has however swung to the point where many people are questioning the benefit of these trends. It is perhaps time for it to be replaced by a campaign for common sense, especially when criminals appear to have more rights than their victims.

Religious conflict.

Religion continues to cause problems in the world. Differences in religious opinion have been the source of many conflicts and atrocities in the past. People who believe that God is on their side tend to be convinced that they are right. These convictions are enhanced by the positive loop that results from communal worship and the rituals that support it. These beliefs apparently continue when people of the same religion are at war with each other and call upon the same God to support them against their enemy.

Where religions differ it is evident that there are so many opposing beliefs in the world that very many people are wrong. Conviction is, however, contrary to humility. If different religions are to coexist then it is as necessary that believers consider they could be wrong as it is for the terrorist and suicide bomber to question that they will go to paradise for their acts. The need to coexist requires a measure of etiquette where at the very least it is considered bad manners to question other beliefs. The antagonism that may otherwise occur can give rise to escalation in conflict - a positive loop that arises when an insult generates greater retaliation. The loop gain in this case is antagonism and appropriate etiquette is likely to be one method of reducing it to the point where it ceases to be regenerative.

Movements in democracy.

There is a trend for people to be more understanding of the problems of others. Whether this is due to the evolution of the democratic process or due to the influence of the media the effect is similar. The power of authoritarian opinion is declining and is likely to continue to do so with the advent of the Internet. The power of the Internet to influence opinion may be two sided insofar as fanatics also have the opportunity to make their views heard. It must be also borne in mind that the ability to address multiple people easily and at low cost via email and the Internet means that a positive loop with enormous gain is available. The opportunity for public discussion of current affairs in the future is nevertheless likely to generate a more democratic society -subject to governments not censoring communications or closing down sites that are critical of them. The technology should be able to provide the opportunity to utilise a continuous negative feedback loop where differing views are considered and modified in accordance with the consensus of public opinion. The power of the media to hype up news and cause unnecessary worry is likely to be reduced if responsible web sites are set up to debate and give considered opinions.

At a national level, however, there is evidently a trend away from democracy at present. Politicians in power are able to disregard the opinion of the electorate without apparent retaliation. A factor is possibly the number of career politicians who are dependent for their livelihood on obeying the dictates of their leader. Such dependence seems to override any moral authority to represent the views of the electorate that should be expected of an elected member. Without counteracting feedback an evolving dictatorship may be inevitable.

Protectionism.

Of equal importance will be the delayed negative loop resulting from the pendulum action to reverse some of the trends. Some such trends are the Nanny State, the litigious society and religious conflict. If we suppose that the mean position of the pendulum to represent the optimum state of society to progress amicably then we must seek a means of reversing the pendulum when it moves to excess. Large damages have been awarded following on litigation (which, as discussed elsewhere, has caused a positive loop). These awards are often high-lighted by the press because the extent of the awards is so high as to be newsworthy. The fact that they are newsworthy means that they are uncommon. It will be a different matter when health services and other public institutions become bankrupt as a result of the excess. As noted the social services have been excluded from liability because it was judged that the penalties for errors could prejudice the service's ability to perform their duty. This absence of a corrective influence is of course a disaster for many families who are wrongly penalised. It is necessary for a penalty to remain but remain within reasonable bounds.

Litigation and the nanny state come together to influence the treatment of children.
A danger is that children are not being prepared to be self-reliant. Some exposure to danger is necessary to educate children in the art of survival. The trend to aversion of risk means that there is little adventure and more spirited children are likely to seek outlets for their energy by less conventional means. In some parts of the community this is manifested by the street gang culture and many children are becoming street-wise.

The aversion to risk does not bode well for future prosperity. The standard of living currently enjoyed arose because of the work of previous generations who took the necessary risks. There is a trend to choose easy options at university. Such a trend must be reversed to encourage a preference for the sciences and engineering if the UK is to compete with Asian countries. China, for example, is quoted as having 10 times the number of engineering graduates.

A factor in the falling education standards must be the restrictions on the methods available to keep discipline. The difference in disciplinary procedures between private and state schools can only exacerbate the differences in attainment. Such differences between nations could be even more important.

As long as terrorism is contained within acceptable limits it is likely that the status quo will continue. If the terrorism escalates to the point where it overwhelms the security services then an uprising would seem inevitable. A trend to multi-nationalism reduces patriotism and alienates the native population.

There is the danger that modern means of communications can spread erroneous opinions too fast for correcting action to take place in time, especially when the facts are exaggerated by the media (for example the lynch mobs who mistook paediatricians for paedophiles).

It is likely that trends, however they are supervised, will be influenced by people who have an axe to grind and are enthusiastic enough to infiltrate and organise positions of power. The groupthink problem will remain unless the silent majority take more interest and organise a more democratic system.

Complexity and interdependence.

As society becomes ever more complex and interdependent so it becomes more vulnerable to problems in one section that can cascade into others [1]. The potential for a pandemic to destroy society, as we know it, lies in our dependence on relatively small groups of people who provide vital services.

The Just in Time system (JIT), which has been important in increasing the economy world wide, is subject to serious penalties if one of the supply chains fails. The cost of storing goods in warehouses, and the refrigeration of perishable items, has meant that storage is kept to a minimum on the basis that they can be replenished by the next delivery. Such a system falls down if there is a pandemic that causes the people in the supply chain to fall ill in large numbers.

Jarad Diamond [2] has reviewed societies that have failed in the past. The dependency on a small group of people has been an important factor. In 1348 the Black Death killed about one third of the European population, but a population survived because it was a feudal hierarchy. More than 80% were peasant farmers so that as each death removed a producer it also removed a consumer so there was little effect on the whole. The Roman Empire was also a hierarchy but with a huge urban population, which depended on peasants for grain, taxes and soldiers. When they fell ill, essential people were not sufficiently available to maintain supplies and defend the city.

Similarly this situation could arise in modern society because of the complexity and interdependence of different sections of industry and commerce. People in the transport and distribution centre are hubs upon which most people depend. Also the complexity inherent in the logistics requires the services of key individuals who would not be easy to replace in the event of illness or death [3].

McKinnon [4] noted that in a pandemic lorry drivers may be sick, dead, too scared to work, stay at home to care for the sick or look after children because schools are closed. This situation would be worse than the UK strikes that blocked petrol delivery for 10 days. On that occasion:

- *One third of motorists ran out of fuel.*
- *Some train and bus services were cancelled.*
- *Shops began to run out of food.*
- *Hospitals were reduced to running minimal services.*
- *Hazardous waste piled up.*
- *Bodies went unburied.*

In such a situation the JIT problem would be exacerbated because:

- *Stocks are kept low to maximise profit.*
- *Need frequent deliveries.*
- *Cities have about 3 days supply of food (not if there is a panic).*
- *Hospitals have daily supply of drugs, blood and gases and only 2 days reserve supply of oxygen.*

There is a significant likelihood of major breakdowns in the freight transportation sector under the more severe influenza scenarios as a direct result of large-scale worker absenteeism [5]. Transport is needed to provide fuel for coal power stations, and all power stations are dependent on healthy staff to run them, Figure 1.

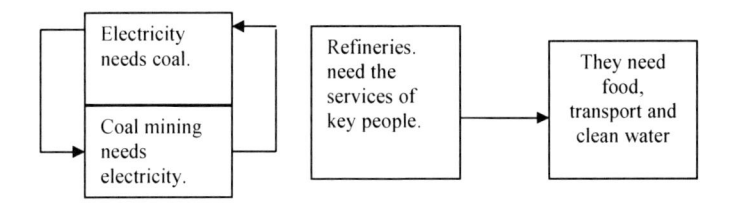

```
┌──────────────┐
│ Electricity  │◄──┐   ┌──────────────┐
│ needs coal.  │   │   │ Refineries,  │   ┌──────────────┐
├──────────────┤   │   │ need the     │   │  They need   │
│ Coal mining  │   │   │ services of  │──►│    food,     │
│ needs        │───┘   │ key people.  │   │ transport and│
│ electricity. │       └──────────────┘   │ clean water  │
└──────────────┘                          └──────────────┘
```

Figure 1. The dependence on key people.

It is interesting to note that some United States authorities call for people to keep 3 weeks of food and water (but people may need 10 weeks worth).

Contingency plans to cope with a pandemic are drawn up to cope with a drop of 25% in the work force. Whilst this issue is considered manageable a 50% drop would put the nation in crisis. Lack of electricity would highlight the dependence of the community on power, Figure 2.

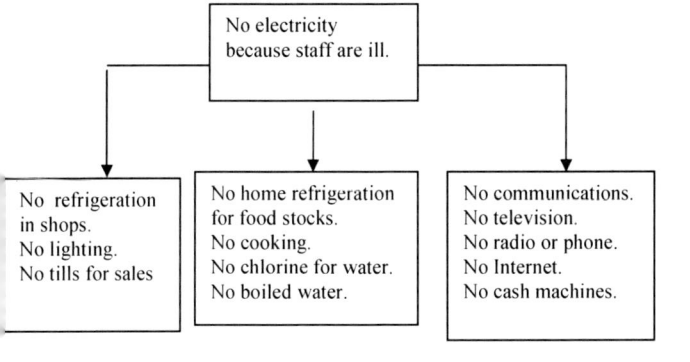

```
                    ┌──────────────────┐
                    │  No electricity  │
         ┌──────────│ because staff    │──────────┐
         │          │ are ill.         │          │
         │          └────────┬─────────┘          │
         ▼                   ▼                    ▼
┌─────────────────┐ ┌─────────────────────┐ ┌──────────────────┐
│ No refrigeration│ │ No home refrigeration│ │ No communications│
│ in shops.       │ │ for food stocks.    │ │ No television.   │
│ No lighting.    │ │ No cooking.         │ │ No radio or phone│
│ No tills for    │ │ No chlorine for     │ │ No Internet.     │
│ sales           │ │ water.              │ │ No cash machines.│
│                 │ │ No boiled water.    │ │                  │
└─────────────────┘ └─────────────────────┘ └──────────────────┘
```

Figure 2. Dependence on essential workers.

The consequences, of one problem, cascade into other essential areas of work. The health of the community depends on clean drinking water and food that has been adequately preserved and distributed.. Numerous feedback loops can develop if essential power is interrupted for a substantial time, Figure 3.

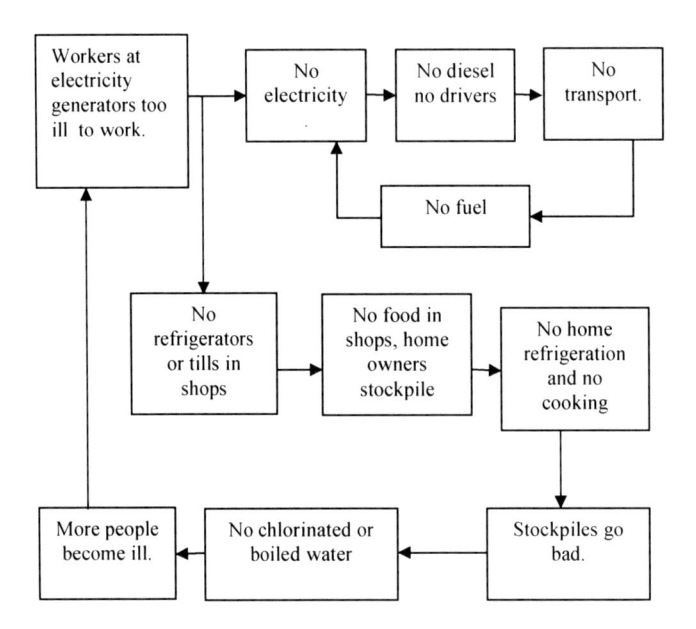

```
┌─────────────┐   ┌──────────┐   ┌──────────┐   ┌──────────┐
│ Workers at  │   │          │   │ No diesel│   │   No     │
│ electricity │──▶│    No    │──▶│    no    │──▶│transport.│
│generators too│   │electricity│   │ drivers │   │          │
│ ill to work.│   │          │   │          │   │          │
└─────────────┘   └──────────┘   └──────────┘   └──────────┘
       ▲               │                              
       │               │         ┌──────────┐         
       │               └────────▶│ No fuel  │◀────────┘
       │                         └──────────┘         
       │               │                              
       │         ┌──────────┐  ┌──────────┐  ┌──────────┐
       │         │    No    │  │ No food in│  │ No home  │
       │         │refrigerators│ │shops, home│ │refrigeration│
       │         │ or tills in │─▶│  owners  │─▶│  and no  │
       │         │   shops  │  │ stockpile│  │ cooking  │
       │         └──────────┘  └──────────┘  └──────────┘
       │                                          │
┌─────────────┐  ┌──────────────┐  ┌──────────┐   │
│ More people │  │No chlorinated│  │Stockpiles│   │
│ become ill. │◀─│  or boiled   │◀─│  go bad. │◀──┘
│             │  │    water     │  │          │
└─────────────┘  └──────────────┘  └──────────┘
```

Figure 3. Some feedback loops arising from power shortage.

The problem is illustrated by Osterholm [6] with the packaging and distribution of milk. If there are enough people to milk the cows, deliver the fuel for trucks, drive the trucks, provide the power for refrigeration, manufacture and deliver the cartons then there will be milk for breakfast. A similar situation arises with oil refineries and countless other commodities

Having reviewed some of the problems can we apply the Scoldent list to suggest themes for limiting the spread of infection? The quantity circulating around loop is *"susceptibility to infection"*:

Saturation would imply reducing the size of the channel for conducting the disease. E.g. minimise the extent of infection by using only one person to act as an intermediary between groups.

Cut-off would be achieved by preventing contact between intermediaries. E.g. the lorry driver stays in an insulated cab and does not get out at delivery point.

Open loop. The infected individuals would not be allowed contact with the population - so quarantined.

Low gain. Limit contacts, disinfect, vaccinate and use masks.

Delay. No contact with suspected cases until declared free of infection.

External influence. Use robots or automated delivery.

Negative feedback. Planning and advice on prevention of disease.

Theme change. Parallel supplies to reduce interdependence.

For a scoldent list on electricity supply, the quantity circulating around the loop is "shortage of electricity"

Saturation. Limit supply to general public and prioritise essential services.
Cut-off. No supply for non-essentials.
Open loop. Alternative supplies.
Low gain. Supportive supplies using various alternative energy sources.
Delay in use of services until essential.
External influence by using supplies from continent.
Negative feedback. Energy saving methods and public education.
Theme change. Distributed energy sources e.g. wood burning for heat and local solar panels & wind generators for electricity.

It should be noted that many authorities have assessed the problems as indicated in the references. Nevertheless the mutation of a deadly virus into a human form could still be a problem. The earthquake in Haiti in January 2010 has provided a horrifying illustration of the dependence of a population on necessary services.

Summary.

1. Legislators must anticipate the future.
2. Litigation is in a positive loop of damaging influence.
3. Consumption will be subject to compensating influences
4. New technology will be in a race to compensate for demand.
5. Over-correction of past injustices must be limited.
6. Etiquette must replace bigotry.
7. The Internet is a force for democracy – unless censored by government.
8. The feedback of reality is being replaced by excessive risk aversion.
9. The speed of information dissemination can exceed the power to correct errors.
10. Groupthink must give way to informed democracy.
11. The complexity and interdependence of modern society makes it vulnerable to a pandemic.

References.

[1] Mackenzie, D,"The End of Civilisation", New Scientist, 5 April 2008, p 28
[2] Diamond J, "Collapse: How societies Choose to Fail or Succeed", Viking books.
[3] Scalingi P, "Pandemic simulations for the Pacific North West"
[4] McKinnon A, Heriot Watt University.
[5] Jones DA, et al, "Pandemic influenza, Worker Absenteeism and impacts on Freight Transport"
[6] Osterholm M, Center for Infectious Disease Research and Policy (CIDRAP), www.pandemicpractices.org
[7] Sly T, Ryerson University.

Copyright Derrick Grover 2005-2011

Index

Absence of feedback 21 62 71 147 216 269 280 284
Absolute power 62 71
Accountability 69 139 148 172 198 219
Achievement 75 178 267 276
Actuarial fairness 173
Adaptation 111 281
Addiction 80 107
Adventure 69 103 284
Advertising 30 73 85 123 163 186 225 269
Aircraft 264 269
Alcoholism 106
Ambulance chasing 223 280
Anticipation 25 34 133 144 165 189 184 196 205 261 280
Anti-social behaviour 72 82 216
Antisocial 72 83
Anxiety 90 113 239
Arbitrage 208
Argument 31 94 133
Army 22 179 227 184
Asbestos litigation 227
Asimov I 255
Authorities 64 79 126 188 216 227 289
Auto-control 269
Automatic 10 37 57 235
Bad money 172
Badge of honour 116
Bailey S 117
Baker and Henderson 230
Baker 145 34 138
Bang-bang control 54
Bank rate 24 168 204
Banks 141 166 178 188 194 261
Banman 113
Bantock G 127 136
Bateson G 107 109
Bath 56
BBC 71 146 198 203
Bear market 162 168
Beneficial loop 8 19 32 61 79 99 117 121 147 168 179 192 264
Benevolence 78 86 112 165
Betamax 170 177

Biofeedback 99 237 239
Bistable systems 15
Black Monday 208
Blood glucose 235
Bonds 204
Bonfire 15 36
Book distribution 263
Boulding K E 169 188 199
Bouncers 82 229
Boxing 49
Bridge 22 184
British Association 113 124 132 171 265 282
Buffet W 121 124
Bulk buying 51
Bull market 193 206
Bureaucracy 24 28 34 39 125 142 164 182 216 228 279
Butterfly economics 169
CAD 269
Call option 210
Capital gain 205
Car 8 23 69 80 103 186 246 253 271
Carbon dioxide 243
Career politicians 284
Cash flow 140 144
Central heating 10 54
Centre of gravity 59
Chaos 104 109 170 262 270
Chicago futures market 208
Child development 47 68 76 104 134
Child support agency 64
China 87 118 181
Civil Service 70 87 123
Clock 22
Cochrane P 265
Cocktail party 44
Compensation 8 16 52 60 103 152 173 217 225 230 273
Competition 15 47 95 133 144 163 180 216 257
Complexity 65 111 136 168 188 205 218 264 285
Compound interest 198
Computer aided design 269
Computer illiteracy 265
Computer literacy 265
Computer spam 265

Computer trading 208
Computer virus 265
Confidence 26 47 74 87 96 148 166 188 261 269
Conflict 49 87 107 134 175 256 283
Confucius 92
Conkers 28
Connectors 115
Coombs A 109
Copycat 72 82 114
Cost 45 64 141 151 171 182 188 198 209 222 227 249 276
Coupon 204
Crane 28
Credit cards 198
Cricket 46 47
Criminal Justice and Public Order Act 220
Criminal 72 115 220 226 280
Crowd behaviour 41 98 114 170
Culpaphilia 226
Curriculum- education 125
Cycle of deprivation 117
Cyclist 8 20
Cyclones 245
Damping 13 28 31
Danger 14 39 51 68 94 103 112 136 165 207 222 236 242 250 260 284
Daniels A 99
Dasgupta P 120 124
Decline of companies 70 139 153
Decline of nations 87 258
Delay 21 70 94 111 125 148 158 190 195 203 217 247 272 284
Delayed assessment 125
Delinquents 62 116
Democracy 50 62 113 118 283
Demonstrations 65 107 116
Desentisize 63
Detached 64 120
Developing situations 50 117 153 178 199 281
Deviation 8 12 70 81 231 282
Diabetes 200 235
Diamond J 285
Digital systems 269
Disability 173 228
Disaster 32 62 79 106 198 256 284
Disease 64 200 226 256 289

Disruptive pupil 128 130
Distortion 67 82 154 202
Dominant 35 42 119
Double bind 107
Dow Jones 208
Dropdown list 135
Drug baron 79
Drug dealer 81
Drunk 9 148
Due diligence 102 194
Ecology 71 243 260
Economics 20 50 83 119 141 158 161 182 196 216 228 258
Economy 24 40 80 143 150 160 178 194 217 248 279 285
Efficiency issues 34 48 126 139 156 180 258 271
Efficiency of transfer 157 271 274
Electroencephalograph 239
Electromyogram 238
Element of surprise 75
Elitist 86
Elsworth C 71
Email 116 266 283
Embarrassment 89 149
EMG 238 239
Encapsulation 111
Energy use 271 281
Energy 22 31 44 130 260 271 284
Engineering graduates 154 285
Engineers 28 48 132 151 178 281
Euthanasia 63
Excessive consumption 281
Expectations 31 46 85 113 123 151 169 197 209 279
Explosion 14 35 63 93 256
Extinction - of incentive 102
False data 218
Fashion 23 41 73 114 134 175 184 226 248 281
Fear 71 82 88 105 107 194 221 227
Financial systems 176 204
Finite element analysis 269
Fire 8 14 19 32 37 54 63 183 223 273
Fishermen 29 214
Flexibility 26 147 249
Fluctuation 13 28 70 196 204
Fluid resistance 58

Football 72 398 119
Footpath 59 68 82
Forced vibrations 184
Forecasting 25 34 104 139 143 176 198 205 229 261 268
Forest 32 36 243
Forgotten evidence 81
Forgotten lines 89
Free market 12 157 161 168 201 217 228 261 276
Freighter management 264
Fulcrum 28 31
Future the 50 93 119 165 197 218 251 268 280
Futures 208 261
Gain of loop 36 41 98 118 138 167 186 197 248 283
Gang culture 104 116 221 284
Gearing 93 132 142 166 194 211 224
Genetically modified foods 282
Genetics 199 223 282
Ghouls 119
Gladwell M 115 124
Global Positioning System 251
Golf 47
Good money 172
Gosling W 24 25
Government reports 267
Government 24 34 51 62 71 81 117 150 163 171 192 199 219 248 267 283
Governor 11 23 34
GPS 251
Graham J 127 137
Gravity 8 19 21 32 59 242
Groupthink 63 105 285
Gynaecologists 223
Heat exhaustion 233
Heckler 89 91
Hedging 208
Helmsmen 24 25 150
Hitting bottom 107
Home ownership 188
Homeostasis 231 237
Hooliganism 73 229
Hot water 54
Housefire 34 54
Human rights 72 83 129 216 229 282
Hunting 23 49 70

Hurricanes 245 260
Hutton W 127 176
Huxley A 133
Hydraulic system 26 58
Hype 17 67 269 283
Hyperthermia 233 237
Hypoglycaemia 236
Hypothalamus 231 234
Hysteresis 44
Immediacy 11 28 57 69 76 80 118 150 165 182 219 273
Inadequate feedback 126 175
Inequality 46 129
Information amplifier 72
Information 20 25 51 66 79 91 108 115 135 164 181 196 231 254 261 272
Insolvent thrifts 166 188
Insomnia 239
Insulation 63 97 118 289
Insulin 234
Insurance premiums 83 223
Insurance 83 183 190 199 223 246 280
Interactive programs 264
Interdependence 79 285
Interest rate 150 168 188 204
Internet 51 116 135 250 265 283
Investment 34 50 78 99 121 139 158 171 189 193 204 211
Involvement 75 93 105 128 225
Irving Janus 109
Janus I 109
Jesus 92
JIT 182 285
Jude Graham 127
Judiciary 74 126
Judo 44
Juries 223 280
Just in time 182 285
Kennedy J 52 94
Kitchen 55
Knight J 88 95
Knowledge loop 106
Kudos 76 83
Leader 31 85 96 105 156 284
Learner 9 148
Legislation and planning 280

Legislation 50 62 72 82 105 128 156 173 183 199 216 228 261 277
Legislators 70 126 217 261 280
Liability insurance 223 226
Litigation 74 172 183 223 280
London ambulance case 262
Loop holes 220
Lord Justice 77
Loudspeaker 14 271
Mafia 79
Magnification 8 170 211 274
Malpractice 223 281
Management level 70
Mandarin class 87 181
Market 23 42 51 76 99 110 144 151 187 201 216 261 272
Marks & Spencer 70 139
Maslow A H 148
Matching concept 151 201 271
Maternal 88
Maximisation of inequality 47 53 72
McHughen A 279
McKinnon A 286
Meade R 243 260
Media hype 17 67
Media 17 50 63 72 114 123 132 186 195 218 229 248 281
Members of Parliament 64 70 219
Meter 25 237 239
Methane 243
Microelectronics 156 176
Microphone 14 72 91
Military aspects 48 74 181
Mindset 107
Minimum wage 151 216
Minority groups 62 118
Minority issues 8 118
Misreporting 67
Modelling 25 57 169 203
Monopoly 19 34 45 50 86 163 199 216
Motivation 75 102 120 192 248
Mugging 74 80
Murder 69 82
Muscle control 231
Nanny state 136 284
National Health Service 200 226 280

Negative equity 166
Negative feedback 8 23
Negative reinforcement 99
Negotiation 31 53 63 94 143 152 164 198 274 282
Net worth 188
Neuro-feedback 240
New York Stock Exchange 208
Newspapers 72
NHS 200 226 280
No-hopers 51 77 81 96 112
Norm 13 100 282
Nursing homes 64 217 282
NYSE 208
O'Loughlin J 124
Obstetricians 223
Oil crisis 17
Old age 185 217 257 282
Old boy network 86
Older generation 82 110 119 150 173 185 228 271
Ormerad P 169
Opinion poll 68 229
Opt out 111
Optimisation 272
Oscillation 9 22 28 70 80 100 110 132 151 184 196 258 273
Osterholm M 288
Overheads 51 139 157 267
Oxygen control 19 32 54 286
P/E 207
Paedophilia 69 285
Pancreas role of 235
Pandemic 260 285
Panic 68 89 98 195 206 236 286
Paranoia 69
Parkinson C Northcote 147
Participation 81 113 187 219
Partnerships 92 259
Patents 183
Paternal 88
Paul Revere 115
Peer groups 81 97 105 113
Peer pressure 81 104 113 186
Pendulum 13 21 58 80 93 100 117 125 147 217 258 282
Pensions 118 156 171 198 282

Perceval J 107 109
Permafrost 245
Personality 82 85 229
Pituitary gland 234
Plowden report 126 136
Pneumatic system 58
Political correctness 72 92 282
Political 51 66 85 123 165 182 198 216
Population 62 118 133 154 177 216 249 255 281
Positive behaviour 128
Positive feedback 8 13
Positive reinforcement 100 148 155
Poverty trap 116 201 216 222
Power and influence 81
Pressure group 81 118
Price of perfection 276
Price to earnings 207
Prison 75 115
Private education 105 133 285
Probability of crime 82
Production 30 51 102 115 163 182 206 235 256 272
Professions 24 48 82 126 133 158 178 220 227 280
Project MAC 263
Proportional influence 11 35 42 51 81 93 100 142 256 276
Psychosis 108
Public speaking 88 239
Put option 210
Queue 8 17 195 223 254 263
Qwerty keyboard 171
Rachmanism 221
Radiator 10 54
Radio 23 60 72 115 223 255 287
Rain forests 243
Rape 82
Ratchet effect 86 114 123 281
Ratcliffe J 89
Realistic accounting 83 155 160
Reasonable force 75
Rebellion 65 97 175
Recognition 44 128 153
Reinforcement 62 61 88 93 97 100 109 128 148 241 248
Religion 63 80 92 97 257 283
Remoteness 63 217

Rent (Control of Increases) 1969 Act 221
Rentier society 176
Reporting 48 68
Resources 34 51 64 78 138 180 216 257 281
Retrospective sanctions 148 219
Return on funds 188
Reward 78 113 128 178 201 240
Rigidity 26 233
Risk benefit 213
Risk 69 80 93 112 126 140 165 176 188 199 224 277 284
Robertson R and Combs A 109
Rote learning 125
Rozenberg J 84
Rumour 48 188 206 261
Run on banks 188 195
Runaway behaviour 39 104 230
Salam A W 188
Sales 30 51 138 161 170 180 201 268 272
Sanctions 50 78 83 97 111 129 147 155 172 183 219
Scoldent list 33 52 89 94 130 144 164 195 199 225 249 256 267 289
Sea level 243
Seed farmer 38
Self-compensation 60
Self-confidence 41 87 96 110
Self-correction 97
Self-effectiveness 113
Self-esteem 113 118
Self-fulfilling 261
Self-limiting 32 61 79 254
Self-perpetuating 75 133
Self-regulating 161 163
Self-reinforcement 62
Self-righting 12
Self-supporting 158
Sensationalism 82 282
Shaw G B 92 95
Shipping 9
Shower 56
Sigmoid loop 41 256
Signpost 44 106
Silent majority 118 285
Simulation 258 290
Single parents 117 123

Skinner B F 99 102 109 136
Slop in system 152 274
Smith Adam 161 183
Snow 55 243
Snowball 8 32
Soap box speaker 89
Social aspects 30 65 76 85 109 120 141 162 178 216 227 257
Social benefits 120 157 173 223
Social capital 120 124
Social conventions 116
Social interaction 92
Social relations 87
Social services 81 223 284
Social unrest 76 115 123 220
Solvency 166 172 188 190
Speculators 207
Staff 28 48 69 127 179 223 262 286
Start-up companies 138 159
Start-ups 145 179
Starving chicken 15 19 49 76 140
Steam engine 10 23 34
Stiction 56
Stitch in time 35 60
Stock market 23 68 99 162 205 261
Straitjacket 28 93 147 165
Stress 23 48 60 127 227 256
Submarine 25
Sub-prime liabilities 193
Subsidies 141 151 192 226 250
Successful 19 35 48 70 85 113 151 163 258 281
Suicide bombers 283
Supermarket 8 68 141 164
Supervisor 64 236
Surveillance 80 180
Swing 21 27 80 117 128 168 184 196 217 273 282
Switch 28 43 54 135
Symbiosis 49 53 187
Tanker 9 25 164
Taxation 34 117 123 151 167 216 222 279 286
Teachers 82 97 126 229 273
Technology 51 65 70 87 110 119 125 133 143 155 172 176 251 261 269 282
Telephone answering 106 269
Television 50 60 72 98 112 119 130 176 271

Temperature 10 17 25 37 54 231 244
Tennis 46 272
Terrorists 283
Thalamus 232
Thermometer 25
Thermostat 10 37 54
Tipping point 19 115 124
Toast 55
Toffler A 65 110 127 150 267
Toilet-roll 57
Tornadoes 245
Totalitarian 113
Tournament ploy 46 54 133
Trade union 150 216
Traffic 69 82 248 254
Transfer of information 273
Transport 120 141 164 246 286
Trauma 77 223 227
Tsunami 21
Turney J 276
Typhoons 245
Undamped 28 100
Unemployment 111 120 150 166 223
Unequal opportunities 133
Unfairness 48 88 175 182
Unrest 66 77 115 123 220
Unruly pupils 129
Unstable system 23 59 207 233 235 264
Urban renewal 65
US department of agriculture 276
Vandalism 229 246
Verhulot P F 256
VHS 170 177
Vicarious existence 119 135
Vicious 14 32 106 114 198 246
Vickers G 65 110 134
Victim 64 74 98 106 181 195 230 283
Video 73 80 91 114 170 177
Vigilance 128 219
Vigilantes 76
Virtual reality 119
Walker S 99
War 49 87 92 119 181 256 283

Warren Buffett 121 124
Waves 184 237 242
Web 284
Welfare 65 117 147 197 221
Wisdom 112 261
Wise David 171
Witnesses 76 227
Worker performance 100
Wragg E C 128
Yacht 13 28 271
Yield 39 108 168 204 282
Young T R 109
Youth club 85

Lightning Source UK Ltd.
Milton Keynes UK
UKOW052029280612

195211UK00001B/260/P